SCOTLAND'S MERLIN

SCOTLAND'S MERLIN

A Medieval Legend and its Dark Age Origins

TIM CLARKSON

First published in Great Britain in 2016 by
John Donald, an imprint of Birlinn Ltd

West Newington House
10 Newington Road
Edinburgh
EH9 1QS

www.birlinn.co.uk

ISBN: 978 1 906566 99 9

British Library Cataloguing-in-Publication Data
A catalogue record for this book is available on request from the British Library

Typeset by Hewer Text UK Ltd, Edinburgh
Printed and bound in Britain by TJ International Ltd, Padstow, Cornwall

CONTENTS

PLATES

MAPS AND GENEALOGICAL TABLE

Maps

Genealogical table

INTRODUCTION

Few characters from the legendary lore of Britain are more recognisable to a modern audience than Merlin. Like King Arthur and Robin Hood, he is both familiar and mysterious – an enigmatic figure who seems to stand on the shadowy frontier between history and myth. In common with Arthur and Robin, he has made the transition from medieval folklore to modern popular fiction, and from page to screen. Indeed, it is through cinema and television that most people probably encounter Merlin today. Such media usually visualise him as a wizard at King Arthur's court – a trusted counsellor and mentor. On screen he is frequently portrayed as an old man with white hair and beard, like Tolkien's Gandalf, but the most popular characterisation of recent years shows him as a young sorcerer at the start of his career. Both images can be traced back to different strands of a richly layered medieval legend.

Did Merlin really exist? Many people who are fascinated by his legend see this is an important question, yet the answer is not a straightforward *Yes* or *No*. The question itself is too simple, for the legend of Merlin is complex and multi-layered. As a major component in the broad genre of Arthurian literature, Merlin's story has a long pedigree reaching back nearly a thousand years. As a subject for serious academic study, it has generated a lot of discussion and a large number of scholarly publications. How Merlin has been represented in various literary forms, from the Middle Ages to our own era, is a large topic in itself. Much of it lies outside the scope of this book, which is chiefly concerned with the origin of the legend. Here, the question of Merlin's historical existence is seen as having three parts: When did the Merlin legend begin? To where can its roots be traced? Is Merlin based on a real person? All three are explored in the following chapters. They are discussed against the backdrop of a widely held belief that the legend originated in the story of a real person who lived in Scotland in the sixth century AD.

Terminology: chronology and geography

Throughout this book, the term 'medieval' is used in relation to a period known as the Middle Ages. In its broadest sense, and in a European context, this period encompasses one thousand years of history from c. AD 400 to c. AD 1500. The first six centuries to c.1000 are often described as the Dark Ages, a label coined to reflect the decline of Roman civilisation in western Europe and the resurgence there of indigenous 'barbarian' cultures. Although not a particularly accurate term it is at least a familiar one and is therefore used in this book. Many historians prefer the less judgmental 'early medieval' and this term also appears here. For the twelfth century onwards, as far as the beginning of the modern era in the sixteenth, the term High Middle Ages is used.

The book's geographical terminology is intended to avoid ambiguity and anachronism. Here, the name 'Britain' has no political connotation and refers solely to the island of Britain and its associated smaller isles (though not, of course, the separate land-mass of Ireland or any part of it). 'British' is here used mainly of the Britons, the native Celtic people who once inhabited the whole island. In the early medieval period or Dark Ages, they increasingly lost control of their ancestral territory to other peoples such as the Scots and Anglo-Saxons. By c.800, at the start of the Viking Age, the territories under British rule had been reduced to three enclaves in the far west: Cornwall, Wales and the valley of the River Clyde. The original homeland of the Scots lay in north-west Britain, in modern Argyll and the neighbouring isles, in a region they called Dál Riata. They spoke Gaelic, the language of the Irish, with whom they had long had a close relationship via the narrow seas that connected rather than divided them. Like the Britons, the Scots were a Celtic people. The same cannot be said of the Anglo-Saxons or English, whose ancestors had arrived in Britain from the North Sea coastlands of Continental Europe in the fourth and fifth centuries. They were a Germanic people, speaking a language very different from the native Celtic tongues of the island. Their takeover of much of the south pushed the frontier of British-ruled territory westward. By c.800, a small group of powerful English kingdoms controlled a very large area. One of these, Northumbria, stretched from the Firth of Forth to the Humber and Mersey estuaries and from the east coast to the west. Its northern neighbours were the still-independent Britons of the Clyde and also the Picts, another Celtic people who inhabited much of the highland region of the far north-east. As the ninth century progressed, the Picts began to merge with the Scots to form a single people – the embryonic

Scottish nation – living within a single, Gaelic-speaking kingdom called Alba. Before c.900, however, the terms 'Scotland' and 'England' did not exist in any meaningful political sense. Not until the Viking Age got well under way in the tenth century did the idea of two large, unified realms begin to emerge. Both terms are therefore used cautiously throughout this book, usually in reference to broad geographical topics such as 'the landscape of Scotland', with no political connotation unless required by the context. The more neutral terms 'northern Britain' and 'southern Britain' tend to be preferred. Another term used here is the Old North, a translation of Welsh *Hen Ogledd*, this being a useful umbrella label for the lands of the North Britons in the Dark Ages. The region itself corresponds roughly to what is now southern Scotland below the Forth–Clyde isthmus, together with some adjacent parts of what is now England. It was the homeland of the aforementioned Clyde Britons and their compatriots in other northern kingdoms until the latter were absorbed into Anglo-Saxon Northumbria (a process completed before AD 700).

Terminology: literature and language

At the heart of this book is an investigation or quest: the search for the origins of Merlin. This is primarily a journey through the literature of the legend in the hope of tracing its roots. The key objective is to identify the 'real' Merlin, the historical figure upon whom the original version of the legend was based. The prime candidate was first put forward in the Middle Ages, in a Latin text called *Vita Merlini Silvestris*, 'Life of Merlin of the Forest'. His name, however, was not Merlin, even though the *Vita* observes that he was already regarded in medieval times as the original figure behind the legend. The *Vita* instead calls him Lailoken, a name that many readers of this book will find strange and unfamiliar. More will be said of him later but, in the meantime, we can call him a 'Merlin-archetype'.

The name Merlin appears to be unknown before the twelfth century. It seems to have been invented by Geoffrey of Monmouth, a writer of Anglo-Norman stock, who essentially created the legends of both Merlin and Arthur in the forms we know them today. Geoffrey drew information on these characters from older traditions of Celtic (mostly Welsh) origin but distilled them into something new and different. His bestselling work *Historia Regum Britanniae* ('History of the Kings of Britain') was completed c.1139 and provided a template for other writers to use and adapt. Through Geoffrey and those who came after him, Merlin became part of a much larger body of legend and pseudo-history known as the Matter of Britain, within which Arthur played a central role. In France, *Le Matiere de Bretagne* became a popular literary theme from the late twelfth century onwards. This was a period when French authors celebrated the ideals of chivalry and courtly love in 'romances' composed in verse or prose. They produced some of the greatest works of Arthurian literature and, in doing so, were instrumental in enhancing Merlin's fame. Because their interpretation of Britain's legendary history owed so much to Geoffrey of Monmouth, the romances and the later works derived from them are sometimes referred to as 'post-Galfridian' (i.e. after Geoffrey) to distinguish them the older 'pre-Galfridian' material that included Geoffrey's own Celtic sources.

In this book, the term 'Celtic' is mostly used in a cultural sense, primarily with regard to the languages and literatures of the Celtic regions of the British Isles. It is rather less useful as an ethnic label, except in broad contexts where, for example, Celtic and Anglo-Saxon cultural zones need to be distinguished from one another. The Celtic languages of Britain and Ireland can be described collectively as Insular (from Latin *insula*, 'island') to distinguish them from Continental Celtic languages such as Gaulish. Modern, still-active Insular Celtic languages fall into two groups: Goidelic (Irish Gaelic, Scottish Gaelic and Manx Gaelic) and Brittonic or Brythonic (Welsh and Cornish). To the Brittonic group also belong an active Continental language (Breton) and two dead Insular ones (Cumbric and Pictish). Cumbric was the language of the North Britons but it had completely disappeared by c.1200, being displaced north and south of the Solway Firth by Scottish Gaelic and English respectively. Pictish, although usually assigned to the Brittonic group, might actually have been a separate language. It, too, was displaced by Scottish Gaelic and had died out before the end of the first millennium.

Overview

The first chapter of this book looks at the development of the Merlin legend in its familiar guise, as an element within the large corpus of Arthurian literature. Geoffrey of Monmouth provides the starting-point and his influence on later writers is duly acknowledged. The chapter then follows the Merlin legend to the end of the Middle Ages when Sir Thomas Malory's monumental *Le Morte d'Arthur* conjured a vivid picture of the world described in the French romances. At the beginning of Chapter 2, the focus returns to Geoffrey of Monmouth and, more particularly, to his Celtic sources. Here we encounter a mysterious character called Myrddin Wyllt, 'Wild Merlin', who appears in a group of old

Welsh poems that seem to have their roots in the Dark Ages. Chapter 2 ends by looking behind the poems to gain a glimpse of the equally enigmatic Lailoken upon whom Myrddin seems to be based. A closer look at the Lailoken legend and its connection with St Kentigern of Glasgow is the main theme of Chapter 3. Both Myrddin and Lailoken are part of an ancient story about a great battle fought on what is now the border between Scotland and England. In Chapter 4, this battle is studied more closely and its location is pinpointed. In Chapter 5, the reasons behind why it was fought are discussed. One popular theory interprets it as the climax of a religious war between Christians and pagans, seeing the real Merlin or 'Merlin-archetype' as a pagan druid and as one of the leaders on the losing side. This theory is questioned and challenged. The sixth chapter considers the fate of the Merlin-archetype in the aftermath of the battle, from which he is said to have fled in madness and terror. His subsequent existence in the deep forests of southern Scotland as a 'wild man of the woods' is discussed, as is his similarity to other 'wild' figures in Celtic literature. The narrative of the book then takes a short detour as Merlin's traditional companion King Arthur steps into the foreground. Just as Merlin's historical and geographical origins form the main topic of the book as a whole, so Arthur's roots in a real time and in a real landscape become the main topic of Chapter 7. A case for seeing the legends of both characters as originating in Scotland is made, although the question of Arthur's existence is left open. Merlin returns to centre stage in Chapter 8, which looks at how both his legendary and historical manifestations have been represented by various 'Scottish Merlins' over a broad span of time, from the twelfth century to the twenty-first. This theme carries over into the final chapter, which draws all the threads together to conclude that the roots of the Merlin legend do indeed lie in Scotland.

1

GEOFFREY OF MONMOUTH'S MERLIN

Historia Regum Britanniae

The traditional image of Merlin as the great wizard of Arthurian legend can be traced back to the twelfth century when he appeared in Geoffrey of Monmouth's *Historia Regum Britanniae* ('History of the Kings of Britain'), a work that quickly became a medieval bestseller. Geoffrey was a cleric – later a bishop – and a native of Wales, although his ancestry was most likely Norman or Breton rather than Welsh.[1] He was born c.1100, possibly at Monmouth in south-east Wales, but spent much of his life in England. In the early 1130s he published his earliest known work under the title *Prophetiae Merlini* ('The Prophecies of Merlin'). This marked the beginning of the Merlin legend in the form familiar to most people today. It is essentially a collection of obscure prophecies supposedly uttered by Merlin, some of them predicting events that had already happened in Geoffrey's own lifetime. Merlin was partly based on the young prophet Ambrosius or Emrys who appears in *Historia Brittonum*, a ninth-century 'History of the Britons' written in Wales. Ambrosius was in turn based on an even earlier figure – a historical military leader called Ambrosius Aurelianus who defended Britain against Anglo-Saxon invaders in the late fifth century. In a preface to the *Prophetiae*, Geoffrey claimed that Merlin and Ambrosius were one and the same, although his reasons for conflating the two are unclear. He first introduced this composite character in a story about the native British ruler Vortigern, another historical figure from post-Roman times who may have been a genuine contemporary of Ambrosius Aurelianus.[2] According to Geoffrey, Vortigern grew angry when his attempts to construct a new fortress were mysteriously thwarted. Each night, the newly-built foundations mysteriously disappeared. Vortigern was told by his counsellors that the problem could only be solved by locating a fatherless child and pouring its blood over the site. A suitable sacrifice, in the person of 'Merlin Ambrosius', was duly found at the town of Carmarthen in Wales and brought before Vortigern. Merlin, here depicted as a youth, informed Vortigern that the source of the problem was an ongoing fight between two dragons – one red, the other white – in a subterranean pool beneath the fort's foundations. He further explained that the red dragon represented the Britons while the white represented their Saxon foes, before prophesying that the Saxons would ultimately emerge victorious as conquerors of Britain. The core elements of this episode were not invented by Geoffrey but were already well-known in Wales from a story about Vortigern and the boy-prophet Ambrosius. A version of this older tale had appeared in *Historia Brittonum* (hereafter *HB*), in which Ambrosius was found not at Carmarthen but in the kingdom of Glywysing (now Glamorgan).[3] *HB* did not mention Merlin but provided a storyline for Geoffrey who borrowed it for his *Prophetiae*.

Prophetiae Merlini was distributed widely, gaining popularity not only in Britain but in Continental Europe. Many of the prophecies alluded to twelfth-century politics and were much discussed by Geoffrey's contemporaries at home and abroad. It is little surprise that he incorporated the same material into his larger work *Historia Regum Britanniae* (hereafter *HRB*) where it appears as part of the narrative in Book VII.[4] *HRB* gave additional information on Merlin, crediting him with magically transferring Stonehenge from Ireland to Britain and assigning him a role in Arthurian legend. This marked an important stage in his evolution as a literary character, for it connected him to King Arthur for the first time. His involvement with Arthur in *HRB* was, however, indirect: he used sorcery to enable Arthur's father Uther Pendragon to spend a night with another man's wife. The lady in question was Igerna, a Cornish noblewoman. She was unaware that she was sharing her bed with Uther, whom Merlin had cunningly disguised as her husband Gorlois. From this deceit the mighty Arthur was conceived. However, Merlin made no more appearances in *HRB* and is thus absent from the main Arthurian section which takes up a large part of the book.

Geoffrey's skill as a writer, coupled with his ability to weave fragments of folklore into a dramatic story, made *HRB* an instant bestseller. It has been described as 'the most influential book ever to have come out of Wales'.[5] To the medieval reader it offered an exciting account of two thousand years of British history, presented as a narrative peppered with all kinds of political intrigue. Among the kings whose exploits it describes are Brutus the Trojan (from whom Britain was supposedly named), the Roman emperor Constantine the Great, the tragic King Lear of Shakespearean fame and, of course, the mighty Arthur himself. The reader soon realises that this is not history but pseudo-history, a work of imagination in which the real and the legendary are seamlessly interwoven. However, while its value as a historical source might be minimal, *HRB*'s impact on medieval literature cannot be overstated. Geoffrey's colourful version of Britain's early history was eagerly received and widely disseminated by the literate circles of the day. The fact that more than 200 medieval copies of *HRB* still survive is a testament to its popularity. In the mid 1150s, Geoffrey's original Latin text had become the basis for another work, the *Roman de Brut* ('Romance of Brutus'), a verse chronicle in French composed by the Norman poet Wace. This held particular appeal for twelfth-century audiences by highlighting virtues such as chivalry and courtly love, hence its influence on later Arthurian romances. Wace also introduced significant new elements such as King Arthur's Round Table but chose to omit the prophecies of Merlin. His work provided the basis for Layamon's *Brut*, an adaptation written in English in the early years of the thirteenth century. Layamon added more new material to the story devised by Geoffrey but neither he nor Wace developed the character of Merlin much further.[6]

Sometime around the year 1200, the Burgundian poet Robert de Boron used Wace's Merlin for his own narrative poem *Merlin*, the second part of a verse trilogy on the legend of the Holy Grail. The first part, *Le Roman de l'Estoire dou Graal*, tells of how the sacred cup that once held Christ's blood was brought by Joseph of Arimathea to the 'Vales of Avalon'. It is the only part of the trilogy that survives complete and was later rendered into prose with the new title *Joseph d'Arimathie*. Of the sequel, *Merlin*, only the first 504 lines have survived but the rest of the narrative is known from a prose version, perhaps written by Robert himself, which still exists in a number of manuscripts. Nothing of the third item in the original verse trilogy – an account of the Grail knight Perceval – has been preserved but it, too, was rendered into a prose version which is extant today. Although Robert's Merlin has much in common with the character in *HRB*, he takes a more central role in Arthur's story, becoming mentor and guardian to the young king.[7] Robert developed Merlin's personality more fully, giving him a somewhat light-hearted aspect and casting him not only as a master of prophecy but also as a trickster and shapeshifter. Throughout Robert's work, the underlying theme is Christian, with Merlin being divinely appointed to encourage mankind's obedience to God's will. It is Merlin who initiates the holy quest for the Grail, the cup used by Jesus Christ at the Last Supper. Familiar elements from *HRB* include the two dragons engaged in subterranean combat, the ruler Vortigern (here called 'Vertigier'), the transfer of Stonehenge from Ireland and the conception of Arthur. Arthur's father Uther ('Uter') also appears, becoming king after defeating the Saxons in battle and – at Merlin's instigation – ordering the Round Table to be made. The new elements include a magical sword firmly embedded in an anvil on a block of stone. Fixed there by Merlin's sorcery, the sword bore on its blade an inscription saying that only the rightful king would be able to draw it out. Despite many men taking up the challenge, only Arthur was successful. The episode of the sword in the stone marked the end of Robert de Boron's original *Merlin* poem, but the narrative continues in the prose version. The contents of the final part of Robert's verse trilogy, the lost *Perceval*, are similarly known from its retelling in prose. Perceval was a knight of the Round Table who embarked on a quest to find the Grail, having various adventures along the way. In some of these he was assisted by Merlin. Later, after Perceval had taken up residence in the Grail castle, Merlin told him about Arthur's military victories and tragic death before he himself retired to a nearby forest.

Continuations of Robert's works on the Matter of Britain included a retelling of the Perceval legend – possibly a prose version of his own *Perceval* poem – together with *L'Estoire de Merlin*, 'The Story of Merlin' (hereafter *EM*), the *Suite de Merlin* and *Livre d'Artus*, 'The Book of Arthur'. However, in the *Suite de Merlin* and *EM* the Merlin story has a rather different ending. These two texts introduced a new female character, the wily maiden Viviane, with whom the wizard fell in love. Completely infatuated, the elderly Merlin divulged the secrets of his magic to his much younger lover, who then used her new-found skills to imprison him in an enchanted cave or tomb. *EM* represents one of the five volumes of the Vulgate Cycle, a major prose collection of Arthurian romance compiled in the early thirteenth century by one or more anonymous authors. The other volumes of the Vulgate are *L'Estoire del Saint Graal*, *Queste del Saint Graal*, *L'Estoire de Lancelot* and *La Mort Artu*.[8] Written in French, the entire collection became hugely popular across Europe and survives today in more than 140 copies, not all of which are complete. In England, the Vulgate material on Merlin inspired home-grown adaptations such as *Of Arthour and of Merlin* – an anonymous poem of the late thirteenth century written in Middle English – and the prose *Merlin* (c.1450) which was essentially an English translation of *EM*. The publication of such works suggests that Merlin continued to attract interest as a significant character in his own right and had not been pushed into the background by King Arthur.[9] He plays a significant role in Sir Thomas Malory's *Le Morte d'Arthur*, an eight-part work written in Middle English prose and completed c.1470. What Malory gave his readers was an English version of the whole Vulgate Cycle, with additional material of his own. In 1485, some fourteen years after Malory's death, the work was published by printing pioneer William Caxton. It went on to enjoy widespread fame and has exerted a profound influence on subsequent Arthurian literature.[10] It nevertheless diminished Merlin's role at Arthur's court, turning the powerful wizard and prophet of the French romances into little more than an adviser. However, it is to Malory that we largely owe the portraits of Arthurian characters still recognisable today: the chivalric king, his wife Guinevere, Sir Lancelot of the Lake, Sir Gawain and other knights of the Round Table. Alongside them stands Merlin in what is, to the modern observer, his most familiar guise: a wise counsellor and minister, yet one somewhat reduced in potency. The mighty seer and sorcerer of the older tales seemingly had no place in Malory's vision.[11]

Vita Merlini

The previous section considered Merlin's popularity in medieval literature from the twelfth century onwards and noted his emergence as an important figure in the Arthurian legend. It brought the story up to the fifteenth century and to Malory's *Le Morte d'Arthur*. We saw that Merlin's international fame can be traced back to Geoffrey of Monmouth's *Historia Regum Britanniae* which lay at the root of subsequent retellings. We now turn to another of Geoffrey's works, the *Vita Merlini* ('Life of Merlin'), a narrative poem that failed to gain the same wide acclaim as *HRB*. It appeared a dozen or more years later, probably around 1150, and cast its central character in a different light. In *HRB*, the reader was presented with the prophet and sorcerer Merlin, a young Welshman from Carmarthen who performed such feats as moving Stonehenge across the Irish Sea and arranging King Arthur's conception. In *Vita Merlini* (hereafter *VM*), we meet Merlin in later life, in a time when 'many years and many kings had come and gone'.[12] Moreover, with this new version of the legend Geoffrey introduced the concept of a northern Merlin, shifting the primary geographical setting from Wales and south-west England to the Forest of Calidon and the kingdom of Cumbria. These two places, as we shall see, lay in Scotland. How Merlin came to be involved in northern affairs is explained at the beginning of the poem. Indeed, *VM* is such a significant text for our present study that a detailed summary of its narrative is required here. Geoffrey's verses not only tell us about his new 'Scottish' Merlin but give a number of important signposts to the original legend that lay in the background.

VM begins by telling us that 'Merlin the Briton' was famed around the world as a king and prophet. The geographical context is initially similar to that in *HRB*, for we are told that Merlin served the leaders of Demetia – the kingdom of Dyfed in South Wales – as their chief seer and law-giver. However, the focus

soon moves northward, to a war between the Britons and the Scots. On one side
of this conflict stood Peredur (*Peredurus*), ruler of the North Welsh kingdom of
Gwynedd and paramount leader of the British forces. Against him marched
Guennolous, the ruler of Scotland. A date and venue for a decisive battle was
arranged and, when the time came, the opposing armies met on the field. The
location is not named but it clearly lay somewhere in the North. Alongside
Peredur marched his three brothers, together with his ally Rodarch (*Rodarchus*),
king of the Cumbrians. In the same entourage was Merlin who, having left his
home in Wales, had 'come to the war with Peredur'. The ensuing clash of arms
turned into a ferocious bloodbath, with heavy losses on both sides. Peredur's
brothers were slain during a brave charge through the Scottish line, while
Peredur and Rodarch 'killed the enemy before them with their dread swords'.
Witnessing so much carnage proved too much for Merlin. Overcome by grief
and horror, he lamented for the young warriors who had been cut down in their
prime: 'O glory of youth, who will now stand by my side in battle to turn back
the princes who come to do me ill and their hordes that press upon me?' The
slaughter ended when the Britons eventually chased the Scots from the field.
Merlin, now weeping inconsolably, ordered his companions to bury Peredur's
brothers in a chapel. This did nothing to assuage his grief. Indeed, he became
even more distraught. 'He threw dust upon his hair, tore his clothes and lay
prostrate on the ground, rolling to and fro.' No comfort would he take from
anyone, not even from Peredur and the other leaders.

Merlin's grief continued for three days, until 'a strange madness' compelled
him to seek solitude in the forest. Alone and in secret, so that his departure
went unobserved, he vanished among the trees. There he began to live as a
wild creature, foraging for roots and berries and observing the ways of animals.
'He became,' wrote Geoffrey, 'a Man of the Woods, as if dedicated to the
woods [. . .] forgetful of himself and of his own, lurking like a wild thing.' For
an entire summer, Merlin dwelt in the forest, surviving on plants and fruit,
until the onset of winter deprived him of food. He lamented the fact that he
could no longer pick apples from the trees that had formerly sustained him.
Even the leaves that had previously sheltered him from the rain were now
fallen. Wild pigs and boars snatched freshly-dug turnips out of his hands. He
compared his plight to that of his 'dear companion', an old grey wolf so weak-
ened by hunger and age that it could no longer hunt for meat. Eventually, the
sound of Merlin's mutterings reached the ears of a traveller passing through
the forest. This fellow attempted to make contact, but Merlin evaded him and
disappeared.

Meanwhile, a number of men from King Rodarch's court were scouring the countryside in search of Merlin. They had been sent out by Ganieda, the king's wife, who was Merlin's sister. Understandably concerned for her brother's welfare, Ganieda hoped to bring him to the safety of her house. One member of the search-party encountered the traveller who had seen Merlin and learned that the crazed fugitive was lurking 'in the dense-wooded valleys of the Forest of Calidon'. The searcher at once headed off into the trees, eventually finding Merlin on top of a mountain. There, among a dense growth of hazels and thorns, he saw the wild man sitting on the grass beside a spring, bemoaning the cold grip of winter and wishing for a change of season. Keeping hidden from view, the searcher began strumming a guitar and singing a lament, hoping this might soothe Merlin's strange mood. He sang about the grief of Guendoloena, Merlin's wife, for the husband whom she missed. He compared Guendoloena's tears to those of Ganieda, who likewise wept for a beloved brother. The tactic worked, for Merlin gradually emerged from his madness and 'recollected what he had been'. He wished then to be escorted to King Rodarch's court, where both his wife and sister were waiting for him. There was much joy and celebration at his arrival, which *VM* describes as a 'homecoming'. The nobility turned out in great numbers to welcome him. Unfortunately, the clamour and the crowds completely overwhelmed him, pitching him back into madness. He felt an urge to return to the woods, so Rodarch ordered that he be put under secure guard to prevent his escape. The king begged Merlin to calm down 'and not hanker after the forest and an animal life under the trees, when he might wield a royal sceptre and rule a nation of warriors'. Lavish gifts of clothes, horses and treasure were presented as inducements, but Merlin refused them all, insisting that they should be given instead to poorer men than he. Then he said: 'But I put above these things the woodland and spreading oaks of Calidon, the high hills, the green meadows at their foot – those are for me, not these things. Take back such goods, King Rodarch! My nut-rich forest of Calidon shall have me. I desire it above all else.'

Frustrated by Merlin's stubbornness, the king clapped him in chains. The additional restraint only served to increase Merlin's despondency. He did, however, laugh unexpectedly when he saw the king remove a leaf that had got caught in Queen Ganieda's hair. Rodarch insisted on knowing the cause of this sudden mirth, but Merlin refused to explain. Only when his chains were removed and he was granted permission to go back to the woods did he give the reason for his laughter. To the king's dismay, Merlin explained that the leaf in Ganieda's hair had come from the undergrowth in which she had met an illicit lover for a tryst. Upon hearing this, Rodarch cursed the day that he and his wife had been wed. She, however, 'hid her shame behind a smile' and calmly protested that her brother's accusation was false. Seeking to demonstrate that he was accustomed to telling lies, she devised what she thought would be a clever trap. First, she pointed out a young boy and asked Merlin to foretell the manner of his death. 'He will die by falling from a high rock,' came the reply. Next, she sent the boy away, but secretly told him to return in disguise, whereupon she asked her brother to predict 'what the death of this one will be'. After Merlin replied that this boy would suffer a violent death in a tree, Ganieda felt that she had sufficient proof of his false prophesying. To convince her husband, however, she offered a third demonstration, this time presenting the same boy disguised as a girl. Once more she asked Merlin to foretell the manner of death. King Rodarch laughed when he heard that the child would die in a river. Three different prophecies for the manner of one boy's death were enough to persuade him of Merlin's falsehood – and of Ganieda's faithfulness.

Having already been given permission to leave, Merlin now headed for the gates, only to find his sister blocking the exit. She did not want him to go and tried to persuade him to stay, even summoning his wife Guendoloena to implore him with an extravagant display of grief. 'I shall remain clear of both of you and undestroyed by love,' said Merlin, adding that he hoped his wife would one day remarry. Then he went out into the wild lands. His three prophecies about the death of the boy were at first dismissed as proof of his deceitful nature. Surely, if his words were to be trusted, he should have prophesied only one death, for nobody dies thrice? He was eventually vindicated when, in adulthood, the same boy suffered a triple demise. Falling from a cliff into a river, he caught his foot in a tree in such a way that his head went under the water, which caused him to drown. He thus perished by rock, tree and river – the threefold death foretold by Merlin.

And so the years passed. Merlin still dwelt in the Forest of Calidon, living like a woodland beast, 'yet that satisfied him more than administering the law in cities and ruling over a warrior people'. News eventually reached him of Guedoloena's betrothal to another, so he assembled a herd of deer and goats and set off to attend the wedding. When he reached the venue, riding on a horned stag, the bridegroom laughed at him. Merlin promptly wrenched the antlers from his steed's head and hurled them at the bridegroom, killing him outright. He then turned about and rode with all speed back towards the forest, pursued by a posse of servants. While crossing a river he fell off the stag and was taken captive, being brought back to Queen Ganieda as a bound prisoner. As before, however, he refused to abandon his yearning for the wild woods. This made the queen and her husband sad, for they both wanted him to stay at their court by his own volition. Instead, he spurned the fine food laid before him and sank into a sullen mood. King Rodarch thought a walkabout in the bustling royal city might help, but even this failed to lift Merlin's spirits. The forest-longing remained as strong as ever. For Ganieda, a particular concern was the coming winter, for then the trees would be bare and her brother would be at the mercy of cold and hunger. Merlin responded by saying that he was happy to endure such hardship, for which the delights of summer were more than adequate reward. In the end, a sort of compromise was worked out: Merlin asked his sister to build him a woodland hall and to provide him with servants who would keep him well-fed. He also asked for a team of secretaries 'trained to record what I say, and let them concentrate on committing my prophetic song to paper'. Ganieda agreed to these requests and a hall was duly built. Merlin then returned to the forest, but dwelt in the open until winter began to bite. When the weather worsened, he moved into his new hall, where Ganieda often visited him. There he wandered through the rooms, gazing out of the windows at the stars, and singing 'in the manner of the future that he knew would be'.

At this point in the narrative, *VM* includes a list of prophecies in the form of a lengthy quote attributed to Merlin. The list takes up more than a hundred lines of verse and most of the prophecies relate to political events. Among them are predictions of war between rival groups of Britons – such as the Welsh and Cornish – and of the deaths of contemporary kings, one of whom is Rodarch. Events on a more distant horizon are also foretold: the Anglo-Saxon conquest of Britain, the Viking raids in the ninth century and the Norman invasion in 1066. The list concludes with a reference to the prophecies of Merlin Ambrosius whose story Geoffrey had already told in *HRB*: 'All this,' said Merlin, 'I once predicted to Vortigern when I was explaining to him the mystic battle of the two dragons as we sat on the bank of the drained pool.' Ganieda, who had been visiting him, returned home, having learned that Rodarch was dying. Before she left, Merlin asked her to summon Taliesin (*Telgesinus*), a figure not previously mentioned. 'I have much I wish to discuss with him,' said Merlin, 'since he has only recently returned from Brittany where he has been enjoying the sweets of learning under the wise Gildas.' Taliesin duly arrived in the forest, whereupon Merlin asked him to explain what had caused the wind and rain. What follows is another lengthy interlude, a blend of science and superstition, attributed to the wisdom of Taliesin. This includes a description of various islands: Britain 'first and best', Thanet off the Kentish coast, Orkney, Ireland, Sri Lanka

(*Taprobana*) together with some that remain unidentifiable such as *Thule* (Iceland?) and *Insula Pomorum* ('Island of Apples', also known as *Fortunata*, 'Fortunate Island'). Taliesin observed that *Insula Pomorum* was ruled by nine sisters, one of whom was Morgen, a renowned healer and shape-shifter. He went on to say that 'it was there we took Arthur after the battle of Camlan, where he had been wounded'. Merlin's reply indicates that the period since Arthur's fall has not been a happy one: 'how great a burden has the kingdom borne since then'. Britain was now being ravaged by Saxon invaders who 'violate God's law and his house'. In fact, as he points out, these depredations were allowed by God because of the wickedness of the Britons and 'as a punishment for our folly'. Taliesin hoped that the mighty Arthur would recover from his wounds and return from the Island of Apples to defeat the Saxons, but Merlin foresaw that the enemy would eventually conquer Britain and retain it for a long time. Merlin then gave an account of how the Saxons came to Britain as mercenaries invited by Vortigern, consul of Gwent in South Wales, against whom they subsequently rebelled. They were opposed by Vortigern's son, Vortimer, who drove them back to their homelands in Germany, but this was only a brief respite before they once again invaded Britain. Leadership of the Britons had then been taken up by the brothers Uther and Ambrosius, returning from exile. Rivals of Vortigern, they slew both him and the Saxon warlord Hengist. Ambrosius then became king of Britain and, for a while, there was an uneasy peace. When Ambrosius died, the kingship passed to Uther, who soon had to face a new Saxon invasion. Once again, the invaders were defeated and expelled. Uther's son, Arthur, eventually became king. He, too, defeated the Saxons, and also the Scots, Irish, Norwegians, Danes, French and Romans. During his overseas campaigns he left Britain in the care of his nephew, Modred, who treacherously began an affair with the king's wife. Returning in wrath, Arthur defeated Modred, who promptly mustered an army of Saxons. In the ensuing battle, Modred was slain by his own troops. Arthur, mortally wounded, was borne to the Fortunate Island. The kingdom then fell into turmoil, as Modred's two sons fought one another for the crown. They were eventually destroyed by Constantine, another nephew of Arthur, who in turn was overthrown by his kinsman Conan. Merlin ended this survey of recent history (or, rather, pseudo-history) by noting that Conan was still in power, though his rule was 'weak and witless'.

This conversation between Merlin and Taliesin was interrupted by the news that a new spring had appeared at the base of a nearby mountain. When Merlin went to drink from it, he found that his madness was miraculously gone. He felt like his old self again. After praising God, he asked Taliesin to explain how the waters of the spring had cured him. This allows the narrative to move off into another long digression, with Taliesin describing a number of rivers, lakes and springs that were reputed to possess healing powers. People came to see the new spring for themselves and to congratulate Merlin on his return to sanity. Some came from his own country in Wales to ask him to return and resume his kingship, but he told them he preferred to remain in the North 'under the green leaves of Calidon'. At that moment, a flock of birds flew overhead in an unusual formation, and Merlin was asked to explain how this could happen. Another digression into the wonders of nature then follows – a list of various birds and their habits – until the main narrative resumes with the sudden appearance of a madman. This fellow was very noisy and threatening but was quickly caught and restrained. Merlin recognised him at once as Maeldin, a friend from his own younger days in Wales. 'At that time,' Merlin explained, 'he was a strong handsome soldier, in whom the nobility of royal descent was patent.' He added that Maeldin's madness had been caused by eating poisoned apples originally intended for Merlin himself. The fruit had been placed beside a spring 'in the high mountains of Arwystli' by a woman whom Merlin had loved and discarded. Needless to say, as soon as Maeldin drank from the newly-formed spring in the Forest of Calidon, his madness was instantly cured. Merlin invited him to remain in the woods as his companion 'in the service of the Lord', an offer that was eagerly accepted. Taliesin then said that he, too, would stay. The recently widowed Ganieda also decided to remain in the woods. There she dwelt with her brother in the hall she herself had provided for him. She even began to utter prophecies of her own. In one of these she had consecutive visions of the city of Lincoln being besieged, of four men engaging in combat, of two stars fighting wild beasts, of famine striking Britain and, lastly, of terrible depredations wreaked by Norman invaders. Merlin, who witnessed this prophecy, congratulated his sister on her new-found talent, adding that the gift of foresight had now passed from him to her. With that, the story comes to an end.

The Merlin of *VM* is clearly not a duplicate of his namesake in *HRB*. One of the main differences between them is that the former migrates to northern Britain while the latter remains in Wales and the South. Many of Geoffrey's readers, whether in the twelfth century or later, may have wondered why this major geographical shift occurred. Those with a broad experience of literature might have recognised Rodarch, king of the Cumbrians, as a namesake of Roderc, 'king of the Rock of Clyde', who appears in a *vita* or Life of Saint Columba written c.700 by Abbot Adomnán of Iona. Roderc is depicted by Adomnán as Columba's contemporary in the late sixth century.[13] Columba had founded a monastery on Iona in 565 and died there forty-two years later. Adomnán's *vita* used eyewitness testimony and is accepted by modern historians as a generally reliable historical source. There is thus no reason to doubt that a king called Roderc really did rule at Clyde Rock, now the site of Dumbarton Castle, in the late 500s. A medieval reader of *VM* who was also acquainted with the story of Columba would have deduced that Geoffrey's Rodarch and Adomnán's Roderc were one and the same. Had this same reader been familiar with Welsh literature he or she would have realised that the identification was absolutely secure, for the same king appears as *Rhydderch* (pronounced 'Hrutherkh') in half a dozen poems from which Geoffrey obtained material for his depiction of Merlin. The primary geographical context of these poems is northern Britain, a setting borrowed for *VM* but not for *HRB*. The Welsh poems also provided Geoffrey with additional material on political prophecy. Their influence can be seen in both of his visualisations of Merlin: the boy-wizard of southern Britain and the crazed fugitive of the North, each of whom possesses prophetic power. Geoffrey's reasons for creating this dual character are closely bound up with the nature of his sources which included not only the Welsh poems but other texts that became available to him during the course of his career. The next chapter will consider these sources and will examine how Geoffrey employed them.

2

MYRDDIN WYLLT

The Myrddin poems

Geoffrey of Monmouth was born in Wales in the first decade of the twelfth century. How much of his early life was spent there is unknown. By the time he reached his early thirties he was living in Oxford as a non-ordained member of a religious community attached to a church. It is likely that he returned to Wales on a number of occasions. Monmouth, his presumed birthplace, lay in the hands of Breton lords who had arrived in the wake of the Norman invasion of England in 1066. Geoffrey's own family background may therefore have been Breton and French-speaking.[1] The sources from which he obtained his information on early British history are hard to identify. He was evidently familiar with the ninth-century *Historia Brittonum*, which included the Ambrosius-Vortigern story, but the extent of his knowledge of other texts from Wales is unknown. Much mystery surrounds his claim in *HRB* that he used an ancient book written in the native British tongue. How old this book really was, what it contained and whether it even existed are unanswerable questions. Nevertheless, we can be fairly sure that he acquired various pieces of Welsh historical and legendary lore during his early life, especially during his time in Wales. At some point he learned of an enigmatic figure called Myrddin, a famous prophet who featured in the Welsh poems mentioned at the end of the previous chapter. These were supposedly Myrddin's own compositions and contained a mixture of prophecy and autobiography. Geoffrey used this same Myrddin as the template for his own creation Merlin, the seer of *Prophetiae Merlini* and *HRB* who reappeared in *VM* as a forest-dwelling madman. At no point did Geoffrey explain why he changed the name Myrddin (pronounced 'Mir-thin') to Merlin but it may have been due to the former's slight similarity to the French word *merde*, a slang term for excrement. An additional possibility is that the name Merlin was not invented by Geoffrey but merely borrowed by him from a story that already included it. This seems rather unlikely, given the absence of any conclusively earlier instances.[2]

The Merlin of *HRB* owes little to the Myrddin of Welsh tradition and far more to Geoffrey's creativity as an author. In *VM*, however, we do catch glimpses of Myrddin and of the contents of the poems attributed to him. The poems are 'pre-Galfridian' – a term based on the Latin form of Geoffrey's name – because they existed before the publication of his works. The same term encompasses his known sources of information, such as *HB*, as well as other early material on the Arthurian legends and on the Matter of Britain. Some material can be described as pre-Galfridian even when the oldest manuscript in which it survives was written after the publication of Geoffrey's writings, because the material itself can be traced back to before c.1130. This is evidently the case with the Myrddin poems. Although none is preserved in a manuscript older than the thirteenth, fourteenth or fifteenth centuries, detailed analysis has shown that some portions are based on earlier compositions from the tenth century or possibly even the ninth.[3] The poems have individual titles: *Yr Afallennau* ('The Apple Trees'), *Yr Oianau* ('The Greetings'), *Ymddiddan Myrddin a Thaliesin* ('Dialogue of Myrddin and Taliesin'), *Cyfoesi Myrddin a Gwenddydd ei Chwaer* ('Conversation of Myrddin and his Sister Gwenddydd'), *Gwasgargerdd Fyrddin yn y Bedd* ('Separation-Song of Myrddin in the Grave') and *Peirian Vaban* ('Commanding Youth'). *Yr Afallennau*, *Yr Oianau* and the *Ymddiddan* are preserved in 'The Black Book of Carmarthen', a manuscript written c.1250 and formerly housed at Carmarthen Priory.[4] The Black Book gets its name from the dark binding that encased its contents. In addition to the Myrddin material, it contains several other poems and also a number of 'triads' or bardic mnemonics. Versions of the *Cyfoesi*, the *Gwasgargerdd* and *Peirian Vaban* are preserved in other texts such as 'The Red Book of Hergest' (c.1400) and 'The White Book of Rhydderch' (fourteenth century), as are variants of the Black Book items. All the Myrddin poems incorporate a first-person narrative in which the speaker is Myrddin himself. They contain a mix of biographical story and political prophecy, the former comprising the central character's allusions to his own life, the latter foretelling important events. The biographical element gives what is essentially a Welsh account of the Merlin legend, in a version older than Geoffrey's and unaccompanied by the trappings of Arthuriana. How much older is a question that will be addressed later in this chapter. In the meantime, our attention turns to the contents of the poems. Their narratives are linked by a number of common themes, one of which is a great battle in which Myrddin participated and from which he fled in madness. This was fought at Arfderydd, a place clearly located not in Wales but in northern Britain. In the poems, the battle is described as a scene of terrible slaughter. So terrible, in fact, that it overthrew Myrddin's mind, compelling him to flee in madness to the Forest of Celyddon (*Coed Celyddon*). There he became a solitary fugitive, living among the woodland creatures. He acquired the power of prophecy, this being a major theme in the poems along-side the tragic tale of his life. In the following summaries, the northern element in each poem is identified, thus drawing together the strands of Myrddin's biography or back-story as perceived in medieval Wales.

Yr Afallennau is a poem of ten stanzas addressed to apple trees. Myrddin tells the trees that he was once a warrior who fought for a king called Gwenddolau. The latter perished in the battle of Arfderydd where the carnage was so great that Myrddin went mad with grief. Fleeing from the field of slaughter, Myrddin eventually reached the Forest of Celyddon. There he dwells in solitude as a wild man of the woods, enduring many hardships while trying to hide from a king called Rhydderch Hael who has sent men to hunt him down. He is especially fearful of Gwasawg, one of Rhydderch's associates, who is full of anger towards him. In addition to these troubles, Myrddin must also bear a burden of guilt for causing the death of Gwenddydd's son, who is otherwise unnamed. Myrddin bemoans the fact that Gwennddydd, a woman who had formerly shown affection to him, now shuns him ('she loves me not and she welcomes me not'). She is not here identified as his sister but we know from another poem that this is the connection between them. He also regrets losing the companionship of a slender maiden with whom he used to sit beneath an apple tree. The prophecies in this poem include one relating to northern Britain ('And I will prophesy battle in Pictland, defending their borders with the men of Dublin') but the rest refer to conflict between the Welsh and English. In one of these, Myrddin fore-sees the Welsh defeat at Machafwy Vale, a real battle fought in 1198, thus giving a useful clue as to when the poem in its present form was composed.

In *Yr Oianau*, each stanza begins with Myrddin's greeting to a small pig whom he cherishes as a woodland companion. He tells the animal that they are both in danger of being caught by King Rhydderch's hunters. He also points out that Rhydderch's comfortable life is in stark contrast with his own. Gwenddolau, the king whom Myrddin once served, is remembered fondly as the most gener-ous of all the kings of northern Britain. This is as much as we learn from this poem of Myrddin's life in the North. The remainder is mostly concerned with prophecies relating to Wales, some of which refer to actual events of the twelfth century and possibly of the thirteenth.

Gwenddolau is not mentioned in the *Ymddiddan*, even though the battle of Arfderydd takes up the second half of the poem. Nor is there any reference to Rhydderch Hael or his vengeful henchman Gwasawg. The first half deals with a conflict in Wales – a raid on the southern kingdom of Dyfed by King Maelgwn of Gwynedd. This is not prophesied as a future event but as one already witnessed by Myrddin and Taliesin. Maelgwn was a historical figure who died in 547, so the 'dialogue' of the poem's title is clearly taking place around the middle of the sixth century. The dialogue itself takes the form of a commentary by Myrddin and Taliesin, each speaking in turn. In their alternating account of Maelgwn's raid they name various warriors, most of whom are otherwise unknown. Halfway through the poem, while Taliesin is speaking, the focus switches quite abruptly to the battle of Arfderydd, which lies in the future. Both Taliesin and Myrddin receive prophetic visions of the carnage that will ensue in the northern battle. Some of its participants are mentioned: the unnamed 'seven sons of Eliffer' and a warrior called Cynfelyn. In the poem's final stanza, Myrddin speaks of the battle as if it has already been fought, informing Taliesin that 'seven score generous nobles went mad; in the Forest of Celyddon they ended'.

The nature of Myrddin's relationship with Gwenddydd, the woman mentioned in *Yr Afallennau*, is made clear in the *Cyfoesi* where she is identified as his sister. The 'conversation' in the title is actually a series of prophecies given by Myrddin in answer to questions posed by Gwenddydd. She asks him about political events of the recent past – such as the death of his patron Gwenddolau in the slaughter at Arfderydd – and those of the distant future. He mentions three other kings of the North Britons – Rhydderch Hael, Morgant the Great and Urien Rheged – but the rest of his prophecies concern Wales. He lists the rulers of the North Welsh kingdom of Gwynedd, naming each in sequence from the sixth century to the twelfth, before alluding to dealings between the Welsh and the Norman rulers of England. The prophetic element then turns to the legendary hero Cadwaladr who will 'scatter the English to the sea's edge'. In this poem, there is no hint of the ill-feeling shown by Gwenddydd towards Myrddin in *Yr Afallennau*. Here, she is on friendly terms with him and expresses a fear that his solitary existence in the forest is taking a heavy toll on his mind and body. From her we learn the names of Myrddin's father (Morfryn) and of his four brothers (Morgenau, Morial, Mordaf and Morien). Throughout the poem she addresses him as 'Llallawg' and, in one stanza, uses the diminutive form Llallogan ('Little Llallawg'). The significance of these names will be discussed at the end of this chapter.

Like the *Cyfoesi*, the *Gwasgargerdd* or 'Separation-Song' is mostly a series of prophecies uttered by Myrddin. However, in this instance he is dead and buried, speaking from the grave. He foresees a period of hardship and woe for the Welsh, who will languish under the Anglo-Norman yoke: 'A world there will be in which the love-tryst will end; the young will fail in the face of misery; in May cuckoos will die of cold.' However, the final prophecy is more optimistic: 'Battle there will be on the River Byrri and the Britons [i.e. Welsh] will overcome. The men of Gower will perform deeds of valour.' There is little of a North British back-story in this poem, but Myrddin's sister Gwenddydd is mentioned at the end, as is the vengeful Gwasawg. These two characters also appear in *Peirian Vaban*, a poem preserved in a manuscript of the fifteenth century, which likewise mentions the northern kings Rhydderch and Gwenddolau. However, the key figure in *Peirian Vaban* is Áedán, son of Gabrán, a powerful king of the Scots in the late sixth century. Áedán's power-base lay in Dál Riata, a large maritime region encompassing Gaelic-speaking groups in north-west Britain and north-east Ireland. In the poem, he brings an army across 'the broad sea' to fight a battle either against or in alliance with Rhydderch Hael. The battle is called the Devil's Encounter and is usually assumed to be the one at Arfderydd where Myrddin's patron Gwenddolau was killed. Myrddin himself is mentioned in the third stanza:

> 'Myrddin son of Morfryn was a white hawk
> when the fierce battle would be fought,
> when there would be joyous death, when there would be a broken
> shoulder,
> when there would be heart's blood before he would be put to flight.
> Because of the memory of Gwenddolau and his companions,
> woe to me for my death – how slowly it comes.'[5]

This is one of the clearest portrayals of Myrddin as a warrior. The last two lines of the stanza clearly identify him as the narrator of the entire poem. In the next stanza, he refers to the wild state that he adopts after fleeing from the battle and recalls with regret the luxuries of his former life:

> 'There was a time when I sat in a court;
> my covering was red and purple.
> And today neither my cheek nor my body is fair;
> for a comely maiden [it is] easy to spare me.
> I call upon Christ; my cry will be heard.
> May the gates of heaven be open for me.'[6]

The fifth stanza refers to 'the death of my brothers and Gwenddolau', together with four other men whose names are not elsewhere associated with the battle

of Arfderydd: Llewelyn, Gwgon, Einion and Rhiwallon. Llewelyn and Einion
are names more often associated with people in Wales rather than in northern
Britain and were probably added quite arbitrarily by the Welsh poet. It is possible, of course, that the entire poem is not about Arfderydd at all and that the
Devil's Encounter is a different battle – whether historical or legendary – in
which Áedán mac Gabráin took part.[7] The 'commanding youth' of the title is a
young warrior who, with Myrddin's encouragement, is about to go to the battle.

Taken together, the references to northern Britain in the Myrddin poems go
some way to providing the biography of a forest-dwelling prophet who had fled
in madness from the battlefield of Arfderydd. To what extent this material
constitutes the surviving remnant of an older story is uncertain. None of the
poems survives in a manuscript written before 1100. Some parts might preserve
fragments of verses composed in the tenth century or earlier, but the manuscripts are too late to enable a more precise dating. One observation that can
however be made is that the poems in the oldest manuscripts seem to contain
more of the biographical North British element than those in manuscripts of
later provenance.[8] Whether the Myrddin of the poems is real rather than
fictional is, of course, another matter altogether.

Geoffrey, Myrddin and Carmarthen

Even from the brief descriptions given above, it is clear that the contents of the
Myrddin poems were borrowed extensively by Geoffrey of Monmouth. The
most obvious borrowing was the theme of political prophecy, this being encountered in all three of his works featuring Merlin. Another borrowing was the
fugitive in the northern woods, a figure copied directly from the poems to reappear in *Vita Merlini* with little alteration. Geoffrey also used much of the
geographical and political context that forms a setting for the poems: the Forest
of Celyddon (*Silva Calidonis* in *VM*), King Rhydderch (*Rodarchus*), King
Gwenddolau (*Guennolous*) and a ferocious northern battle (described in *VM*
but unnamed). Other borrowed themes include the madness that afflicts the
central character, his relationship with his sister Gwenddydd (*Ganieda* in *VM*),
Taliesin (*Telgesinus*) and the significance of apples and apple-trees.

Aside from this liberal copying, Geoffrey took other material from the Welsh
poems but added particular twists of his own, sometimes forging new connections between key characters. Thus, in *VM*, Merlin's sister Ganieda is the wife of
King Rodarch, whereas Gwenddydd's husband is not named in the Myrddin
poetry and she is not explicitly connected with Rhydderch Hael. Likewise, we

see Merlin and Guennolous on opposite sides of the great battle at the beginning of *VM*, with Rodarch and Merlin as allies. This reverses the relationships between Myrddin, Gwenddolau and Rhydderch in the poems, which portray the first two as foes of the third. Geoffrey does, however, retain a separate Welsh tradition of hostility between Gwenddolau – his 'Scottish' king Guennolous – and the figure whose name he Latinises as *Peredurus*. The original Welsh version of this name is 'Peredur' and, although he is absent from the Myrddin poems, one line of the *Ymddiddan* does make an anonymous reference to a North British ruler whom we know from other sources was a bearer of this name. More will be said of this Peredur in Chapter 4. Some of Geoffrey's other ideas sprang from his own imagination. Thus, in *VM*, Merlin is a king in his own right – the ruler of Dyfed – and has a wife (*Guendoloena*). The Myrddin of the poems is simply a soldier in the service of King Gwenddolau. His wife – if he had one – is not mentioned.

The six poems were not Geoffrey's only sources of information on Myrddin. In *HRB*, he related how King Vortigern's men went in search of a fatherless youth, a quest that brought them to Carmarthen where they eventually found Merlin. At that time, the boy was living in a convent. He was of Welsh royal blood, the son of a Dyfed princess, upon whom he had been sired by a demon. He did not therefore have a real, human father and, as far as Vortigern's henchmen were concerned, was therefore fatherless. From his demon parent he had acquired the supernatural powers that would save him from being sacrificed at Vortigern's fortress. Geoffrey called the boy Merlin and equated him with the famed fifth-century warlord Ambrosius Aurelianus whose story he already knew from *Historia Brittonum*. In *HB*, however, Vortigern's men discover the fatherless youth Ambrosius in Glamorgan in South Wales. The link between Ambrosius and Carmarthen was actually Geoffrey's own invention but he did not choose the place randomly or by chance. Indeed, Carmarthen's own folklore probably gave him his first encounter with Myrddin. According to local legend, the name Carmarthen means 'Myrddin's Fort' (Welsh: *Caerfyrddin*, with 'm' softening to 'f'), having been named from a famous seer who is said to have dwelt there. The antiquity of this tradition is unknown but it may have originated as far back as the sixth century to explain how the place-name arose.[9] It is, in fact, a false etymology, for *Caerfyrddin* does not derive from a personal name at all. It originally referred to a Roman fort established in the first century AD. The Romans called their stronghold *Moridunum* or *Maridunum*, Latinising a native British name that was probably something like *Moridunon*, 'sea-fortress'.[10] After the end of Roman rule in the fifth century, the native Brittonic language underwent significant changes and, by c.600, local people had shortened the place-name to *Merdin* or *Myrdin*. To this they subsequently added the prefix *caer*, 'fort', being unaware that the -*din* suffix already preserved the same meaning. What happened next is uncertain but it seems likely that the *caer* in question was assumed to have been the stronghold of an ancient hero whose name it commemorated. The same figure was duly given the name *Myrddin* and may have been imagined as a seer who had founded Carmarthen in some remote past. It seems that this foundation-legend did not develop much further but, in the twelfth century, it reached the ears of Geoffrey of Monmouth. The town's eponymous founder was a ready-made figure with whom Geoffrey could merge the fatherless youth Ambrosius of *Historia Brittonum*. He borrowed Myrddin's name, changed it to 'Merlin' and created an entirely new character. Geoffrey himself devised false etymology of the Carmarthen kind to explain the name of Caerleon in South Wales. Caerleon means 'Fort of the Legion' but, in *HRB*, it becomes the *caer* of King Lleon, a mythical figure and eponymous founder whom Geoffrey simply invented.

There is, it should be said, a counter-argument, an alternative to the conventional view that Myrddin is nothing more than a fictional eponym. It sees him as a North British figure who was already known as Myrddin long before his story came to Wales. It proposes that he originally had no connection with Carmarthen, seeing the town's foundation-legend as a later development created after stories about him came down from the North.[11] Support for this argument comes from the absence of a developed version of the legend in Carmarthen's own traditions which say surprisingly little about Myrddin. Indeed, a medieval alternative to the town's conventional etymology appears in an old Welsh tale that certainly pre-dates *HRB*. This tells how the famed Maxen Wledic, a legendary hero based partly on the fourth-century Roman general Magnus Maximus, employed a *myrdd* ('myriad') of men to build Carmarthen, which thus acquired its Welsh name Caerfyrddin (*caer* + *myrdd*).[12] What the counter-argument struggles to explain is the absence of the name Myrddin in an independent North British version of the Merlin legend which refers instead to a character called Lailoken. As we shall see in the next chapter, Lailoken is almost certainly the 'Merlin-archetype', the historical figure at the root of the legend. The northern version makes no mention of Myrddin, in spite of the fact that its surviving manuscripts recognise Lailoken and Merlin as being one and the same. Supporters of the counter-argument must also explain a strange coincidence required by their theory: the creation of the name *Myrddin* in two different places, with two different meanings. In other words, how did a place-name suffix at Carmarthen arise independently as a personal name in faraway northern Britain? The most rational answer is that the odds against such a coincidence are indeed too high, and that the name Myrddin must therefore have arisen in one place only – at Carmarthen, where it provided a spurious etymology. This remains the conventional view among scholars. It removes any need to imagine that Lailoken of the North was already known as 'Myrddin' before his story migrated to Wales.

Why, we might ask, did Geoffrey present his readers with two quite different Merlins? The answer surely lies in the timing of his access to – or his awareness of – the two Welsh strands of the Myrddin legend. The undeveloped Carmarthen foundation-story probably came to him via oral folklore in Dyfed, with Ambrosius coming via the Vortigern legend in *Historia Brittonum*. These sources almost certainly provided him with his basic material for the new character of Merlin. Later, but perhaps only a few years after the publication of *HRB*, he encountered another Welsh Myrddin – the fugitive from the battle of Arfderydd – who eventually became the main character in *VM*. In later Welsh tradition the northern Myrddin of the poems was known as Myrddin Wyllt ('Wild Myrddin'), a name apparently coined by the sixteenth-century chronicler Elis Gruffudd. Reconciling this forest-dwelling seer with his own creation Merlin Ambrosius required some juggling on Geoffrey's part and the result was far from satisfactory. Geography posed less of a problem for him than chronology, for the Myrddin poetry makes a number of references to places in Wales. It was relatively straightforward for Geoffrey to depict *VM*'s Merlin as a Welshman who travelled to the North. However, *HRB*'s young wizard was a contemporary of Vortigern in the mid-fifth century, whereas the wild fugitive of the poems was clearly around in the late sixth. In *VM*, Geoffrey attempted to bridge this chronological discrepancy by giving Merlin an extraordinarily long life of more than 120 years, so that his career spanned both the fifth and sixth centuries. Not all of Geoffrey's contemporaries found this acceptable, even for a character of semi-supernatural birth. Some regarded the gap between the two Merlins as all too visible and, as we shall see in Chapter 6, they began to devise their own solutions.

Myrddin and political prophecy

We have seen that the legend of Myrddin pre-dates Geoffrey of Monmouth by several centuries, having almost certainly sprung from folklore at Carmarthen in the kingdom of Dyfed. There is little doubt that this first Myrddin was a

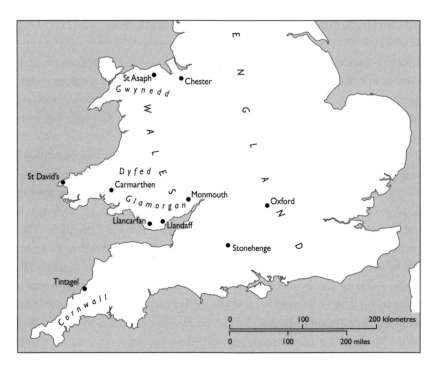

Map 1 Wales and the Merlin legend

fictional character. Originating in legend as an eponym to explain the name of the town, he was presumably portrayed at some point as a famous local seer.[13] We then see this prophetic theme developed more fully in the Myrddin poems, albeit with the primary geographical setting now transferred from Wales to a far northern land. Casting a legendary figure as a prophet was a fairly common tactic in early medieval storytelling. In Welsh tradition, moreover, political prophecy played an important role in defining a sense of national identity, especially with regard to the long struggle against English domination. It can be traced back to the end of Roman Britain in the fifth century, when power reverted to native elites as the imperial administration collapsed. Anglo-Saxon immigrants from across the North Sea – the ancestors of the English – took advantage of the upheaval to establish small kingdoms of their own. Their subsequent rapid expansion caused dismay among some, though by no means all, of the indigenous Britons. Native interests were vested in the political leaders of the day, among them the historical Vortigern, but none of these individuals was capable of halting the Anglo-Saxon advance. Even when they came together as a national council, supposedly to organise an effective defence, the

Britons allowed temporary unity to give way to petty rivalry. In despair, some began to see Anglo-Saxon domination as inevitable, or even as a punishment sent by God. Subsequent history seemed to confirm this pessimistic view and, by c.800, British-ruled territory had been reduced to three areas on the western periphery: Wales, Cornwall and Clydesdale. In Wales, people began to look in hope towards a brighter future where strong leaders might yet emerge to win back the lost lands. Out of this optimism came the literature of political prophecy, a genre vividly represented by the tale of two dragons fighting beneath Vortigern's castle.[14] In this famous story, recounted by the Welsh author of *Historia Brittonum* in the early ninth century, the young seer Ambrosius – not yet transformed into Geoffrey's Merlin – identified the red dragon as the Britons and the white as their Saxon foes. Ambrosius interpreted the fight between these creatures as the vision of a future in which 'our people will arise and valiantly throw the English people across the sea'.[15] A hundred years after the publication of *HB*, probably around the year 940, another Welsh writer produced a long poem called *Armes Prydein Vawr*, 'The Great Prophecy of Britain', which envisaged a time when the English would be overwhelmingly defeated by a grand alliance of Celtic natives and Viking settlers. The poem is indeed 'great' for it runs to almost 200 lines. Near the beginning we come across a reference to Myrddin:

> Myrddin prophesies – they will meet
> in Aber Peryddon agents of a Great King,
> and though it be not in the same way, they will lament death.[16]

In the first line, 'they' are the Celtic and Scandinavian forces whom the poet hopes will join together in an anti-English coalition. The poem's first stanza lists them individually: Welsh, Irish, Scots, Cornish, Clyde Britons and Dublin Vikings. *Aber Peryddon*, 'mouth of the River Peryddon', is evidently the site of a battle between these allies and the forces of an unnamed Great King. The latter is almost certainly Athelstan of Wessex (reigned 924–39) while the River Peryddon, although unidentified, seems to be in South Wales.[17] Myrddin is here cast solely as a prophet rather than as a forest-dwelling wild man. If the reference to him is part of the original tenth-century poem, we should assume that he was already a figure of legend whose prophetic powers were so renowned that he could be employed without further explanation as an authoritative mouthpiece for Welsh political hopes.[18] Unfortunately, there is no evidence that the reference is not a later interpolation.

Myrddin as bard

In the Welsh poems associated with him, Myrddin frequently takes the role of narrator, thus giving the narrative an autobiographical tone. The clear implication is that he is also the composer, hence the belief among later Welsh poets that he was a member of their profession. This accounts for his appearance in a 'triad' listing the three premier bards of Britain, a triad being a type of text in which objects sharing a common attribute are grouped in threes. Triads were a popular device in medieval Celtic literature from Ireland and Wales and are thought to have originated as mnemonic aids for poets and storytellers.[19] In an age when much literature was preserved and disseminated orally rather than in written form, triads assisted in the retrieval from memory of poems and tales on specific topics. A large number of triads, each one carefully memorised, served a useful purpose as a subject index of oral literature. Eventually, the triad seems to have become a literary form in its own right, to be recited like a single stanza of poetry. Triads were gathered together into collections and some of these have survived. In Wales, the oldest collection is contained in 'Peniarth 16', a manuscript of the second half of the thirteenth century. This includes some forty-two triads, a little under half of the total known from Wales. Most are very brief, simply listing three items under a subject header, but others give additional detail explaining a context that would otherwise be quite obscure. Indeed, one frustrating aspect of the Welsh triads is that some of them refer to things – people, places, events or whatever – that are not mentioned elsewhere. Such unique references are undoubtedly the ghostly imprints of tales and poems that have not themselves survived. A similar observation can be made of those triads which mention familiar or recognisable things in contexts not described elsewhere but which, we can assume, were once present in texts that are now lost.

Although apparently a well-known figure in Welsh tradition, Myrddin appears in only one triad: 'Three Principal Bards of the Island of Britain: Myrddin, son of Morfryn, Myrddin Emrys and Taliesin'. A variant appears as 'Three Skilful Bards of Arthur's Court' but 'Three Principal Bards' is regarded as the older heading.[20] Both versions, in any case, belong to the post-Galfridian era when a distinction could be made between the two Merlins, namely Merlin Ambrosius (Myrddin Emrys) of *HRB* and the Wild Merlin (Myrddin Wyllt, son of Morfryn) of earlier Welsh tradition.[21] It is interesting to note, in the context of this triad, that a tale recorded in the sixteenth century attempts to merge the three bards as one by having Myrddin Emrys reincarnated first as Taliesin, then as Myrddin son of Morfryn.[22]

Son of Morfryn

The triad of the Three Principal Bards is not the only medieval Welsh text in which Myrddin is identified as a composer of verse. Among the verses of *Y Gododdin*, a work of uncertain date discussed in more detail below, one line seemingly refers to Myrddin's 'fair song'. From the twelfth century onwards, this theme was echoed in the works of later bards. A stray anonymous verse from the late 1400s, scribbled in a margin of the Black Book of Carmarthen, provides an illustrative example. It gives a nod to the North British Myrddin of the poems, the crazed seer who lived in a forest with a piglet as his companion:

> Myrddin the Wild, with a repulsive and mad sickness,
> son of Morfryn, of doubtful ancient status[?],
> sang a very similar, exceedingly frivolous poem
> long ago in the wood from his enclosure
> to his nasty, strange little pig
> and his birch tree, like a fool.[23]

Welsh tradition grouped Myrddin alongside Taliesin and Aneirin as one of the Cynfeirdd or 'Elder Bards' who created the earliest heroic verse in the sixth century.[24] All three, although revered in medieval Wales, were chiefly associated in Welsh tradition with the Old North. Some modern scholars have accepted Myrddin as a historical Elder Bard, seeing his poetic ability as part of the original or 'real' story at the root of the Merlin legend. Thus, just as the historical Taliesin is commonly assumed to have been the real bard of King Urien of Rheged, so the historical Myrddin or 'Merlin-archetype' is seen as serving Gwenddolau in a similar role.[25] The main difference between the two is that a small number of the poems traditionally attributed to Taliesin are often seen as genuine sixth-century compositions, whereas no similar claim can reasonably be made for the Myrddin poems. Some portions of the latter may, as previously noted, be as old as the ninth century but we should be wary of pushing this date any further back. However, late composition is not fatal to a belief that the Myrddin poetry incorporates older traditions in which the historical Merlin-archetype was indeed depicted as Gwenddolau's personal bard or court-poet. Early medieval kings often had bards in their entourage, employing them in what might be described in modern parlance as a 'public relations' role. The bard was expected to compose and recite panegyric verses highlighting the king's achievements in battle or praising his generosity towards loyal henchmen.[26] A king who rewarded his bard with lavish gifts would be praised as a patron of poetry. We may note the following line from *The Dialogue of Gwyddno Garanhir and Gwyn ap Nudd*, a poem from the Black Book of Carmarthen: 'I was present where Gwenddolau was slain, the son of Ceidio, pillar of songs.'[27]

Although this line may have been composed hundreds of years after Gwenddolau's death, it is more than likely that he did have a personal bard, from whom he would have expected to hear recitations of praise-poetry in the royal hall. It may be tempting to identify this bard as the Merlin-archetype and to see traces of his work in the later Welsh poems. Unfortunately, we cannot pursue such a suggestion very far, beyond acknowledging it as a possibility.[28] What we can believe with more confidence is that Gwenddolau's fall at Arfderydd would have become the subject of an elegy, perhaps even a composition by a personal bard who had survived the slaughter. No such poem is known, so perhaps there was nobody left to sing it or to hear it sung in the wake of the battle. Nonetheless, four lines of the poem *Yr Oianau* capture the sentiment that would probably have been expressed:

> 'I saw Gwenddolau on the track of the kings,
> collecting booty from every border.
> Now indeed he lies still under the red earth:
> the chief of the kings of the North, greatest in generosity.'

It has been suggested that these lines look as if they were once part of an actual elegy.[29] If such an elegy existed, it need not have been a contemporary *marwnad* ('death-song') from sixth-century northern Britain. It could have been composed much later, in eighth- or ninth-century Wales, at a time when tales of famous North British kings were widely popular. A number of poems commemorating Urien Rheged originated in this way, as Welsh compositions of the 800s.[30] Perhaps a *marwnad* for the long-dead Gwenddolau was indeed composed at the same time?

The idea that Gwenddolau's bard was the historical Merlin-archetype represented by the fictional Myrddin of the poems is actually quite hard to sustain. Although regarded by later Welsh tradition as one of the Elder Bards, he is notably absent from the only known list of them. This appears in *Historia Brittonum*, in a section relating to northern events of the sixth century: 'Then Talhaearn, father of inspiration, was famed in poetry; and Aneirin and Taliesin and

Bluchbard and Cian – known as 'Wheat of Song' – were all simultaneously famed in British verse.'[31]

Poems attributed to Aneirin and Taliesin have survived but nothing composed by Talhaearn, Bluchbard or Cian is known today. Nevertheless, all five were evidently recognised in Wales as the greatest bards of the Old North. If Myrddin had been accorded equal status, whether in early northern tradition or among the poets of ninth-century Wales, he would surely have appeared in the same list. His absence suggests that his elevation to the rank of Elder Bard was a later development, coming after the Myrddin poems were composed and after the publication of *HB*, in a period when he was retrospectively identified as a creator of ancient verse. Present-day proponents of the 'Bard Myrddin' idea might point out, quite rightly, that the *HB* list of northern poets is unlikely to be complete or definitive. On the other hand, we may note that the list might reasonably be expected to include any poet who was assumed to have fought at the famous battle of Arfderydd. We may also observe that Myrddin undoubtedly became well-known in Wales during the hundred years between the publication of *HB* (c.830) and the composition of *Armes Prydein* (c.940). If he really was a renowned North British poet of the sixth century, then *HB*'s author would already have been aware of his existence and would have added him to the list of Elder Bards. Myrddin's absence suggests that his casting as a bard was indeed a later development or afterthought, devised long after the Myrddin poems were composed in Wales and prompted by their first-person perspective.

Clas Merdin

One of the most important collections of early Welsh lore is *Llyfr Gwyn Rhydderch*, the White Book of Rhydderch, a manuscript written in the fourteenth century. Among its contents are the mythological stories known as the Four Branches of the Mabinogi, together with the Arthurian tales *Peredur* and *Culhwch and Olwen*, both of which may have pre-Galfridian origins.[32] Another item from the White Book, also dated to the period before c.1130, is *The Names of the Island of Britain*, a short triad that mentions Myrddin (under the alternative spelling 'Merdin'):

'The first name that was upon this island before it was seized or settled: *Clas Merdin*. And after it was seized and settled: "The Honey Island". And after it was conquered by Prydain, son of Aedd the Great, the name "The Island of Britain" was given to it.'[33]

The Welsh word *clas* is usually translated as 'cloister' or 'precinct'. Such meanings often have a religious connotation, calling to mind a monastic community, but the word can also simply refer to an enclosure. Why the island of Britain should be regarded as Myrddin's *clas* is a question that has vexed the minds of Celtic scholars for a very long time. In the nineteenth century, Sir John Rhys considered this triad to be 'the echo of an ancient notion'.[34] It may be connected with the original meaning of the name Myrddin or Merdin if, as is generally accepted, this derives ultimately from *Moridunum*, the ancient name of Carmarthen. As we have seen, Latin *Moridunum* and its presumed native precursor *Moridunon* both mean 'sea-fortress'. The later personification *Merdin* or *Myrddin* may, in local folklore, have been seen as a supernatural protector of the entire coastline of Britain. In this sense, the *clas* of Merdin would indeed be sacred, like a monastic precinct, being an enchanted island (Britain) protected by magical defences.[35] If Carmarthen's legendary founder was indeed elevated to the rank of national coastguard, we should not be unduly surprised. Such an idea could have arisen at local level, in the folk-lore of Dyfed, before spreading to other parts of Wales. There is no need to take this further by envisaging Merdin/Myrddin as some kind of pan-British god, a protective deity in the ancient pagan pantheon, or that the original 'sea-fortress' was not Carmarthen but the whole island of Britain itself.[36]

Myrddin in *The Gododdin*

Llyfr Aneirin, the Book of Aneirin, is a Welsh manuscript written in the second half of the thirteenth century. It contains two versions of what appears to be a single poem with the title *Y Gododdin* ('The Gododdin'), the composition of which is attributed to Aneirin.[37] The two versions were written by two different scribes and today are usually designated as the 'A' and 'B' texts. They have a number of features in common, but A has more than twice as many verses. However, B is written in an older form of the Welsh language and was most likely copied from a text of the tenth century, or possibly even the ninth. Nothing in either A or B can be conclusively shown as having been composed before c.800, despite the attribution to Aneirin whom the *Historia Brittonum* identifies as a sixth-century 'Elder Bard'. The main theme of the poem is the slaughter of warriors from Gododdin, a North British kingdom centred on Edinburgh. Many of these warriors are named, in one or more verses which extol their bravery and martial prowess. Some verses refer to a battle at *Catraeth*, seemingly fought against Anglo-Saxon enemies at the end of the sixth century. Others are more vague or allusive, while a few deal with topics only loosely connected to the main narrative. One verse in the A text mentions Myrddin:

> For the battle, a sorrowful disaster,
> for the fair but devastated land,
> for the falling of hair from the head,
> for his warriors, Gwyddien was an eagle.
> Fiercely he protected them with his spear,
> its owner planned its use with skill.
> Morien defended
> the fair song of Myrddin and laid the head
> of a chief of the earth, with support and sanction.
> The equal of three men, for the favour of a maiden, was Bradwen;
> of twelve, Gwenabwy son of Gwen.[38]

This verse was once thought to contain the oldest surviving reference to Myrddin.[39] However, Myrddin is absent from a parallel verse in the older B text, which instead describes Morien fighting heathens, Gaels and Picts.[40] Most specialist scholars now regard the Myrddin reference in A as an interpolation, a later addition that was not part of the original version of *The Gododdin*. It was presumably added at a time when stories about him were already popular among the bards of Wales. Whether this was the northern prophet Myrddin Wyllt or the legendary founder of Carmarthen is hard to say, though the former seems a more likely presence in poetry associated with a North British kingdom. This brings us to the heart of an ongoing debate about the antiquity of *The Gododdin*. As long as the chronology of their composition remains uncertain, none of the verses can be dated to any period before the ninth century. In the case of the Myrddin reference, some scholars have noted that the name is actually written as *Mirdyn* in the manuscript of *Llyfr Aneirin*, an archaic spelling which might possibly suggest an earlier date.[41] However, an alternative is that *Mirdyn* is simply a scribal error for *Myrddin*, with 'i' and 'y' in the wrong places.[42] Another point of debate is the Welsh term *gwenwawd*, translated here as 'fair song' but elsewhere as 'blessed inspiration'.[43] If 'inspiration' is the more accurate meaning, the reference might be to Myrddin's gift of prophecy, an attribute that may not have become attached to him until the Myrddin Wyllt poems were composed. If the poems did not take shape in Wales before c.800, the *Gododdin* reference can hardly be earlier than this date. The idea of Myrddin as a prophet was, however, sufficiently developed for inclusion in the poem *Armes Prydein* of c.940. Based on these two approximate dates, we could tentatively suggest that the line mentioning Myrddin replaced one that didn't at some point between the late eighth century and the early tenth. It is possible that the older line was discarded because it used an archaic idiom that rendered it obscure or unintelligible to a Welsh audience.[44]

Llallogan

Both the Myrddin of the poems and the seer of *Vita Merlini* were depicted as prophets and wild madmen. Each is shown being caught up in a ferocious battle which overthrows his mind, causing him to flee into the depths of a forest where, barely surviving on the edge of subsistence, he lurks in constant fear of capture by armed men. They are clearly the same character in two different guises: a North British 'wild man of the woods' whose name (Myrddin -> Merlin) was borrowed from the foundation-legend of Carmarthen. An important question then arises: is this wild man based on a historical figure, a real fugitive who fled from the sixth-century battle of Arfderydd to dwell alone in the wilderness? In this book, a case is made for the answer being a cautious *Yes*, which in turn raises a second question: do we get a glimpse of him – and a hint of his real name – in the Welsh poems?

Our attention returns to the *Cyfoesi*, where Gwenddydd addresses Myrddin as *llallawg* (*llallawc* in the manuscript) and *llallogan*. The latter seems to be a diminutive of the former, with the suffix *-an* giving a word meaning 'little llallawg'. The context suggests a nickname or pet-name bestowed by Gwenddydd on her brother. In Welsh, *llall* means 'the other', so *llallawg* and *llallogan* are usually interpreted as descriptive names or labels meaning 'the other one'. The sense is of 'another who accompanies', like a friend or close companion. In the context of the relationship between Gwenddydd and Myrddin, the even more specific meaning 'twin sibling' has been proposed, with the 'other' being a companion at birth. Thus, a line from the *Cyfoesi* given in Welsh as *cyfarchaf i'm llallogan fyrddin* has been translated as 'I will greet my twin brother Myrddin'.[45] The diminutive form *llallogan* raises the possibility that Gwenddydd is here gently mocking Myrddin as 'little', perhaps in the sense of his reduced social status in the wild forest, unless she simply means 'my younger brother'.

Alternatively, she might be using *llallogan* as a term of endearment. It is worth observing that the term *llallawg* does not occur in the other Myrddin poems. Indeed, it makes only one other appearance outside the *Cyfoesi*, appearing in a line of ninth-century verse attributed to the bard Llywarch Hen (*ac ni wn ai hi llallawg*, 'and I do not know if she is a twin sister'). In the case of *llallogan*, the single occurrence of this word in the *Cyfoesi* is unique: it is not found anywhere else in medieval Welsh literature. Did the poet who composed the *Cyfoesi* – perhaps in the tenth century – invent this word, or did it already exist in whatever older material he used or recycled? The second of these possibilities seems the likelier. It suggests that the word *llallogan* may have been present in the North British 'back-story' glimpsed behind the Myrddin poems. Moreover, it draws our attention away from Wales to the forests and hills of southern Scotland. There, among traditions preserved in Scottish medieval texts, we encounter a wild, forest-dwelling seer called *Lailoken*. This character has so much in common with Myrddin Wyllt that their respective legends look like branches of the same tree. The close parallels allow us to go even further by identifying Lailoken as the 'Merlin-archetype', the original figure whose story lies at the root of the Merlin legend. In the next chapter, we shall take a much closer look at him.[46]

3

LAILOKEN

The saint of Glasgow

In the early twelfth century, a large part of southern Scotland was ruled as a semi-independent princedom by David, younger brother of the Scottish king, Alexander I. Much of this area had formerly been the heartland of the old kingdom of Strathclyde, the last realm of the native Britons of the North, which had been conquered by the Scots sometime before 1070. At the height of their power, the kings of Strathclyde had ruled an extensive territory stretching from the northern end of Loch Lomond to the Eden Valley south of Carlisle.[1] This large kingdom was known as Cumbria, the land of the *Cumbri* or North Britons. Its rulers and many of their subjects spoke a language similar to Welsh, both languages being descended from a single ancient tongue that had once been spoken across the whole of Britain. Today, the language of the Cumbri is commonly referred to as 'Cumbric'. It no longer survives as a living language and was already in serious decline by c.1113 when David began to rule his princedom.

As a member of the Scottish royal family, David's main language was Gaelic. The Scottish nobles in his entourage – to whom he allocated lordly estates in the old Strathclyde lands – likewise spoke the same language. Gaelic thus became the new medium of power in post-conquest Clydesdale. Cumbric speech quickly became redundant before eventually disappearing altogether by c.1150. However, David's princedom continued to be known by its former name Cumbria, at least for a while. In contemporary Latin documents, David was described as *Cumbrensis regionis princeps*, 'prince of the Cumbrian kingdom'.[2]

One of David's most important acts after taking up his princedom was the revival of a bishopric at Glasgow. This had seemingly lapsed for a number of years, perhaps since the conquest of Strathclyde by his father, Malcolm Canmore, king of Scots from 1058 to 1093. David had spent a considerable part of his youth in Norman England and had acquired many influential contacts there.

He was a close friend of King Henry I, son of William the Conqueror, and the two became kinsmen when Henry married David's sister.[3] In 1114 or thereabouts, David asked the English archbishop of York to appoint a new bishop to Glasgow. The appointee was a man called Michael who may have held the position in name only – he is said to have been buried in northern England and might never even have set foot in Scotland. His tenure of the Glasgow bishopric was brief, being over by 1118. He was succeeded by John, a monk of the Tironensian order, who had previously been David's personal chaplain. John held the bishopric for some thirty years until his death in 1147. He is credited with the founding of Glasgow Cathedral, a stone-built edifice formally consecrated in 1136 by David. By then, the erstwhile prince of Cumbria had been crowned as King David I of Scotland. The cathedral was dedicated to Kentigern, otherwise known as Mungo, the patron saint of Glasgow. According to the traditional story of his life, Kentigern was a Briton from Lothian, born out of wedlock to a royal princess called Teneu or Thaney. He is credited with founding Glasgow's earliest church in the late sixth century, on a site later occupied by the cathedral, where his tomb can still be seen in the lower crypt. Tradition identifies him as the first bishop of Glasgow and as a friend of a certain 'King Rederech' who had a palace nearby.

The main sources of Kentigern's story are two Latin *vitae* or 'Lives', both of them written in the second half of the twelfth century. The earlier of these has not survived intact, being preserved in an incomplete copy containing only a preface and the first eight chapters. Its author's name is unknown but he was evidently not a native of Scotland. In the preface he describes himself as a 'cleric of St Kentigern' – a member of the ecclesiastical community at Glasgow Cathedral – who had previously travelled through many lands. He states that he was commissioned by Bishop Herbert, the successor of Bishop John, to write a *vita* in the style of a recently-published Life of the English saint Cuthbert (died 685) produced at Durham. He implies that no earlier *vitae* of Kentigern were in existence, hence his use of oral testimony as a source of information. The only written source at his disposal, or the only one mentioned by him, was a *codicello* ('little volume') in which Kentigern's miracles were recorded. He gives no further detail about his sources but his primary informants are likely to have been fellow-monks at Glasgow. It is possible that their contributions were supplemented by stories preserved in the oral folklore of Clydesdale.[4] The resulting work, now usually referred to as the 'Fragmentary' or 'Herbertian' Life, was completed c.1150. It was superseded thirty years later by another *vita* that has survived virtually intact. This new work was commissioned by Bishop

Jocelin who held the Glasgow episcopate between 1175 and 1199. Its author, also called Jocelin, was a monk at Furness Abbey in north-west England and a competent writer of hagiography (biographical literature on saints). Such was his talent that he later received a commission from the archbishop of Armagh to write a new Life of St Patrick. His *vita* of Kentigern, completed around the year 1180, is our main source of information on Glasgow's patron saint. In the preface, Jocelin refers to one of his sources as an older Life that the cathedral brethren had been using for some time. He regards this as flawed on a number of grounds, judging its literary quality to be poor and questioning its inclusion of a story he regarded as blasphemous. There is little doubt that he is referring here to the Herbertian Life and that the offensive tale was an account of Kentigern's birth in which Teneu was depicted as a virgin.[5] Although the traditional folk-motif of a fatherless child was not unfamiliar to medieval audiences, its attachment to a Christian saint raised uncomfortable issues that Jocelin felt were better avoided. Needless to say, he left the virgin-birth episode out of his *vita*. As well as the Herbertian Life, he also consulted another which he rediscovered after it was thought to be lost. This text, which he describes as a *codicilus*, was probably the same 'little volume' of miracles that the Herbertian author had used thirty years earlier. Jocelin notes that it was written in a 'Scottic style', by which he presumably meant that its language was Latin but with characteristics that looked odd to a non-Scot such as himself. It contained 'uncouth diction' and a number of grammatical errors that he was able to identify, so it was certainly not written in Gaelic or Cumbric, neither of which he is likely to have understood in sufficient depth. Whether the *codicilus* was really as badly written as he suggests is open to doubt: his criticisms may have more to do with promoting his own work as the definitive *vita* of Kentigern. As far as chronology is concerned, Jocelin gives no indication of when the *codicilus* was written. If, however, we take 'Scottic' at face value, we can reasonably assign its composition to the last three decades of the eleventh century when the former kingdom of Strathclyde was brought under Scottish control.

In addition to the two Glasgow *vitae*, our sources on Kentigern include brief accounts contained in two 'breviaries' – collections of hagiographical information on early Scottish saints. The oldest of these is a thirteenth-century text, the Sprouston Breviary, comprising a prose section on Kentigern's childhood with verses alluding to later events in his career. The other breviary was produced at Aberdeen in the early 1500s and also includes a mix of prose and poetry in its account of Kentigern, together with a separate entry on his mother Teneu. Both breviaries seem to have taken information from Jocelin's *vita*, while the entry for

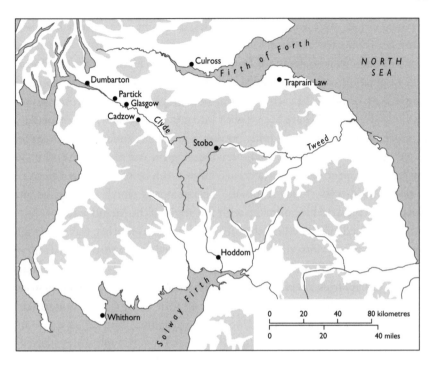

Map 2 St Kentigern and Strathclyde

Teneu in the Aberdeen text plainly derives from the Herbertian Life.[6] A final source on Kentigern is a shortened version of Jocelin's work by the fourteenth-century chronicler John of Tynemouth. The main value of this text is that it includes a brief summary of a lost chapter, missing from the surviving copies of Joceline's *vita*, telling of a corn-mill erected by Kentigern on the banks of the River Clyde.[7]

Kentigern's career

Historians generally agree that the information on Kentigern presented in the *vitae* and breviaries is based on much older traditions from the kingdom of Strathclyde.[8] How much of this ancient lore existed in textual rather than in oral form is uncertain, for the written record of the North Britons is essentially a lost literature. Whatever documents still existed in the mid-eleventh century, when the Clydesdale heartlands finally fell to the Scots, must have been destroyed as soon as any useful data had been abstracted by the conquerors. We may reasonably assume that one or more *vitae* of Kentigern, written in Latin by Cumbric-speaking clerics, were among the casualties. These, in turn, would have been compiled from even earlier traditions, some of which may have been passed down through many generations from the saint's own lifetime. Factual information originating with his disciples and with other contemporaries would, of course, have been overlain with an array of hagiographical motifs. Accounts of his actual deeds would have been turned into miracle-tales in which a supernatural aspect demonstrated his saintly powers. Somewhere amid this much-embellished narrative lay a historical core representing the real story of the saint. We can here attempt to tell this story, in so far as it can be reconstructed from the hagiographical texts at our disposal. The attempt is worth making, because Kentigern is inextricably bound up with the origin of the Merlin legend.

The Herbertian Life tells us that Teneu, Kentigern's mother, was the daughter of a semi-pagan king called Leudonus who ruled from a fortress on Traprain Law, a distinctive hill in what is now East Lothian. We are told that the name Lothian derives from the name of this king. Leudonus wanted Teneu to marry a fellow-Briton from another kingdom, the suitor being Owain, son of King Urien of Rheged. Teneu refused, so Owain disguised himself as a girl and gained access to her chamber. There he seduced her, though she remained a virgin despite becoming pregnant. Her father, evidently assuming that Owain was not the culprit, became enraged and condemned the unfortunate maiden to death. First, she was thrown from the summit of Traprain Law but miraculously survived. Then she was cast upon the Firth of Forth in a small boat, the intention being that she would drift out to sea and perish along with her unborn child. However, the vessel beached on the further shore, at Culross in Fife, and Kentigern was born on the beach. At this point the surviving fragment of the Herbertian Life ends abruptly, but the story is continued by Jocelin and the breviaries. We are told of the rescue of mother and baby by St Serf (or Servanus) who had a monastery at Culross. Serf baptised the refugees and placed them under his care, becoming Kentigern's foster-father and mentor. The boy was raised at Culross as a young member of the monastic community, receiving from Serf the pet-name Munghu (Mungo) which – according to Jocelin – meant 'dear friend' in Gaelic. It is actually a Cumbric name whose true meaning is unknown.[9] At this point, we may pause briefly to comment on the story so far, noting that almost none of it is likely to be authentic. Fictional elements from a common stock of hagiographical motifs abound, making genuine history difficult to identify. Thus, we find Kentigern being given a royal parentage appropriate for his later fame. His maternal grandfather, supposedly the founder of Lothian, appears in other tales as 'King Loth' and is nothing more than a figure of legend. Owain of Rheged, although undoubt-edly a real person, was probably selected by the hagiographers as a suitable father for Kentigern because of his fame in sagas of the Old North. Teneu's narrow escapes from peril and death likewise conform to a standard template for miracle-stories. Serf of Culross was a well-known saint in his own right and therefore an ideal patron for the young Kentigern. Of all these characters, Teneu is probably the only one who was present in the real story of her son's conception and childhood.

The narrative resumes with Jocelin's *vita* where Kentigern leaves Culross to make his way towards Clydesdale. According to the Sprouston Breviary, he crossed a river marking the frontier between the Scots and 'the kingdom of the Britons'. The river is undoubtedly the Forth, in its lower reaches around Stirling, but it is interesting to note that the Breviary describes the Britons as a separate people. Its author was probably drawing on source-material compiled when Strathclyde was still an independent realm, before it became part of Scotland, in which case the ultimate source may have been one of the lost Kentigern texts produced by the Britons themselves.[10] As he drew near the Clyde valley, Kentigern came to a place called *Kernach*, to the house of a certain Fergus, who promptly died. Kentigern put the dead man on a cart and continued his journey, eventually arriving at *Cathures*, which was also known as Glasgow. There he buried Fergus in an old cemetery consecrated by Ninian, a North British saint usually associated with Whithorn in Galloway. At Glasgow, Kentigern lived with two brothers, Telleyr and Anguen. He was respected by Anguen but scorned and insulted by Telleyr, who subsequently perished in an act of divine retribution. Kentigern established his first church and monastery at Glasgow, the forerunner of the twelfth-century cathedral. According to Jocelin, the king of Cumbria (i.e. Strathclyde) at that time was Morken, who refused to donate food to Kentigern's monastery and even aimed a kick at the saint. This tyrant was suitably punished with an ailment from which he eventually died. He is not named in the Aberdeen Breviary, which simply refers to him as a *regulus* or 'petty king'. No king bearing the name Morcant – the Cumbric name behind Jocelin's 'Morken' – is recorded in any other text as a ruler on the Clyde. However, a sixth-century King Morcant is depicted in *Historia Brittonum* as an enemy of Urien Rheged and may be the individual mentioned by Jocelin.[11] If so, then we have another example of a figure from North British saga being drawn into the Kentigern hagiography. As we shall see, this kind of literary connection between famous characters who probably had no real contact with one another may explain Kentigern's link with the Merlin legend.

Jocelin's *vita* now makes a long detour southward, bringing Kentigern to Wales by way of Carlisle. We see Kentigern meeting the Welsh national saint David and founding a monastery at Llancarfan in the diocese of Llandaf. It hardly needs saying that we are not dealing here with genuine history. According to Llancarfan's own traditions, the monastery was not founded by Kentigern but by a Welsh saint. Jocelin's version is hagiographical invention of the most blatant kind and can probably be connected to twelfth-century rivalry between the neighbouring bishoprics of Llandaf and St David's.[12] Elsewhere in Wales, in the kingdom of Gwynedd, Kentigern supposedly built a monastery beside the River Elwy, entrusting it to his disciple Asaph when he himself returned to northern Britain. This place is now St Asaph (Llanelwy) but it is unlikely to have any real connection with Kentigern, for none is recorded before the monastery's refounding under Norman patronage in the 1100s. The alleged connection between Asaph and Kentigern, and likewise between Kentigern and Wales, probably also originated in the twelfth century. As we shall see in Chapter 8, the background to this fictional interlude may be sought in twelfth-century ecclesiastical politics rather than in sixth-century history.[13]

Kentigern arrived back in the North, having been summoned by Rederech, the new king of Cumbria. The family of the tyrant Morken no longer held power, so it was safe for Kentigern to return. He had plenty to do, for paganism had made a comeback while he had been in Wales. Rederech – a devout Christian – wanted to stamp it out. He and Kentigern met at Hoddom in Dumfriesshire where the saint gave a sermon against the pagan Germanic god Woden, whom Kentigern declared to be a king of the Saxons and therefore a mortal man. After building churches in the locality, including an episcopal centre at Hoddom, Kentigern travelled north to Glasgow where he took up residence as bishop. At Hoddom, Rederech had paid homage to the saint, giving him supreme authority over the kingdom and setting a precedent that all kings of Strathclyde would always be subservient to the bishop of Glasgow. As with the Welsh interlude, much of this part of Jocelin's narrative is fiction. Rederech is the historical king Rhydderch Hael from the Rock of Clyde at Dumbarton, while Hoddom was a major monastery in the Dark Ages, albeit one under English control from the late seventh century to the end of the ninth.[14] But the rest is mostly invention. The Saxon god Woden cannot have been worshipped in Dumfriesshire in Kentigern's time, for the Anglo-Saxons did not extend their power so far west until several decades later. When they did eventually reach the Solway lands in the mid 600s, they were already embracing Christianity. Nor should we assume that the supposed 'pagans' around Hoddom were native

Britons clinging onto or rediscovering the old religion of their ancestors, still less that Jocelin's Woden represents a deity venerated by them. Archaeological evidence from Whithorn and other sites along the northern Solway coast indicates that these lands were firmly controlled by a military aristocracy proud of its Christian credentials.[15] Moreover, as one esteemed scholar once observed, 'no traditions of Celtic gods *as such* seem to have survived in Britain in the Dark Ages', by which he meant the preservation of active cults rather than vague folk-memories of pagan beliefs.[16] The entire theme of residual sixth-century paganism in Dumfriesshire may have been invented by Jocelin himself, to add drama and urgency to Kentigern's work among the North Britons. By depicting the natives of the area as pagans, Jocelin was presenting the saint with a major challenge that could be turned into a great achievement. Whether he also invented Kentigern's association with Hoddom is a matter of debate, but the original monastery there was indeed established in the sixth century and by Britons.

Jocelin calls Rederech's queen 'Languoreth' and says that she bore him a son, Constantine, who became a priest. We are told that Constantine eventually succeeded his father on the throne, earning praise for subduing the enemies of the kingdom without spilling blood. After his death, the people acclaimed him as a saint. Nothing more is said of him, nor is he identifiable outside the *vita* as one of the several Constantines commemorated in church dedications and in hagiographical fragments.[17] His namesakes are connected with churches beyond the borders of Strathclyde, in places such as Kintyre and Cornwall, but one of them is found within the kingdom itself. This is the mysterious saint allegedly entombed in a stone sarcophagus at the old parish church of Govan on the western side of Glasgow. Little is known of him but the church is dedicated to St Constantine and stands on the site of an ancient foundation reaching back to Kentigern's era.[18] It is highly likely that Govan's saint and Rederech's son are one and the same. Constantine's mother Languoreth is similarly obscure, being unheard-of outside Jocelin's narrative. She takes a prominent role in a miracle-tale about a lost ring – a gift from her husband – that unexpectedly turns up inside the belly of a salmon fished from the River Clyde. Nowadays, this tale is remembered in the coat of arms of the city of Glasgow. It is unlikely to have been invented by Jocelin as it occurs in the Aberdeen Breviary in what seems to be an independent, slightly different version. It may have been present in the older Kentigern hagiography of the Strathclyde Britons. However, the theme of a love-token being found inside a fish is found in Irish literature as far back as the seventh century so it is not unique to the Kentigern tradition.[19] The Aberdeen Breviary version does not name either the king or his wife, instead

referring to the lady as 'queen of Caidzouu'. The place is now Cadzow in South
Lanarkshire, site of a royal stronghold used by Scottish kings from the twelfth
century onwards and arguably by their Strathclyde predecessors.[20]

Both Jocelin and the Aberdeen Breviary include an episode in which
Kentigern meets Columba, abbot of Iona. The two saints exchange croziers and
depart in friendship. Here, as in the account of Kentigern's upbringing by Serf
of Culross, the hagiographers were keen to portray their subject as a significant
player in ecclesiastical circles. A real meeting between Columba and Kentigern
is unlikely to have occurred. Had it done so, Adomnán's *vita* of Columba would
no doubt have mentioned it.[21]

And so we come to Jocelin's final chapter. This is the most significant item of
Kentigern hagiography with regard to the Merlin legend. Under the heading
'Of the prophecy of a certain man, and of the burial of the saints in Glasgow',
Jocelin describes the aftermath of Kentigern's death.[22] He begins by telling us
that Kentigern's friend, King Rederech, 'remained much longer than usual in
the royal town, which was called Pertnech'. Among the king's retainers was a
jester or fool called Laloecen who, after becoming deeply affected by Kentigern's
passing, 'gave himself up to the most extreme grief and would receive no consolation from anyone'. Amid his sadness he uttered a prophecy about King
Rederech and 'another chief of the land, by name Morthec'. Both men, he foretold, would die before the year was out. The prophecy turned out to be true,
prompting Jocelin to draw a comparison with the Roman assault on Jerusalem
in AD 79 which, he observed, was also 'foretold by a madman'. He says nothing
more of Laloecen and moves swiftly to the end of his book.

Laloecen's name has a familar ring. It calls to mind the Welsh word *llallogan*
in the Myrddin poems. Like Myrddin, Laloecen possessed the power of prophecy. Both became grief-stricken and inconsolable. In Myrddin's case, the cause of
grief was a savage battle; in Laloecen's, it was the impending death of a king and
a high-ranking lord. Both Myrddin and Laloecen were social outcasts: the one,
a forest-dwelling fugitive; the other, a court jester whose 'foolish words and
gestures' provided amusement for people of rank. Jocelin of Furness offered no
clues as to where he obtained the Laloecen story. However, he is not our only
source of information on this curious figure.

Vita Merlini Silvestris

Among the medieval manuscripts held by the British Library is a fifteenth-
century text known as 'Cotton Titus A xix'. Its contents include the prologue

and first eight chapters of the Herbertian Life of Kentigern – the sole surviving fragment of this *vita*. In the same manuscript is an abridged version of Geoffrey of Monmouth's *Vita Merlini* together with a unique text entitled *Vita Merlini Silvestris*, 'Life of Merlin of the Forest'.[23] The latter is a work in two parts, the first of which tells of an encounter between Kentigern and a naked, hairy madman called Lailoken. It describes how the saint was praying among trees in the wilderness when Lailoken suddenly appeared 'like a raging beast'. Kentigern greeted the madman and asked him to explain who he was and why he lived alone as 'a companion to wild beasts'. Lailoken then told his story, beginning with the assertion, 'I am a Christian.' He explained that he had committed a terrible crime and must henceforth dwell in loneliness, 'since I do not deserve to suffer my punishment in the company of men'. The crime in question was to cause the deaths of all those who had fallen in a great battle 'well known to all the inhabitants of this country, which was fought in the plain that lies between Lidel and Carwannok'. During the fighting, the sky had opened and a voice from Heaven had spoken to Lailoken, informing him that he alone was responsible for the slaughter and must pay the price. Looking up at the sky, he had seen a dazzling light and an army of celestial warriors brandishing fiery spears. This terrifying vision had so unnerved him that he had been seized by an evil spirit who consigned him to the wilderness. After hearing this tragic tale, Kentigern was so moved by pity that he began to weep. He prayed that Lailoken would find peace and healing in the afterlife. After this initial encounter, the madman frequently appeared to Kentigern. He would emerge from the wilderness to sit on a steep crag 'which rises on the other side of the Molendinar Burn, overlooking Glasgow, to the north of the church of that place'.[24]. Kentigern and his monks were often disturbed by Lailoken's wild shrieking as he uttered obscure, garbled prophecies that none of them could comprehend. On one occasion, amid a cacophony of wailing and shouting, Lailoken demanded the holy sacrament so that he might be 'fortified with the body and blood of Christ before he passed over from this world'. When Kentigern sent a monk to tell the madman to be quiet, Lailoken again begged for the sacrament, prophesying that his death would occur on that same day. This was reported to Kentigern, who sent another monk to ask Lailoken how he would die. The reply came back: 'I shall die today, crushed by stones and cudgels.' But the saint did not believe this, so he told the monk to ask again, hoping that a more truthful answer might be given. Lailoken's response was indeed different: 'Today my body will be pierced by a sharp wooden stake and thus my spirit will fail.' Again he was disbelieved, so a third request was sent. This time the madman said, 'Today I will terminate my present life by drowning,' which brought a furious reaction from the monk, who accused him of lying. Lailoken burst into tears, insisting that he was merely relaying a prophecy given to him by Jesus Christ. He requested that Kentigern come to him in person, bringing the sacred bread and wine that he so fervently desired. As the saint approached the crag, Lailoken came down to prostrate himself on the ground. Kentigern listened while the madman claimed to be now free of the demons that had formerly taken hold of his mind. The saint's prayers, he insisted, had been heard by God. He, Lailoken, had thus been liberated from 'Satan's angels'. He was now a committed Christian and therefore deserving of the sacrament. Kentigern duly offered the bread and wine. Afterwards, Lailoken spoke another prophecy in which he foresaw the deaths of 'the most outstanding of the kings of Britain, the holiest of the bishops and the noblest of the lords' before the year's end. He then dashed off into the wilderness. Sure enough, even as he had foreseen, he died that same day. He was stoned and beaten by shepherds in the service of a king called Meldred. Mortally injured, he fell down the bank of the River Tweed near the fortress of Dunmeller and was impaled on a sharp wooden stake. His head fell forward into the water and he drowned, thus fulfilling his prophecy of a triple death.

The second part of _Vita Merlini Silvestris_ tells of the madman's dealings with the aforementioned King Meldred, by whom he was kept as a bound prisoner at Dunmeller. Meldred is here identified as a _regulus_, a minor king, thus implying subservience to a more powerful monarch. He imprisoned Lailoken because he wanted him to utter prophecies. For three days, the captive stayed stubbornly silent, despite being starved. On the third day, Meldred's wife entered the royal hall while king and prisoner were both present. Her wimple or head-covering had caught a stray leaf, which her husband promptly ripped to shreds. This brought a laugh from Lailoken. Meldred asked him why he was amused and promised to release him if he gave the reason. Lailoken responded by posing a riddle, with the condition that he be freed if it could be solved. The riddle was somewhat obscure: 'From poison dripped sweetness and from honey bitterness, but neither is so, although both remain true.' Completely baffled, the king requested a different riddle, which turned out to be just as puzzling as the first: 'Wickedness returned good with evil, and goodness repaid it the other way round, but neither is so, although both remain true.' A frustrated Meldred once again demanded to know why Lailoken had laughed, but the prisoner answered: 'If I speak openly to you, sadness will be the result for you, and for me death-bearing sorrow.' He then asked the king for a favour, requesting burial in 'a place suitable for a dead believer'. The spot he had in mind lay on the eastern side of

Dunmeller, where the Passal stream flows into the River Tweed. 'For,' he added, 'it will come to pass after a few days that I shall die a threefold death'. He immediately followed this prophecy with one that referred to events of a more distant future: 'at the time when the meeting of the two rivers is close to my grave, the ruler of the British people will hold sway over an adulterous race'. The writer of *Vita Merlini Silvestris* evidently felt a need to explain this second prophecy by informing his readers that it foretold 'the destruction of the Britons, and that there would be a reunification after their separation'. The narrative then resumes with Lailoken being granted his funeral request together with his freedom. Before leaving the royal hall, he explained the meaning of the two riddles, both of which alluded to the queen's adultery with a secret lover in the king's garden. He depicted the leaf as the queen's enemy – for betraying her unfaithfulness – and as the king's friend for providing evidence of it. He then departed from the hall, seeking the wilderness. The queen, meanwhile, urged her husband to dismiss the madman as a liar. She pointed out that everyone dies once, and once only, but nobody dies three times. The prophecy of a threefold death, she insisted, was therefore untrue. Meldred responded by calling her 'the foulest of adulteresses'. In bitterness, she began to plan her revenge on Lailoken. Several years later, on the day when he received holy communion from Kentigern at Glasgow, he was passing near Dunmeller. There he was set upon by shepherds acting on behalf of the queen and suffered death in the triple manner that he had foretold.

So ends *Vita Merlini Silvestris*. It is clear that its central figure is not the Merlin of the title but the North British wild man Lailoken who appears in Jocelin's *vita* of Kentigern as 'Laloecen'. The title *Vita Merlini Silvestris* might therefore seem erroneous, were it not for two brief references in the narrative. The first comes near the beginning of the first section, immediately after Lailoken's name is mentioned. It adds that 'certain people say that he was Merlin (*Merlynus*) who was regarded by the Britons as unique in his powers of prophecy, but the identification is uncertain'. The second is a two-line verse appended to the tale of Lailoken and Meldred: 'Pierced by a stake and having endured stoning and drowning, Merlin (*Merlinus*) is said to have undergone a threefold death.' What these two notes tell us is that the author of *Vita Merlini Silvestris* believed that Lailoken was none other than the famous Merlin. His use of the name-forms *Merlynus* and *Merlinus* show that he was familiar with the works of Geoffrey of Monmouth or with later texts based on Geoffrey. Moreover, there is a close similarity between the unfaithfulness of Meldred's wife and the story of Queen Ganieda's adultery in Geoffrey's *Vita Merlini*. The two royal courts even share the same geographical context, both being associated with places in southern Scotland. In *VM*, King Rodarch's court is somewhere in 'Cumbria' – an alternative name for the kingdom of Strathclyde – while Meldred's fortress of Dunmeller is said to lie only thirty miles from Glasgow. While it is beyond doubt that the author of *Vita Merlini Silvestris* drew the names *Merlinus* and *Merlynus* from a post-Galfridian version of the Merlin legend, the source of his information on Lailoken is unknown. One possibility is that he found it among material relating to Kentigern preserved in documents at Glasgow Cathedral. He may even have found the story of Lailoken and Kentigern in the Herbertian Life, in a chapter lost from the surviving fragment of this text.[25] This could explain why *Vita Merlini Silvestris* and the Herbertian fragments are preserved in the same manuscript. The author presumably found the tale of Lailoken and Meldred among stories relating to Kentigern and combined it with the Lailoken–Kentigern tale to create a sort of rudimentary biography of the wild man. He clearly had an interest in both Merlin and Kentigern and recognised Lailoken as a link between them.

Some scholars refer to the two tales in *Vita Merlini Silvestris* as 'Lailoken A' and 'Lailoken B'. Others prefer to call them, respectively, *Lailoken and Kentigern* and *Lailoken and Meldred*, the style of reference preferred in the present study. As well as being more descriptive of the contents, it draws an important distinction between the tales by highlighting Kentigern's absence from the Meldred story. Of Meldred himself we know only what *Vita Merlini Silvestris* tells us, for he appears nowhere else. Lailoken, however, does appear elsewhere. His encounter with Kentigern was described in *Scotichronicon*, also written in the fifteenth century. *Scotichronicon* was compiled by Walter Bower, a priest at Inchcolm Abbey in the Firth of Forth, in the 1440s.[26] It was a continuation of *Chronica Gentis Scotorum*, 'Chronicles of the Scottish People', written in the late fourteenth century by John of Fordun. In his account of Kentigern, drawn probably from material in the cathedral library at Aberdeen, Fordun had not mentioned the saint's encounter with a mad prophet. Bower, however, not only described the episode but gave what is essentially an abridgement of the tale of Lailoken and Kentigern in *Vita Merlini Silvestris,* omitting the part where Lailoken interrupts Kentigern's preaching at Glasgow. Bower's version has the header *De mirabili paenitentia Merlini vatis*, 'Of the penitential marvels of the prophet Merlin'. He did not copy directly from *Vita Merlini Silvestris* but both narratives clearly drew on the same body of source-material which possibly included a complete version of the Herbertian Life of Kentigern.[27] Some of the differences between Bower and the *Vita* are worth noting. For instance, Bower does not repeat the mis-spelling of the River Tweed, given as 'Traved' in the *Vita*. Also, he renders the name of King Meldred's fortress as Dun Mellis rather than Dunmeller. Near the beginning of his account he has Lailoken telling Kentigern 'I was formerly the prophet of Vortigern called Merlin.' This, he felt, required further explanation at the end:

> Do not be amazed that Merlin and St Kentigern died in one and the same year, since St Kentigern was 181 years old when he died. For we have below in Book 5, Chapter 43 a mention of a certain knight called John of the Times who lived for 361 years. Others say that it was not the Merlin who lived at the time of Vortigern but another miraculous prophet of the Scots who was called Lailoken; but because he was a miraculous prophet he was called a second Merlin.

The stories in *Scotichronicon* and *Vita Merlini Silvestris*, together with Jocelin's abbreviated version, reflect a body of lore that was plainly in existence by c.1150. This must derive ultimately from even older North British traditions pre-dating the Scottish takeover of Strathclyde in the previous century. We are therefore dealing with information of considerable antiquity, an ancient tale of kings and saints and battles and strange prophecies. The central character was identified by later writers as Merlin but, at this stage, it might be premature to describe it as the original version of the Merlin legend. For the moment, we should probably call it the legend of Lailoken.

Alladhan

The geographical setting of the Lailoken tales and their survival in Scottish literature imply that they originated in northern Britain. There is no reason to imagine that their ultimate source is to be found elsewhere. Lailoken does not appear in traditions from other parts of Britain, except perhaps in the word *llallogan*, a nickname for Myrddin in the poem *Cyfoesi*. In any case, Myrddin himself has a North British rather than a Welsh context. Only in Ireland do we encounter what seems certainly to be an account of Lailoken outside the Scottish tradition. This is *Buile Shuibhne*, 'The Frenzy of Suibhne', the story of a legendary Irish wild man called Suibhne Geilt ('Wild Sweeney'). Written in the Gaelic language of Ireland in the twelfth century, it contains material found in much older texts going back to the ninth.[28] At one point, it tells of a journey made by Suibhne to the 'land of the Britons' where, in a great forest, he met a deranged British wild man (*geilt Bhreathnach*). The latter gave his name as Alladhan but said he was also known as *Fer Caille*, 'Man of the Wood'. He spoke of a king whom he feared and whose men were hunting him. Having learned to his relief that Suibhne was not in this king's service, Alladhan explained that he had gone insane during a battle between two other kings, whom he named as Eochaid and Cugua. He himself had supported Eochaid. His madness was due to a curse having been directed at him by Cugua's soldiers, who had yelled 'three shouts of malediction'. Suibhne was immediately reminded of certain similarities with his own situation, for he himself had been hurled into madness during a battle in Ireland after being cursed by a saint. A bond of friendship thus grew between the two wild men, and they dwelt together in Britain for a whole year. Eventually, Alladhan realised his days were numbered, forseeing that he would soon be drowned at 'Blackhouse Falls'. He also predicted that he would be buried in the graveyard of a saint's church and that his soul would ascend to Heaven. Suibhne likewise uttered a prophecy about his own impending death and said that he must return at once to Ireland. And so they parted company, each dying in his own land before the year was out.

The name Alladhan is unknown in Irish literature except for its brief occurrence in *Buile Shuibhne*. It is either a name of Gaelic origin or the Gaelicised form of a name in another language. Given the geographical setting of the Suibhne–Alladhan episode, which takes place entirely in a 'land of the Britons', it seems likely that Alladhan represents a British name altered for a Gaelic-speaking Irish audience. Indeed, although some scholars have proposed an entirely Gaelic origin based on the word *allaidh*, 'wild', the most plausible hypothesis is that it is an Irish rendering of the name we have previously encountered as Lailoken.[29] This would mean that the Lailoken legend was already circulating in Ireland by the early 1100s and may have been known there for a long time previously, having travelled from an origin-centre in northern Britain. Indeed, it seems likely that the very idea of Suibhne going insane after a battle was simply borrowed by Irish storytellers from the tale of Lailoken's madness.[30] Alladhan is almost certainly Lailoken. As we shall see in Chapter 6, Suibhne Geilt might represent an Irish version of the same character, moulded around a historical namesake already known in Irish lore.

Origins: Lailoken and Myrddin

The Lailoken legend appears to have taken shape in northern Britain before the twelfth century. If it provided Irish storytellers with material for their characterisation of Suibhne Geilt, its origins can probably be pushed back much earlier. Indeed, it may have reached a fully-developed stage by c.800, after which date it perhaps migrated across the Irish Sea. Geographical information in the extant versions suggests the kingdom of Strathclyde as a likely origin-centre.[31] The kingdom's heartland around Glasgow is clearly the setting of the tale *Lailoken and Kentigern* and also of Jocelin's final chapter, which is essentially a diluted version of the same story. Strathclyde likewise fits the description 'land of the Britons' in *Buile Shuibhne* where Alladhan met his Irish counterpart. It is where the Lailoken legend's core elements would most likely have been brought together: the main character's name, his madness after a battle, his power of prophecy and his threefold death. Other elements might have featured at the outset or were perhaps added at subsequent stages as the narrative evolved. In the case of Kentigern, his hagiography inevitably attracted famous characters from North British folklore and this no doubt explains his alleged connection with Lailoken. Both were apparently well-known in the folklore of Strathclyde so their coming together would have elicited no surprise to a medieval audience, especially to a Cumbric-speaking one. It is not difficult to imagine Kentigern's early hagiographers in the kingdom of Strathclyde using Lailoken in the way that they used famous saints. Like Columba and Serf, the wild madman of the Old North was recruited to Kentigern's story in a supporting role, having previously taken centre stage in his own tales. The key point is that there is no need to see the encounters between Kentigern and the madman as real. They were no more historical than the alleged meeting between Kentigern and Columba in the Aberdeen Breviary. This is an important point to keep in mind when, in later chapters, we consider modern interpretations of the Lailoken–Kentigern material. There we look at how Kentigern's original or true story was embellished with themes, motifs and characters from elsewhere. We can be fairly certain that Lailoken was one of these borrowings. This does not mean that we should dismiss Lailoken himself as a fictional figure crafted by storytellers. He was quite possibly an actual contemporary of Kentigern, just like Serf and Columba, but like them had no real contact with Glasgow's saint. The case for accepting him as a historical figure of the sixth century is examined at the end of the present chapter.

To the hagiography surrounding Kentigern we owe the preservation of Lailoken's legend. For both saint and wild man, our main sources of information survive in texts of Scottish origin. However, Lailoken's story is also connected in some way with the Myrddin poems with which it shares a number of elements in common. For example, the central figure of a North British wild man is so similar that both the Welsh and Scottish traditions surely refer to the same individual. In the poetry, the wild man's prophecies link him with people and events in Wales, as does the name Myrddin which – as we have seen – is simply the fictional eponym of Carmarthen. The obvious deduction is that the Welsh context in the poems is an overlay grafted onto an original story about a wild northern seer. This effectively strips away much of the historical and geographical detail in the poems to leave a core narrative centred upon a character whose primary setting is the same as Lailoken's. The narrative can be reconstructed as follows: a North British warrior fought alongside King Gwenddolau at the battle of Arfderydd before fleeing in madness to the Forest of Calidon or Celyddon. There he uttered prophecies, some of which alluded to contemporary political events. Straying into the territory of a king (Meldred in the Scottish tales; Rhydderch in the Welsh poems) he was pursued and captured. Later, while wandering freely, he was ambushed and slain. This represents the bare bones of the original story. In removing the Welsh overlay we must necessarily discard the name Myrddin itself, thus leaving the central character of the poems without a name. He would indeed remain in anonymity if we did not already have an alternative name to bestow upon him. That name, of course, is Lailoken.

It seems logical to conclude that the poetry attributed to Myrddin Wyllt represents a Welsh version of the Lailoken legend. The poems were composed in Wales and therefore belong to the rich corpus of medieval Welsh literature, but their basic storyline originated in northern Britain, among the traditions borrowed independently by Kentigern's hagiographers. It is worth noting that Kentigern is not mentioned in the poems at all. His absence suggests that he did not feature in the Lailoken legend in the form that it came to Wales and probably confirms that he played no part in the original North British version of the legend. Supernatural elements in the Myrddin poetry, such as strange visions and magic, were arguably part of the Lailoken legend too, perhaps entering it at an early stage of development in the hands of North British storytellers. This aspect perhaps accounted for the legend's popularity in Wales and the North and in Irish storytelling circles as well. Dating the northern legend's migration to Wales is nevertheless difficult. It may have travelled before the ninth century, this being the earliest period of composition for the Welsh poetry that seems to lie behind certain archaic verses in *Yr Afallennau* and in other poems attributed to Myrddin. Gazing even further back, we may note that the Lailoken material must have arrived in Wales after 573, the year when – as we shall see in the next chapter – the battle of Arfderydd was fought.

We come now to a fundamental question: is the Lailoken legend based on a real person or a fictional one? While there is not enough evidence to provide a definitive answer, there is no reason to doubt that a northern wild man of this name actually did exist. Indeed, some scholars believe that the story presented in the Lailoken tales, the Myrddin poetry and *Vita Merlini* must be based on a historical figure who fought in a savage battle at a place called Arfderydd.[32] Their belief is founded on more than guesswork or wishful thinking, for the battle is part of authentic Dark Age history. It lies at the heart of the legends of Merlin, Myrddin and Lailoken and will be examined more closely in the next chapter.

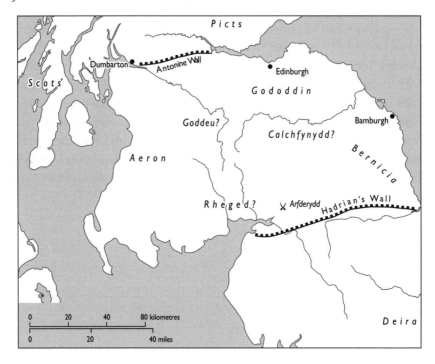

Map 3 The Old North

4

THE BATTLE OF ARFDERYDD

The previous chapter concluded that the North British traditions on which the Myrddin poems were based originally referred to a wild man called Lailoken who may really have existed in the sixth century. Our next step is to identify the historical element in the poems, in the hope of catching glimpses of this enigmatic figure. We begin with one of the most important themes, one that runs through the Welsh tradition and its Scottish counterpart. Both traditions refer to a savage battle in which the central character was involved. It is referred to only briefly in the Lailoken tales but is mentioned a number of times in the Welsh poems. In the fifth stanza of *Yr Afallennau*, for example, Myrddin utters the following words:

'And in the battle of Arfderydd my torc was of gold,
though today I am not treasured by the one of the aspect of swans.'[1]

The final stanza of *Yr Oianau* contains a similar lament:

'Since the battle of Arfderydd I care not
were the sky to fall and the sea to overflow.'[2]

In the *Cyfoesi*, Myrddin mentions the battle while addressing his sister Gwenddydd, though here he calls it 'the battle of Arfderydd and Erydon'. In this poem he also refers to 'Gwenddolau's death in the bloodshed of Arfderydd', using the phrase three times, while Gwenddydd herself observes that the battle has brought a sickness upon her.

The battle was well-known in medieval Welsh literature, not only because of its connection with Myrddin but also as a famous historical event in its own right. It was noted in *Annales Cambriae*, the Welsh Annals, in an entry under the year 573:

Bellum armterid inter filios Elifer et Guendoleu filium Keidiau; in quo bello Guendoleu cecidit; Merlinus insanus effectus est.

('The battle of Armterid between the sons of Elifer and Guendoleu son of Keidiau; in which battle Guendoleu fell; Merlin went mad')

Armterid is simply an older form of *Arfderydd*. The archaic spelling shows that the annalist did not obtain the name of the battle from the Myrddin poems. His information probably came from traditions that had been circulating in Wales since c.800 or even earlier. The oldest surviving manuscript of the Welsh Annals, written in the early 1100s, is a copy of a lost tenth-century original that was itself based on a set of annals compiled in the ninth century.[3] Its entry for 573 is our oldest record of the battle of Arfderydd and would originally have comprised a simple two-word notice: *bellum armterid*. The names of the protagonists and the reference to *Merlinus* appear in a later copy written at the end of the thirteenth century. The scribe of this later version was clearly familiar with the post-Galfridian legend of Merlin, hence his use of Geoffrey's spelling rather than the older Welsh form *Myrddin*.

The name *Guendoleu* in the annal entry is an older form of *Gwenddolau*. This individual is mentioned several times in the Myrddin poetry where his death at Arfderydd is lamented. In *Yr Afallennau*, he is identified as the patron whom Myrddin served:

'For after Gwenddolau, no lord honours me [. . .] Now I sleep not, I tremble for my prince, my lord Gwenddolau, and my fellow-countrymen.'[4]

More information about Gwenddolau appears in *Yr Oianau*, in a stanza we have already encountered. It describes him as a king of renown who plundered his enemies:

'I have seen Gwenddolau, a glorious prince,
gathering booty from every border.
Beneath the brown earth now he is still,
chief of the kings of the North, greatest in generosity.'[5]

The poems do not name Gwenddolau's kingdom, nor do they point us to its precise location. They merely indicate that it lay somewhere in northern Britain. Gwenddolau's relationship with Myrddin is likewise unexplained, although the most obvious interpretation is that Myrddin was a soldier in Gwenddolau's army. The poems are also vague on the identity of Gwenddolau's foes. According to the entry in the Welsh Annals, the enemy force was commanded by the sons of Elifer. Turning back to the Myrddin poetry, we see that these men are briefly mentioned in the *Ymddiddan*, the 'dialogue' between Myrddin and Taliesin:

> 'The seven sons of Eliffer, seven proven warriors,
> will not avoid seven spears in their seven battle-sections.'

The names of the seven sons are not given in the poem but other Welsh sources identify three of them: Gwrgi, Peredur and Arthur. Gwrgi and Peredur frequently appear together, in contexts suggesting that they were close political allies. In one triad they are shown riding to the battle of Arfderydd on a single mount:

> Corvan, horse of the sons of Eliffer, bore the second Horse-Burden: he carried on his back Gwrgi and Peredur and Dunod the Stout and Cynfelyn the Leprous, to look upon the battle-fog of Gwenddolau at Arfderydd.[6]

Although they rode on Corvan, neither Dunod nor Cynfelyn were Eliffer's sons. As we shall see below, genealogical information associates them with other families. In another triad, Gwrgi and Peredur are said to have been abandoned by their army before a battle in which they both perished:

> the warband of Gwrgi and Peredur, who abandoned their lord at Caer Greu, when they had an appointment to fight the next day with Eda Great-Knee; and there they were both slain.[7]

The slaying of the brothers at Caer Greu is presumably the event behind an entry in the Welsh Annals under the year 580, seven years after the battle of Arfderydd:

Gurci et Peretur moritur.

('Gwrgi and Peredur died')

Also from Wales come a number of genealogical texts purporting to show the ancestry of various North British rulers of the sixth century. These 'pedigrees' show Gwrgi and Peredur as the offspring of Eliffer Gosgorddfawr ('Eliffer of the Great Warband'). Welsh tradition also assigns them a brother Arthur *Penuchel*

('High-Head') as well as the sisters Arddun and Ceindrech. Although Arthur is a namesake of the famous king of legend, nothing more is known of him and he is possibly a misprint for Arddun.[8] Nor can much be gleaned of Eliffer himself, not even the most approximate location of his territory. The same can be said of Dunod and Cynfelyn, whom the triad of the 'horse-burdens' describes as allies of Eliffer's sons at Arfderydd. Indeed, of all the named protagonists in the battle, only Gwenddolau can be placed in any kind of secure geographical context. Our ability to pinpoint his kingdom on a map is due largely to the efforts of one Scottish historian in the Victorian era.

Geography of the battle: W.F. Skene

The author of the Myrddin poems gives scant information on the location of Arfderydd. We are left to wonder where exactly the battle was fought, having deduced from the poems that the site lay somewhere in northern Britain. This question began to exercise the minds of Scottish historians in the nineteenth century, with a number of solutions being put forward. George Chalmers, author of the magisterial *Caledonia*, proposed that Arfderydd must be Airdrie in North Lanarkshire, basing his theory on little more than a slight similarity between the names. He was apparently unaware that Airdrie is not a name of Welsh or Cumbric origin but an Anglicised form of Gaelic *An Àrd Ruigh*, 'the high slope'.[9] Later in the century, the mystery of the battle's location was addressed by William Forbes Skene, a respected scholar of Celtic literature who went on to become Scotland's Historiographer Royal. Skene's starting-point was not a modern name that sounded vaguely like *Arfderydd* but a small clue in Walter Bower's *Scotichronicon*. Bower, writing in the fifteenth century, included a version of the tale *Lailoken and Kentigern* in his account of Glasgow's patron saint. As we have already noted in Chapter 3, Bower's version differed somewhat from the one presented in *Vita Merlini Silvestris*. One difference occurs in Lailoken's description of the famous battle in which he claimed to have fought. In the *Vita*, this conflict took place 'in the plain that lies between Lidel and Carwannok', but Bower's version has 'in the plain that lies between Lidel and Carwanolow'. Skene saw this as the key to pinpointing the site of the battle mentioned in the Myrddin poems.[10] He recognised Lidel as the Liddel Water, a river that runs southwestward from Kielder Forest to join the Esk on the border between Scotland and England. The name *Carwannok* in *Vita Merlini Silvestris* defies identification and was rightly dismissed by Skene as a corrupt name but *Carwanolow* seemed to him a possible older form of *Carwinley*, the name of a present-day hamlet near the confluence of Esk and Liddel. Further research confirmed this guess, for documents from the thirteenth century showed early forms of the name Carwinley as *Karwindelhou* and *Carwendelowe*.[11] Skene felt certain that these preserved a memory of a *caer* or fortress of Gwenddolau. He knew that initial *Gw* or *Gu* in the Welsh texts would become *W* in a place-name. From maps of the surrounding area he learned that Carwinley lay on the northern boundary of Arthuret, an ancient parish north of Carlisle. In the late twelfth and early thirteenth centuries, this name was recorded as *Artureth* and *Arturede*, prompting Skene to believe that he had at last discovered *Arfderydd*.[12]

Eager to see these places with his own eyes, Skene took a train from Edinburgh along the old Waverley route towards Carlisle, alighting at Longtown on the English side of the Border. There he found the Graham Arms, an old coaching inn, which he used as a base. First on his itinerary was a visit to the Arthuret Knowes, a pair of low hills near the parish church. These, he felt, must be connected with the battle, especially as the higher of the two showed evidence of earthworks on the top. In reality, the earthworks were probably medieval, but further examination is now impossible because the hill in question has been destroyed. Next on Skene's list was the hamlet of Carwinley, to which he was conveyed in a horse-cart belonging to his hosts. The two-mile journey from Longtown took him past Netherby Hall, the ancestral home of the Graham family, built on the site of a Roman fort. After crossing a stream, the Carwinley Burn, the cart brought Skene within sight of a tree-covered ridge overlooking the Liddel Water. Here, he got out to continue his expedition on foot. At the north end of the ridge he came upon the earthworks of an old fortification known locally as the 'Roman Camp'. This was much overgrown but nevertheless retained an imposing aura. On the far side, the ridge fell away steeply to the railway that at this point ran alongside the course of the Liddel. From the tree-shrouded brink, the great earthen ramparts of the 'Camp' curved out and back in a huge semicircular arc, enclosing in their midst a grassy mound. From the summit of this eminence Skene was able to survey a wide panorama, noticing the distinctive shape of Burnswark Hill on the northern horizon and the waters of the Solway Firth stretching away to the west. Standing in that high place, he felt certain that he had found *Caer Gwenddolau*, the fortress of Myrddin's patron. He further believed that the land around the site must be 'the field between Lidel and Carwanolow' mentioned by Walter Bower. His belief was reinforced when the tenant of the nearby Upper Moat Farm, who had accompanied him to the site, recounted a local folk-tradition of a great battle being fought there in ancient times 'between the Romans, and the Picts who held the camp, in which the Romans were victorious'. This settled the matter as far as Skene was concerned. He eventually returned to Edinburgh where he reported his discovery at a meeting of the Society of Antiquaries of Scotland in February 1865. The title of his paper was 'Notice of the Site of the Battle of Ardderyd or Arderyth'. Few among his audience would have doubted the truth of his assertions. Today's historians are likewise in broad agreement that the battle's geographical context has been correctly identified.

Geography of the battle: Caer Gwenddolau

The earthworks seen by Skene were not, as he thought, the defences of a Dark Age stronghold but the grass-grown remains of Liddel Strength, a medieval castle erected in the twelfth century.[13] This comprised an earth rampart enclosing a courtyard or 'bailey' within which stood an artificial mound or 'motte' with a wooden tower on top. Such a design was typical of small 'motte and bailey' castles in the Anglo-Norman period, but Liddel is slightly unusual in showing traces of an outer bailey, which might be the remnant of an earlier fortification. Whether this was an early Norman ringwork – a rampart without a motte – or something rather more ancient is hard to deduce. Topographically speaking, a high ridge overlooking the confluence of two major rivers would be an appropriate setting for a Dark Age centre of power, but only a modern archaeological survey would be able to shed more light. In the absence of further information, we cannot simply assume that the site of Liddel Strength was occupied in the sixth century.

There is, however, another possible candidate for Gwenddolau's fortress. One mile south of Liddel Strength, and slightly below the river-junction, stands the mansion of Netherby Hall. This was the residence of the Graham family from the fifteenth to the twentieth centuries. Beneath it lie the remains of the Roman fort *Castra Exploratorum*, 'Fort of the Scouts'.[14] Constructed in the early second century AD, probably on the site of an earlier camp, this was garrisoned into the twilight years of the Roman occupation of Britain. It was probably abandoned by c.400, at least in a formal military sense. Whether it lay completely deserted in the ensuing centuries is open to question. At the Hadrian's Wall fort of Birdoswald, some fifteen miles south-east of Netherby, archaeologists have found evidence of post-Roman occupation. Timber halls were erected in the fort's interior in the fifth century, probably by a local warlord whose relationship to the final Roman garrison is unclear.[15] It is possible that something similar happened at *Castra Exploratorum*. A group of native Britons may have settled there after the last Roman troops left, or the soldiers themselves may have 'gone native' after their wages and provisions stopped arriving from the imperial treasury. Archaeological investigations in the future might tell us more but, until such time, we cannot press the case for continuity too far. What cannot be doubted, however, is that *Castra Exploratorum* would have remained a dominant feature in the local landscape for a very long time. It had a footprint of some seven acres enclosed by strong stone walls, with gate-towers and battlements. In the late sixth century, at the time of the battle of Arfderydd, it would have been the largest and most imposing man-made structure in the vicinity. Travellers would have known it as a major landmark, a relic of ancient authority guarding an ancient crossing on the River Esk.

Some historians think *Castra Exploratorum* might be the *caer* of Carwinley. There is little doubt that the latter name derives from Cumbric *Caer Gwenddolau* via intermediate forms such as *Carwendelowe* and *Carwanolow*. In Wales, Roman forts are often known by *caer*-prefixed names such as Caerleon ('Fort of the Legion') and Cardiff ('Fort on the River Taff'). Some, such as Caerphilly ('St Ffili's fort') and Caerhun ('King Rhun's fort') bear the names of historical figures while others commemorate legendary ones. Caerfyrddin (Carmarthen, 'Myrddin's fort') is a prime example of a Roman fort being linked to a fictional character, in this case to explain a place-name whose true origin had been forgotten. The names of forts near the border between England and Scotland frequently have the suffix *chester*, derived from Old English *ceaster*, but others are prefixed by *caer* or its variant *car*. These prefixes denote names coined in an era when Cumbric, not English or Gaelic, was still being spoken in the Anglo-Scottish borderlands. On the English side of the Border, in the present-day county of Cumbria, former Roman sites such as Carlisle and Carvoran (earlier *Caervorran*) fall into this category. The situation is made more complex by the fact that both *caer* and *car* were attached to native hillforts as well as to Roman forts. Moreover, a *car* prefix need not always denote a strongly defended site. In the tenth century, it was bestowed by Cumbric-speakers on smaller settlements that were probably little more than stockaded farms.[16] Whether the first part of the name Carwinley relates to a Roman fort, a native stronghold or a tenth-century farmstead is therefore hard to say. What does seem likely is that the second part refers to the sixth-century ruler Gwenddolau. From this we might deduce that the place-name preserves a genuine historical link between him and the land around Carwinley, but other explanations need to be considered. One alternative is that *Caer Gwenddolau* was a name coined long after the sixth century, in a later period when stories about the battle of Arfderydd were already circulating among local Cumbric-speakers. Indeed, although the approximate location of the battlefield may have been retained in the area's folklore for hundreds of years, the precise whereabouts of Gwenddolau's centre of power might have been forgotten. A hiatus in the transfer of folk-memories from generation to generation could have occurred during the period c.650 to c.900, when the lands around the Solway Firth lay within the Anglo-Saxon kingdom of Northumbria. In this period, both the language and culture of the native Britons were replaced by those of a new, English-speaking elite. Not until the collapse of Northumbria in the Viking Age did this heavy layer of Englishness begin to weaken. In the wake of Northumbria's decline after c.850, Cumbric-speakers from Strathclyde came southward to take power over the land. Their presence revived the Cumbric language in the Solway region and, by the early tenth century, English place-names were being replaced by Cumbric ones.[17] This was the era when many of the *car* and *caer* names of southern Scotland and northern England were formed. It is possible that the original name of Carwinley was one of these. Descendants of the area's native Britons are likely to have been fully Anglicised by then, to the extent that they considered themselves English rather than British. Traditions of their ancestors had no doubt been preserved in some form, perhaps as fragments of folklore, but these would have reflected a culture that had been obsolete for many generations. Detailed information about a sixth-century battle between two armies of Britons is unlikely to have survived 200 years of Englishness. It is rather to the new wave of Britons from Strathclyde, arriving in the region c.870–900, that we should credit the creation of a name like *Caer Gwenddolau*. Stories about the famous battle of Arfderydd were undoubtedly well-known in Strathclyde, having evolved in tandem with the related legend of Lailoken. An opportunity to associate this lore with specific sites in the Solway region certainly arose in the early tenth century. As the only visible stronghold in the area of Arfderydd, the Roman fort of *Castra Exploratorum* may have been selected by new Cumbric-speaking settlers as a likely location for Gwenddolau's headquarters, especially if no other obvious candidates existed. The ridge where Liddel Strength was erected in the twelfth century may, for instance, have been completely bare of earthworks in the tenth. Whether *Castra Exploratorum* played any actual role in the conflict of 573 must remain an open question. We should, in any case, keep in mind the possibility that *Caer Gwenddolau* might not be derived from a personal name but could mean something quite different. 'Fort of the fair dales' has been suggested as an alternative derivation, with Gwenddolau himself being invented later to provide an explanation for the name when its original meaning had ceased to be remembered.[18] The context for this radical scenario would be a period when the Arfderydd saga was still evolving among the North Britons, before its migration to Wales. Such a process would be analogous with the invention of a figure called Myrddin or Merdin to explain the origin of Caerfyrddin, the Welsh name for Carmarthen.

Geography of the battle: Arfderydd

Carwinley lies near the northern boundary of the old parish of Arthuret. If the latter is the ancient *Arfderydd* and the former has a name meaning 'Gwenddolau's Fortress' we can infer that Gwenddolau's core territory included the battlefield itself. Pinpointing the precise location of the fighting requires us to identify Arfderydd more precisely. What does this name mean, and to which part of the local landscape did it originally refer?

A common misconception is that Arthuret has some connection with King Arthur. Local folk-etymology derives the name from 'Arthur's Head' and believes that the king is buried in the parish church. A plaque on the wall of the church asserts this claim and suggests that the present-day building occupies the site of a sixth-century predecessor.[19] These traditions are without foundation. Philologists have sought a more plausible explanation of the name Arthuret, recognising it as being of Cumbric origin. The oldest recorded form is *Armterid* in the Welsh Annals, which appears to be a straightforward compound *arm+terid*. The first element is probably related to Welsh *arf*, a borrowing from Latin *arma* ('arms' or 'weapons'), while the second seems to be the word now rendered *terydd* in Welsh, meaning 'fierce' or 'blazing'.[20] *Armterid* would thus be an appropriate name for a river or stream that gleamed like a sword-blade or spearpoint, as a shining weapon laid upon the land. Is the feature in question identifiable today? The major rivers in Arthuret are the Lyne and Esk which, respectively, define the southern and western boundaries of the parish. Both have names of ancient origin, the former being derived from a Celtic word meaning 'elm trees', the latter meaning simply 'water'.[21] Neither is likely to have been given an alternative Celtic name – there would be no need or reason for it. We should therefore consider other watercourses, specifically those whose original Celtic names have been replaced by later English ones and whose topography matches the characteristics implied by *arm+terid*. Our attention is drawn to one candidate in particular: the Carwinley Burn, a stream flowing roughly midway between Liddel Strength and the Roman fort. Its present name is late, having been borrowed by English speakers from the name of the hamlet through which it travels on its way to join the Liddel Water. The original name of this stream may have been *Armterid*.[22]

Having discussed the place-names, we can now consider their implications for our understanding of the battle. If the Carwinley Burn is the Arfderydd of the poems, then the battlefield itself must lie nearby. Notwithstanding the possibility that 'Gwenddolau's Fort' might have been invented in the tenth century by Cumbric-speaking settlers from Strathclyde, we may nevertheless suppose that the folklore behind it was accurate and that the Carwinley Burn did indeed lie at the centre of what had once been Gwenddolau's realm. The poems identify him as a king, and a mighty one too, so the total area under his authority was no doubt extensive. In addition to his heartland around Arfderydd, he is likely to have held the lower reaches of Eskdale and Liddesdale under his sway, controlling the southern parts of these valleys from their point of confluence.[23] An important crossing of the Esk lay immediately below the river-junction, its position indicated by a *vicus* or civilian settlement attached to the Roman fort. Although the *vicus* is no longer visible, archaeologists believe that it stretched northwestward from the main gate of *Castra Exploratorum*, lining a road running down to the river. This road would have reached the further bank via the ford. As guardian of this crossing in post-Roman times, Gwenddolau would have been able to exert power and influence over local communication networks. Indeed, levying tolls on travellers and traders may have been one of his primary sources of wealth.

Calidon and Celyddon

Geoffrey of Monmouth's Merlin took refuge in the Forest of Calidon, clearly the same place as *Coed Celyddon* in the Myrddin poems. Both names seem, at first glance, to refer to Caledonia, the land of the ancient Caledonian people whose territory spanned a large part of the Scottish Highlands. Roman writers imply that the Caledones or Caledonii were an ancestral group of the people later known as Picts, who are likewise associated with lands north of the Forth–Clyde isthmus. This does not fit the setting indicated by Geoffrey, the Welsh poets or the Lailoken tales. We should instead envisage Calidon/Celyddon as an area of woodland closer to Clydesdale, Tweeddale and Arfderydd, the places most closely associated with the North British seer. A clue is given by the medieval Scottish chronicler Hector Boece who wrote that 'the water of Clyde rises out of the same mountain within the Wood of Calidone, from which rises the Annan'.[24] Boece evidently understood *Calidone* to be a name applicable in southern as well as in northern Scotland, raising the possibility that there were two areas so called – one in the Highlands, the other in the Lowlands. Alternatively, his words might imply that the ancient name *Caledonia* had no precise geographical connotation in the Middle Ages and that any large area of Scottish woodland could be described as 'Caledonian Forest'.[25] To a medieval audience in faraway Wales or southern England, the name Calidon in *Vita Merlini* might have conveyed nothing more than a vague image of northern remoteness and wildness. On the other hand, a Scottish audience may have correctly deduced from the poem that the southern part of their country was meant and that Calidon was here the wooded region in which the three great rivers of Clyde, Tweed and Annan sprang from the hills. In the later French Arthurian romances, the 'Caledonian' connection was abandoned and the site of Merlin's refuge became the mystical forest of Broceliande in Brittany.

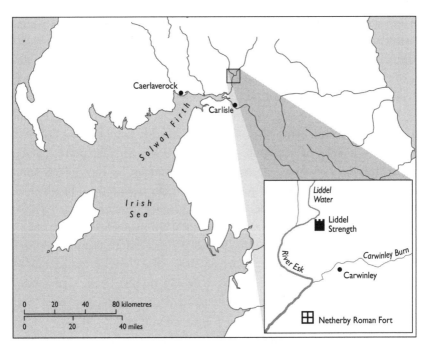

Map 4 The battle of Arfderydd

Gwenddolau's foes

The entry for 573 in the Welsh Annals implies that Gwenddolau's chief adversaries were Gwrgi and Peredur, two sons of Eliffer. In the triad of the horse-burdens, the brothers were accompanied to the battle by Dunod the Stout and Cynfelyn the Leprous. Identifying who these people were and where they came from is no simple task, for the sources give hardly any clues. So sparse is the information that historians can do little more than shoot ideas into the dark, hoping to establish plausible scenarios. Some of the resulting theories have more merit than others but all fall short of providing definitive answers. The most we can say with confidence is that Gwenddolau's enemies – Gwrgi, Peredur, Dunod and Cynfelyn – were real figures of the Old North in the late sixth century. Of the four, only Peredur appears in Geoffrey of Monmouth's retelling of the battle of Arfderydd at the beginning of *Vita Merlini*. However, Geoffrey describes *Peredurus* not as a North Briton but as a leader (Latin *dux*) from the Welsh kingdom of Gwynedd. He is an ally of Rodarch and Merlin against Guennolous and tries to console Merlin after the fighting is over.

One popular theory sees Gwrgi and Peredur as rulers of York. This is based on an assumption that the medieval tale *Peredur*, one of the Welsh Arthurian romances, contains reliable facts about Eliffer's son. *Peredur* is preserved in manuscripts of the fourteenth century and appears to be based on sources similar to those used by the twelfth-century French writer Chrétien de Troyes for his romance *Perceval, le Conte du Graal* ('Percival, the Story of the Grail').[26] In the Welsh tale, the young Peredur strives to become one of King Arthur's knights. At the royal court he is mocked by another knight called Cai, so he undertakes a series of adventures to prove his worth. Chrétien's character Percival follows a similar path: after being ridiculed by 'Sir Kay', he sets out on the road to adventure. At one point, he witnesses a procession in which the Holy Grail is carried by a maiden, but there is no mention of this sacred object in the Welsh tale. In both stories the hero is a Welshman who seems to have no connection with northern Britain. In the Welsh version, Peredur's father is Efrawg Iarll, a name meaning 'Earl of York' (the Romans called the city *Eburacum*). This is frequently seen as a significant clue to the sixth-century Peredur's geographical context. It has spawned an entirely speculative back-story which assumes that Eliffer ruled York when it still lay in native British hands.[27] By c.600 at the latest, the city had become an important centre of power for the Anglo-Saxons of Northumbria. According to the back-story,

Gwrgi and Peredur succeeded their father as co-rulers of York. From there, in 573, they led their army northwestward across the Pennine hills to make war on Gwenddolau. Such is the popularity of this scenario that it is sometimes cited as established fact. Unfortunately, its reliance on a theory that the sixth-century Peredur and his Arthurian namesake must be identical is not always acknowledged. The plain truth is that we have no reason to make any kind of link between the two Peredurs beyond the fact that they happen to share the same name. Indeed, it has been suggested that the Welsh Peredur might be based not so much on a North British namesake as on a mythical hero called Pryderi.[28] The many uncertainties mean that we really have no idea where the sons of Eliffer came from. Their domain might have lain much closer to Arfderydd, making them near-neighbours of Gwenddolau rather than invaders from the other side of the Pennines. If we remain wary of linking Peredur and Gwrgi with York, we should likewise take with a pinch of salt their traditional identification as Gwenddolau's cousins. This alleged kinship appears in the North British pedigrees but should not be taken at face value. The pedigrees are likely to reflect the creativity of later Welsh scribes rather than real family ties in the Old North.[29]

Peredur, son of Eliffer, has also been identified as the warrior Peredur *arfau dur* ('steel weapons') who appears in *The Gododdin*. The latter, as previously noted, is a collection of verses relating to the Britons of Gododdin, a kingdom that emerged in post-Roman times in Lothian. One of its themes is a sixth-century battle at a place called Catraeth where the Gododdin army suffered heavy losses. The collection now survives in a single Welsh manuscript of the thirteenth century, having undergone numerous changes during a long period of transmission. The verse relating to Peredur 'of steel weapons' need not imply that he was a Gododdin soldier, or that he was actually present at Catraeth. It is therefore possible that he is indeed Eliffer's son, selected as a suitable addition to the list of Gododdin heroes because of his own fame in North British lore.[30] No further light can be shed on this matter. Likewise, almost nothing is known of Peredur's brother Gwrgi. One Welsh triad asserts that the slaying of a certain Gwrgi *Garwlwyd* ('Rough-Grey') was a 'fortunate assassination', but we cannot assume that this Gwrgi was Eliffer's son rather than a namesake.

Dunod the Stout was presumably an ally of Gwrgi and Peredur. Like them, he appears in the pedigrees where his father is named as Pabo *Post Prydein* ('Pillar of Britain'). The pedigrees show Pabo and Eliffer as brothers but their kinship might be a product of later textual manipulation in Wales. Like Eliffer and his sons, neither Pabo nor Dunod can be assigned a specific geographical context. Efforts have been made to locate them in what is now the English county of Cumbria, where the place-names Papcastle and Dent have been high-lighted as commemorations of father and son respectively.[31] In both cases, the supporting arguments are wafer-thin. Papcastle, a name of uncertain orgin, perhaps incorporates Old Norse *papi*, 'hermit', rather than *Pabo*. Dent, formerly in Yorkshire, might be the place referred to as *regio Dunutinga* in a seventh-century Life of the Northumbrian saint Wilfrid.[32] Although *Dunutinga* is of Old English origin, it has been seen as containing the British name Dunod, like the similar place-name *Dunoding* in Wales. This raises the possibility that *regio Dunutinga* means 'region (or kingdom) of Dunod's people'. The Dunod in ques-tion would presumably have been a North Briton, perhaps even the Arfderydd protagonist. Alternatively, *regio Dunutinga* could simply mean 'region of the people of Dent' without any reference to the name Dunod. Elsewhere in present-day Cumbria, the name Cardunneth possibly means 'Dunod's fort' but an older form *Cardunnoke* (c.1390) suggests another derivation. None of this really brings us any closer to Dunod the Stout. Even if we could be sure that Cardunneth and Dent owe their names to someone called Dunod, it would still require a big leap to identify him as the man who fought at Arfderydd.

The fourth rider on the horse of Eliffer's sons was Cynfelyn, whose epithet *Drwsgyl* is usually translated 'Leprous'. The pedigrees appear to connect him with a royal dynasty on the Clyde but, as stated before, the reliability of these texts should not be assumed. Like his fellow-riders he is geographically adrift and cannot be linked with confidence to a particular kingdom. Pedigrees asso-ciating his kinsmen Clydno and Cadrod with *Eiddin* (Edinburgh) and *Calchfynydd* (perhaps Kelso) might incorporate authentic data but tell us little about Cynfelyn himself.[33]

Rhydderch Hael

When William Forbes Skene presented his paper on the battle of Arfderydd to the Society of Antiquaries of Scotland in 1865, he identified Gwenddolau's principal adversary as Rhydderch Hael. In Chapter 2, we discussed this same Rhydderch in the context of the Myrddin poetry, where he appears as a king whose men pursue the wild fugitive through the forest. In *Yr Afallennau*, possi-bly the oldest of the poems, a tree provided Myrddin with concealment from his pursuers, one of whom is named:

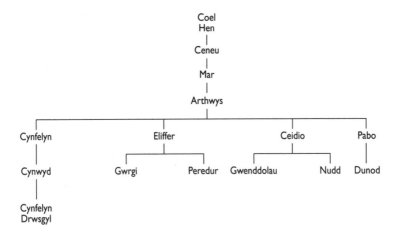

Pedigrees of the Arfderydd protagonists, based on information in the Welsh genealogical tract *Bonedd Gwŷr y Gogledd*, 'Descent of the Men of the North' (c.1250)

'Sweet apple-tree that grows in a glade,
its peculiar power hides it from the lords of Rhydderch;
a crowd by its trunk, a host around it,
it would be a treasure for them, brave men in the ranks.
Now Gwenddydd loves me not and does not greet me
– I am hated by Gwasawg, the supporter of Rhydderch –
I have killed her son and her daughter.'[34]

In *Yr Oianau*, Myrddin advises the piglet to hide from Rhydderch's hounds:

'burrow in a hidden place in the woodlands,
for fear of the hunting-dogs of Rhydderch Hael, defender of the Faith'

Later in the same poem, Myrddin compares the hardships of winter in the wilderness to the comforts of a royal feasting-hall:

'Little does Rhydderch Hael know tonight in his feast
what sleeplessness I suffered last night,
snow up to my hips among the wolves of the forest,
icicles in my hair, spent is my splendour'

In the *Cyfoesi*, Myrddin prophesies Rhydderch's death ('there will be no Rhydderch Hael the day after tomorrow') and in *Peiryan Vaban* he refers to 'the encounter of Rhydderch and renowned Aeddan, so clearly it is heard from the north to the south'.[35] This 'Aeddan' was the sixth-century Scottish king Áedán mac Gabráin who ruled from a power-base in Argyll. Welsh tradition does not explicitly associate him with Myrddin, nor is he directly linked to the Arfderydd campaign, so his 'encounter' with Rhydderch might have no connection with the battle of 573. Nevertheless, some modern commentators take a contrasting view. They deduce from *Peiryan Vaban* that both Rhydderch and Áedán were indeed present and that Rhydderch was Gwenddolau's chief adversary, thus explaining his later harassment of Myrddin. This was the scenario preferred by Skene and it has remained popular ever since.[36] It can be traced back a further 200 years, to the seventeenth-century Welsh antiquary Robert Vaughan who seems to have been the first to connect Rhydderch with the battle of Arfderydd.[37] However, no such connection is hinted at in the Myrddin poetry or in the triads. In the poems, Rhydderch is simply Myrddin's oppressor in a later period, when Gwenddolau was already dead. Vaughan may have assumed that Rhydderch fought at Arfderydd because of the role played by 'Rodarch, king of the Cumbrians' in Geoffrey of Monmouth's *Vita Merlini*. At the beginning of *VM*, Rodarch accompanied Merlin and Peredur 'of the North Welsh' to a battle in which they were victorious over Guennolous 'who ruled the kingdom of Scotland'. Geoffrey was clearly drawing on Welsh traditions of Arfderydd but shuffled the main characters so that Merlin/Myrddin appeared on the winning side as an ally of Rodarch/Rhydderch, the king who had been his oppressor in the Welsh poems. Before Geoffrey, there was no hint that Rhydderch participated in the battle. He should therefore be excluded from it.

Unlike Gwenddolau, Peredur, Gwrgi, Dunod and Cynfelyn, all of whom are cited only in the Welsh sources, Rhydderch Hael appears in literature from other lands. His geographical context is secure and precise, mainly due to the reference in Adomnán's *vita* of St Columba. Writing at the end of the seventh century, Adomnán identified 'Roderc, son of Tothail, king of the Rock of Clyde' as Columba's contemporary and friend. We have already noted that this is the Rhydderch of the Myrddin poems. Not only is *Roderc* an older form of the name, Welsh tradition calls Rhydderch 'son of Tudwal' and associates him with *Alt Clut*, which means 'Rock of Clyde' in Cumbric. Alt Clut was known to Gaelic-speakers as *Dun Breatann*, 'Fortress of the Britons', a name still used today in the Anglicised form Dumbarton. Archaeological excavations in the 1970s showed that the Rock was inhabited by people of wealth and status in the sixth and seventh centuries.[38] The physical evidence matches the testimony of contemporary chronicles, such as the Irish Annals, which frequently refer to the kings of Alt Clut as key players in Dark Age politics. A pedigree preserved in Wales traces the lineage of these kings backwards from the ninth century to a shadowy period in the late fourth or early fifth. Although the list of names omits Rhydderch Hael, a separate pedigree shows him descending from a collateral branch of the main royal line. The Welsh triads refer to his court at Alt Clut, to his horse 'Dun Grey' and to his magical sword. He also appears in Scottish traditions that are independent of the Welsh material. The oldest of these is in Adomnán's Life of Columba while another is found in the Kentigern hagiography used by Jocelin of Furness in the twelfth century.[39] Jocelin's king *Rederech* of the Clyde – obviously Rhydderch Hael – has an important role in the Kentigern narrative as patron and protector of the saint. In Rederech's palace at *Pertnech* (Partick) dwells the madman Laloecen whom the king treats quite well. By contrast, Laloecen's Welsh counterpart Myrddin lives in fear of Rhydderch. Royal hostility is also a theme in the tales of Lailoken, one of which reports his death at the hands of shepherds in King Meldred's service. This same king's hostility is more ambivalent in the other tale where, on the one hand, he holds Lailoken captive in the hope of extracting a new prophecy from him, yet later defends him against the queen's false accusations. In neither tale is there any mention of Rederech. This suggests that two different accounts of Lailoken's dealings with royalty evolved in North British tradition. In one, the king is benevolent and compassionate (Rederech); in the other, he is rather less genial (Meldred) or outwardly hostile (Rhydderch Hael). While it is possible that these reflect two contrasting aspects of a single character, it is perhaps more likely that there was originally only one version of the story and that this featured a hostile king. Having already discussed Rhydderch, the Welsh representation of this character, we now turn to his Scottish equivalent.

King Meldred

Nothing is known of Meldred outside the Lailoken tales. He is not mentioned in Welsh tradition, unless he lies behind its portrait of Rhydderch Hael. Like Rhydderch he has no direct link with the battle of Arfderydd, except via his interaction with one of the survivors. In the story of his wife's adultery he takes the role played by Rederech in the parallel version told by Jocelin of Furness. These two kings are unlikely to have entered the Lailoken legend as separate characters whose respective roles later became conflated and confused. A more plausible scenario is that the one replaced the other, with Rederech arguably the newcomer. Rederech's major presence in the Kentigern hagiography should make us wonder if he, alongside the saint, was parachuted into the Lailoken legend at some point during its evolution. Did he displace an original character called Meldred who was less well-known to a Glasgow audience? We know that Rederech/Rhydderch certainly existed so perhaps Meldred did too. If he was real, we can envisage him as the ruler of a small kingdom in the valley of the River Tweed, the area where his encounter with Lailoken takes place. He is described as a *regulus*, a minor king, the vassal of a more powerful monarch. The latter might have been none other than Rhydderch of Alt Clut, assigning the eastern frontier of his realm to a *regulus* from whom he could expect homage and tribute. At first glance, the name Meldred appears to be of English origin, being similar to the name Maldred borne by an eleventh-century Northumbrian nobleman. The suffix looks like Old English *raed*, 'counsel, advice', seen in names like Aethelred and Uhtred. However, both Maldred and Meldred may represent a Cumbric name in which the first element was *Mael* (as in Welsh *Maelgwn*). Such a name could have been particularly associated with the kingdom of Strathclyde, a possibility worth considering in the light of the name of Maldred's son Gospatric which derives from Cumbric *Gwas-Patric* 'servant of St Patrick'.[40] Alternatively, Maldred might indeed be an English name, albeit one transcribed as Meldred to replace a similar-sounding Cumbric name that the writer of *Vita Merlini Silvestris* found strange or unfamiliar. We can probably assume that 'King Meldred' was a Briton. The *Vita* calls his fortress *Dunmeller* but this name, like his own, does not appear in any other source. Nor will it be found on a modern map. It is now *Drumelzier* (with the 'z' pronounced 'y'), the name of a village in Upper Tweeddale. Older forms of the present-day name include *Drummeiller* (1326), *Dumelliare* (1305) and *Dunmedlar* (c.1200). Their root is commonly assumed to be of Gaelic origin, with the meaning 'bare fort'. Contemporary records show that the medieval forms were mainly associated with a castle on the 'haugh' or low-lying ground on the east bank of the Tweed. The castle's ruins are still visible at Drumelzier Place, a farm situated a little under one mile south-west of the village. In medieval times the castle was the seat of the Tweedie family, lords of the barony of Drumelzier from at least the thirteenth century. In the 1600s, the Tweedies sold their lands to the Hays, who remain lords of Drumelzier to this day.

During their years of prosperity, the Tweedies maintained an outpost on a small, conical hill at the north end of the village. This is known today as Tinnis Castle, a name possibly deriving from Cumbric *dinas* ('fort') if it is not merely a corruption of 'Thane's'. Only a few scant traces are visible today. It seems to have stood on the site of an older stronghold than the castle on the haugh, possibly a tower or keep erected in the twelfth century by a Norman retainer of the Scottish kings. The hill itself is a distinctive feature in the local landscape, a natural vantage point commanding wide views over the Tweed valley. Its strategic potential was recognised as far back as the Iron Age, when a hillfort was erected on the top. The main wall of this ancient settlement enclosed the summit plateau and was of drystone construction laced with timber. No additional defences were needed on the precipitous south-east slope but, where the gradient was less steep, protection was offered by two outer ramparts, one with a ditch on the inner side. The fort was apparently entered from the south-west, via openings in the outer ramparts and inner wall.[41] This is as much as archaeology can presently tell us. In the absence of a modern, full-scale excavation the chronology of occupation and abandonment are unknown. Nevertheless, it is tempting to identify this as the fortress of King Meldred where Lailoken was held captive. The second element of *Dunmeller* may even preserve the king's name, prefixed with Gaelic *dun* to give the meaning 'Meldred's Fort'.[42]

Maelgwn, Taliesin and Arfderydd

The Myrddin poems were composed in Wales and frequently refer to Welsh people, places and events. These references sit alongside those relating to northern Britain and to the 'wild man of the woods' who fought at the battle of Arfderydd in 573. The Welsh material in the poems spans a broad swathe of history, from the Dark Ages to the Anglo-Norman period, much of it presented as political prophecy uttered by Myrddin himself. In one poem, the *Ymddiddan* or 'Dialogue' between Myrddin and Taliesin, the latter mentions the Welsh king Maelgwn Gwynedd:

> 'Maelgwn's host, bravely they came,
> resplendent warriors of battle on a bloody field.
> The battle of Arfderydd (whence comes the cause?)
> all during life they prepare for it.'[43]

The Welsh Annals place Maelgwn's death in 547, nearly thirty years before the battle of Arfderydd. He was a real king rather than a legendary one but, as far as we know, he never waged war in northern Britain. One Welsh tale does, however, claim that his son Rhun launched an invasion of the North in revenge for a raid on Gwynedd by Rhydderch Hael and other well-known northern figures.[44] At first glance, this might seem to provide a possible context for Maelgwn's alleged participation at Arfderydd – a feud spanning two generations of the Gwynedd dynasty. However, the story of Rhun's northern campaign is almost certainly fiction. It was probably invented as political propaganda for later kings who claimed him as an ancestor. Such a tale would have enhanced his status – and therefore that of his descendants in Gwynedd – by pitching him against mighty heroes of the Old North. A similar propagandist motive may account for his father's supposed presence in the northern battle of 573.

The bard Taliesin – Geoffrey of Monmouth's Telgesinus – is a familiar figure in early Welsh literature. He is best-known for giving his name to *Llyfr Taliesin*, the Book of Taliesin, a manuscript of the fourteenth century containing more than fifty poems supposedly composed by him. Tradition assigns him to the sixth century, yet most of the poems in his *Llyfr* are plainly of much later date. Only twelve are considered to be ancient, although even these are not demonstrably older than the tenth century.[45] Eight refer to the North British king Urien of Rheged whose deeds of warfare and raiding are described and praised. Urien is mentioned in *Historia Brittonum* as one of four kings who fought against the Anglo-Saxon kingdom of Bernicia – the northern part of the later realm of Northumbria – in the second half of the sixth century. Another of the four was Rhydderch Hael of Alt Clut. Rhydderch was active in the time of St Columba's abbacy of Iona (c.563–97) and thus provides a secure chronological anchor for Urien. *HB* describes a war in which Urien besieged Theodoric, son of Ida, on the island of Lindisfarne. Theodoric ruled Bernicia from 572 to 579, so his conflict with Urien can be assigned to this period. Taliesin himself also appears in *HB*, as one of the five Elder Bards in the time of Ida (died 547), but is not there associated with Urien. In the eight praise-poems he identifies himself as Urien's personal bard at the royal court of Rheged. Unfortunately, the precise location of Rheged is unknown, in spite of a widely held (and very tenuous) belief that it lay near the Solway Firth.[46] Modern scholars have tended to regard the eight 'archaic' Taliesin poems as reliable sources of sixth-century history, accepting them as the authentic work of Urien's bard. However, a shadow of doubt hangs over such optimism while the date of composition remains uncertain. It has been suggested that Kentigern's role in the Lailoken tales may have been played in *Vita Merlini* by Taliesin.[47] On the other hand, Taliesin is not associated by Welsh tradition with the Arfderydd campaign. The stanza quoted above is therefore unlikely to incorporate genuine North British information relating to the battle. It belongs rather to a later period of composition, long after the Arfderydd lore arrived in Wales, when Taliesin, Maelgwn and other famous characters were drawn into the story.

Summary: Lailoken and Arfderydd

In the previous chapter we noted that Myrddin Wyllt, the mad prophet of early Welsh tradition, owes much of his character to the wild man Lailoken whose story is told in Scottish texts. Myrddin's madness was caused by his witnessing of the terrible carnage at Arfderydd which claimed the lives of many brave warriors. Lailoken's insanity likewise began during a bloody battle fought in a field between Liddel and Carwinley on the northern boundary of Arthuret parish. In Lailoken's case, his mind was overthrown when a celestial voice accused him of being the cause of the slaughter. So similar are the Welsh and Scottish traditions that they are unlikely to have arisen independently. They clearly share the same origin. Names have been changed and details have been altered but the core narrative tells of a great battle at the confluence of Liddesdale and Eskdale. This was a real event that took place in the year 573. The commanders on both sides were North British kings, one of whom was Gwenddolau whose territory included the battlefield itself. It seems quite plausible that one of the few survivors was a warrior who had fought in Gwenddolau's army, a man so traumatised by what he had seen that he fled into the wilderness.[48] If we are seeking one particular event – a single moment in history that provided the spark for the Merlin legend – then the battle of Arfderydd is undoubtedly it.

5

CHRISTIANITY AND PAGANISM

A futile battle

The previous chapter addressed three key questions in relation to the battle of Arfderydd: When? Where? and Who? Having discussed the date, the location and the identities of the commanders, we turn now to a different question: Why? This can be expanded into two parts: What was the cause of the battle and what were the motives of its participants? Once again, we must sift through the various sources, looking for pertinent clues. We begin with an item from Welsh literature: the Triad of the Three Futile Battles:

> Three Futile Battles of the Island of Britain.
> One of them was the Battle of Goddeu: it was brought about by the cause of the bitch, together with the roebuck and the plover.
> The second was the Action of Arfderydd, which was brought about by the cause of the lark's nest.
> And the third was the worst: that was Camlan, which was brought about because of a quarrel between Gwenhwyfar and Gwennhwyfach.
> This is why they were called Futile: because they were brought about by such a barren cause as that.[1]

From this triad we learn an interesting fact about the battle of Arfderydd: Welsh tradition regarded it as a conflict waged for trivial reasons. Like Camlan and Goddeu it was believed to have been fought over a small or trifling matter. The curious detail of the bird's nest is left unexplained but probably refers to a tale or poem that no longer survives. Nevertheless, the triad contains the only direct information on the cause of the battle, hence its exposure to considerable scrutiny by modern scholars. Some have wondered if the 'lark's nest' might be an allusion to a real place that did indeed become a bone of contention in 573. Suitable candidates have duly been looked for in the lands around the head of the Solway Firth, in the hope of gaining an insight into why the battle was fought. Much attention has been drawn to the castle of Caerlaverock, a well-known site on the Dumfriesshire coast. This stone-built stronghold with its distinctive triangular shape has a name that might have been formed from Cumbric *caer* or *car* and the Old English word *laverock* to give the meaning 'Fort of the Lark'.[2] It was built in the thirteenth century on a low-lying position that initially looks unpromising as the site of an ancient fort. We would probably expect the latter to be on higher ground like a typical Celtic hillfort. Moreover, we may note that in medieval times, before the Solway shoreline shifted further away, the land around the castle was prone to flooding.[3] The original *caer* is therefore hard to identify. We do not even know if it was a native British fort or a Roman one. There is a suggestion that a Roman harbour once existed south of the castle, but no such facility has yet been discovered. In the same general location, between castle and shore, a mysterious lozenge-shaped mound can be seen today. Surrounded by a double ditch, this might be a feature of Roman or Dark Age date, if it is not simply an outlying earthwork of the castle.[4] Looking in the other direction, a more likely candidate for the original Caerlaverock is the hillfort of Wardlaw. This seems a fairly plausible 'Fort of the Lark', despite being situated one mile from the castle. It stands in a strategic position above the mouth of the River Nith, which is no doubt why the Romans erected a small fort of their own nearby. The hillfort itself is prehistoric, having almost certainly been abandoned during the Roman period, but archaeological investigation at some future date may yet reveal evidence of Dark Age reuse.[5] We should keep in mind that Wardlaw and Caerlaverock may have no connection with the Arfderydd campaign. The 'lark's nest' in the triad need not be a reference to a real place at all. It might be nothing more than a metaphor for pettiness, to emphasise that the battle of 573 was fought over something small and insignificant. Besides, there is no certainty that the name Caerlaverock does mean 'Fort of the Lark'. It is equally possible that it represents 'Llywarch's Fort', perhaps in commemoration of a North British prince-poet called Llywarch Hen ('Llywarch the Old') who was said to have been a kinsman of Urien Rheged.[6] Like Urien himself, Llywarch Hen lacks a precise geographical context, but he probably existed. He was a famous character in Welsh poetry of the ninth century and his fame, like Urien's, might have originated in the North. His real or legendary association with a site near the shore of the Solway Firth remains a possibility.

Setting aside the mysterious lark's nest, we turn to other possible causes of the battle. One intriguing suggestion is that Gwenddolau was attacked by fellow-Britons because he had formed an alliance with their Anglo-Saxon enemies.

This appeared in 1931 in an article by W.R. Gourlay who, in the previous year, had presented an oral account of the battle to members of the Dumfriesshire and Galloway Natural History and Antiquarian Society outside the parish church of Arthuret. In his article, Gourlay noted that Gwenddolau had a stronghold or *caer* 'in the neighbourhood of Netherby'. Drawing on information in the Welsh pedigrees, Gourlay also noted that Gwenddolau had a brother called Nudd, an obscure figure of whom little is known. He then explained that the most northerly of the Anglo-Saxon kingdoms was Bernicia, on the coast of present-day Northumberland. This was founded by Ida in the middle of the sixth century. According to a passage in *Historia Brittonum*, Urien Rheged and three other North British kings – Rhydderch Hael, Gwallawg and Morcant – fought against Ida's sons. Gourlay observed that neither Gwenddolau nor Nudd is mentioned in this passage and wondered if their absence might be significant: 'It is possible that these two brothers had become friendly with the Saxons, and that this friendliness had made them an object of suspicion to the rest of the Britons. The possibility of the Saxons cutting the Britons' territory in two by settlements on the Solway was a real danger.'[7]

Suspicion then led to an invasion of the brothers' territory and to their defeat at Arfderydd. All in all, an ingenious theory, yet it is based on a particular interpretation of a single passage in *HB*. Gourlay is by no means alone in assuming that the context of this passage was a North British military alliance comprising the armies of four kingdoms in a joint venture against Bernicia. Indeed, this view remains so prevalent that the alliance or 'coalition' is often regarded as an established fact of sixth-century political history. It is worth taking a closer look at the passage to see what it actually says:

> Against them [the Bernicians] fought four kings; Urien, and Rhydderch the Old, and Gwallawg, and Morcant. Theodoric fought vigorously against Urien and his sons. During that time, sometimes the enemy, sometimes the citizens [i.e., the Britons] were victorious, and Urien blockaded them for three days and three nights in the island of Lindisfarne. But, while he was campaigning, Urien was killed at the instigation of Morcant, from jealousy, because his military skill and generalship surpassed that of all the other kings.[8]

The author of *HB* was not necessarily saying that the Britons acted in unison. He simply gave the names of four kings who waged war on Ida's successors and made the point that Urien was the best general among them. There is no real hint that the British kings pooled their forces in a single campaign rather than mounting individual ventures of their own on different occasions. Nor is there any implication that other kings were left out of the list because they had been politically ostracised. The fact that Gwenddolau and Nudd are not mentioned is therefore irrelevant. The absence of these brothers tells us nothing about their relationships with other Britons. At the very most, we could perhaps make a general observation that later Welsh tradition did not regard them as prominent foes of the Anglo-Saxons, but this is as far as we can go.

The Scottish historian George Chalmers, writing in the early nineteenth century, believed that the battle of Arfderydd was a contest between Rhydderch Hael on one side and Gwenddolau on the other, with the Scottish king Áedán mac Gabráin fighting as Gwenddolau's ally. While suspecting that the cause of the battle was irretrievable, Chalmers ventured a theory of his own. He suggested that the main bone of contention may have been 'a disputed boundary' rather than the elusive bird's nest of Welsh tradition. Although he did not say which boundary he had in mind, it was presumably not in the Solway lands but closer to Airdrie in Clydesdale, his preferred candidate for Arfderydd. He believed that the battle was fought in Rhydderch's territory, the kingdom of Alt Clut or Dumbarton, and perhaps imagined that the frontier dispute occurred on the edge of this realm.[9]

A religious crusade?

The plain fact of the matter is that we have absolutely no idea why the battle of Arfderydd was fought. Our scant knowledge of the political history of the Old North sheds little or no light, while the 'lark's nest' might be nothing more than a symbol of pettiness and futility. None of the theories discussed in the previous section brings us closer to the cause of the conflict. One more theory remains to be considered, for it is frequently quoted, especially in the context of the Merlin legend. This sees the battle as a religious contest fought by Christians on one side and pagans on the other. It first appeared in the nineteenth century and was a key theme in the paper presented by Skene to the Society of Antiquaries of Scotland in 1865. Drawing on information in the Welsh triads, Skene proposed that Gwenddolau was a heathen king who stubbornly resisted the advance of Christianity. Skene identified two triads that he saw as containing allusions to Gwenddolau's paganism. In the triad of the Horse-Burdens, the Welsh term *mygedorth* was interpreted by Skene not as 'battle-fog' but as 'sacred fire', thus rendering the line in question as 'to see the sacred fire of Gwenddolau at

Arfderydd'.[10] This immediately added a mystical or supernatural aspect that was certainly not implied by the more literal interpretation of *mygedorth* as 'battle-fog'. In her definitive edition of the Welsh triads, Professor Rachel Bromwich imagined *mygedorth* as 'the rising vapour of cloud or dust which arose from a horse or army in the stress of battle'.[11] Another possibility is that the 'fog' has a more gory explanation, being due to the sheer ferocity of hand-to-hand combat. Bromwich cited the case of an old Irish tale of battle in which 'it is said that in the press and fury of the contest no two persons could recognize each other, because of the wind-driven blood'.[12] The imagery conjured here is of a mist formed by blood-spatter as the warriors hack desperately at each other. Skene's interpretation is therefore not the only one available, nor is there any reason to assign it precedence over others.

Another Welsh triad tells of Three Fortunate Assassinations of the Island of Britain and refers to 'the two birds of Gwenddolau, and they had a yoke of gold on them. They ate two corpses of the *Cymry* [Britons] for dinner, and two for supper'. Skene saw this as evidence of heathen beliefs. He suggested that Gwenddolau 'with his sacred fire, and his birds who devoured men, was surely the type of the old paganism of the country'.[13] Marching against Gwenddolau's pagan enclave, according to Skene's vision of the battle, came a Christian force led by Rhydderch Hael. Like Chalmers before him, Skene regarded Rhydderch as Gwenddolau's main adversary, but imagined him as a zealous crusader who commanded 'the Christian party' in the battle. This was Skene's own idea and is not implied by the sources, which merely confirm that Rhydderch was indeed a Christian king whose contacts included the renowned saints Columba and Kentigern. Skene was familiar with the Myrddin poems and perhaps placed an overly literal interpretation on one line in *Yr Oianau* which refers to Rhydderch as 'defender of the faith'. He certainly believed that the campaign against Gwenddolau must have had a religious dimension, seeing it as nothing less than 'a great struggle between the supporters of the advancing Christianity and the departing paganism, in which the former were victorious'.[14]

Skene's train of thought was picked up by subsequent commentators. In 1892, the year of Skene's death, Arthur Grant offered the following account of the circumstances surrounding the battle:

Druidism, which had well-nigh disappeared among the Southern Britons, still flourished among the Men of the North, as the Scottish Cymri were sometimes called. Many of the noble families proudly held to their ancient belief, and, as Christianity crept in amongst them, the breach between

Christian and pagan Cymri grew wider and wider. The chiefs of two ancient royal houses took opposite sides in this struggle – Rhydderch Hael leading the Christian, and Gwenddolew the pagan factions [. . .] At last the crisis came, when the Christian and pagan forces met on the battlefield of Ardderyd in the year AD 573.[15]

Gourlay, in the article mentioned above, thought Gwenddolau 'belonged to the old British faith, or at least he was not a Christian'. This was no doubt prompted by Skene's 'sacred fire' and the man-eating birds. Gourlay suggested that Christianity had once held sway in the region around Arfderydd but had been forced into retreat 'and in its place had come the influence of the gods of the Saxons'. He nevertheless regarded the battle as having been fought primarily for political reasons, 'one incident in the campaign of the Britons against the Saxons and not a battle of Christians against pagans'.[16]

Skene's influence on later studies of the battle can be seen in the following statement by F.J. Carruthers, writing in the final quarter of the twentieth century: 'History states that it was fought between the Christian and pagan parties, and that Rhydderch led the winning Christians.'[17] History, of course, says no such thing. Indeed, although Skene and others suggested religious warfare as the underlying cause, their theories are modern and do not carry the authority of ancient tradition. Carruthers believed that the battle settled a long-running religious conflict in the Solway region, seeing it as 'a turning point in a struggle which had been waged for years between the advancing forces of Christianity, and the retreating influences of paganism within the British people [. . .] it was nevertheless a local fight: a private fight between two competing religious factions of the same nation'.[18] Notwithstanding this belief, he acknowledged that the cause of the battle remained elusive, adding that it may have been fought 'for possession of Caerlaverock, over a disputed boundary, on religious grounds, or just for the hell of it'.[19]

The notion of Arfderydd as a battle fought over religion was explored by Nikolai Tolstoy in his 1985 book *The Quest for Merlin*. Tolstoy accepted Skene's interpretation of the triads as hinting at Gwenddolau's paganism. He suggested that the birds who ate four people each day might indicate that Gwenddolau's kingdom was home to 'a cult of malevolent otherworld birds'.[20] One triadic allusion highlighted by Tolstoy, but not by Skene, mentions Gwenddolau's ownership of a gold chessboard with silver pieces that played by themselves. Its obviously magical properties led Tolstoy to suggest that it may have had 'a ritual significance'.[21] In the triad of the horse-burdens, Tolstoy preferred the more accurate translation 'battle-fog' to Skene's 'sacred fire' but nevertheless interpreted this phenomenon as 'druidical', seeing it as a magical mist designed to frighten Gwenddolau's enemies.[22] On a broader note, Tolstoy drew a distinction between the Britons of the North and their southern compatriots in the fifth and sixth centuries, seeing the former as less Romanised and therefore less civilised. Such folk, he argued, would have been less receptive to Christianity, the religion of Rome, and more willing to preserve their old heathen ways. Thus, while acknowledging that all North British kings were at least nominally Christian by c.600, he suggested that some merely paid lip service to the new faith. He interpreted 'bull-protector of the Island of Britain', a description bestowed on both Urien Rheged and Gwenddolau in one Welsh triad, as referring to a pagan attribute.[23] He also regarded as non-Christian the practice of burying a king's head separately from the body, citing the cases of Urien and an Irish contemporary, both of whom were said to have been decapitated after death. Taken together, the various hints and allusions led Tolstoy to propose the following scenario:

> It would seem, then, that paganism was openly practised in the North in the second half of the sixth century, and that stories circulating in later centuries remembered Gwenddolau in particular as a figure associated with heathen practices. There is thus some reason for believing that the battle of Arderydd was fought between a pagan prince and his Christian adversaries.[24]

Dark Age druids

Celtic paganism is frequently associated with the druids, an elite social class in the pre-Roman Iron Age of Britain, Ireland and Gaul.[25] The term 'druid' seems to have encompassed various custodians of knowledge and lore – bards, healers and judges – but the most familiar image is of a pagan priest or sorcerer. Antiquarian writers of the seventeenth, eighteenth and nineteenth centuries showed a particular fascination with druids, nurturing a romanticised view that fitted with broader contemporary ideas about ancient Celtic society.[26] These ideas were popularised by works such as the Ossian saga, an edition of supposedly ancient Celtic poems that was actually little more than a late eighteenth-century invention. Such romanticism encouraged the growth of a detailed but largely fictional reconstruction of druidical beliefs and practices. It led, for example, to labels such as 'druid temple' being bestowed on mysterious prehistoric sites whose age and purpose could not otherwise be explained.²⁷ The primary example of this creativity is Stonehenge, which was popularly associated with druids. Indeed, the term 'druidism' itself was used in a rather casual way as a synonym for Celtic paganism and as a convenient umbrella for any non-Christian religious practices in the old Celtic lands. This was an erroneous view, for the word 'druid' originally had a much narrower meaning. It first appeared in Classical literature in a Greek text of c.300 BC and was later used by Latin writers after the Roman conquest of Gaul in the first century BC. Rome regarded the druids as members of a powerful priesthood drawn from the upper levels of Celtic society and as practitioners of magic.²⁸ It saw them as a political threat, a rallying-point for native resistance. There is, however, no indication that druids were present in every Celtic region, nor that their 'order' was a formal, international institution like the Christian priesthood of later times. Usually male, the druid was portrayed in Roman writings as an intermediary between the people and their gods and as an overseer of religious rituals such as sacrifice. The famous general Julius Caesar, our main source of information on druids, noted the contemporary belief that druids originated in Britain. He also stated that Gallic druids were accustomed to travelling to Britain when they wanted to further their knowledge. Aside from these references, Caesar tells us nothing about British druids and leaves us to assume that they were similar in most respects to their Gallic brethren. Some hundred years later, we learn from another Roman text of the destruction of a major druidical centre on Anglesey in AD 61. The writer in question, Cornelius Tacitus, conjured a dramatic scene of fire and slaughter accompanied by the cries of dying priests and the screams of black-robed women.²⁹ The attack on Anglesey broke the power of the druids, thus removing a potential major obstacle from Rome's path to the eventual conquest of Britain.

Outside the realm of literature, the druids are largely invisible. Nothing in the archaeological record can be conclusively associated with them, not even a single site or inscription. It has even been suggested that they were invented by Classical authors as stereotypical 'noble savages' – an imaginary order of barbarian priests whose primitive rituals were untouched by Roman sleaze. Such scepticism may be unwarranted but we should nevertheless be wary of imagining druidism as a formal set of religious beliefs, or of its practitioners as members of a monolithic, pan-Celtic priesthood organised along formal lines like the clerical orders of Christian times.

Druids slipped out of the documentary record for a while before reappearing in the post-Roman 'Dark Ages' when they turn up in British and Irish texts written by Christian monks. It may be more accurate to say that the term 'druid' was now applied to certain sages, sorcerers and seers who performed various roles in Celtic society. Irish law-codes written c.700 referred to 'druids' casting spells but it is hard to see what these magicians had in common with the high-status, politically powerful priests of earlier times.[30] Contemporary with the law-codes was Adomnán's account of St Columba's clash with a heathen Pictish sorcerer called Broichan. This probably occurred c.570 in the vicinity of modern Inverness and is discussed further below. Although some English translations of Adomnán's work call Broichan a druid, we should not be too quick to assume that the druidical order of pre-Roman times survived, or was revived, in sixth-century Pictland – or, for that matter, in any other Celtic region. In tenth-century Wales, more than 200 years after Adomnán's death, the author of the poem *Armes Prydein* mentions druids (Welsh *dryw*) but this is either a reference to the ancient priesthood of Roman times or to contemporary folk who possessed prophetic powers.[31] There is, in fact, no evidence that druidism of the type mentioned in Classical texts was still being practised anywhere in Britain or Ireland in the Dark Ages. Vague similarities between the supernatural prac-tices described in Irish or Welsh texts and the religious rituals performed by the druids of the pre-Roman period do not substantially challenge this view.

Myrddin the druid

The notion of Arfderydd as a showdown between paganism and Christianity enjoys widespread popularity. From such a standpoint, it is only a small step to cast Myrddin in the role of pagan priest or 'druid'. The basic premise seems, at first glance, to be quite rational and logical. Just as a pious Christian king had Christian priests and bishops in his entourage to perform sacred rituals, so a non-Christian king would surely have assigned this role to pagan equivalents. Moreover, there appears to be a historical analogy from the very era in which Gwenddolau and Myrddin were active. Adomnán of Iona, in his Life of Columba, reported an encounter between the saint and the pagan sorcerer Broichan at the stronghold of a Pictish king. Broichan is described by Adomnán as a *magus*, a Latin term translated in some English versions of the Life as 'druid' but in others as 'wizard' or 'magician'.[32] Adomnán portrays him as a key figure at the royal court, a man with strange powers who serves as counsellor and foster-father to the king. His pagan beliefs are reflected in bitter hostility towards Columba, whose entry to the royal fortress Broichan attempts to thwart with sorcery. Some modern scholars see the historical Myrddin undertaking a similar role as Gwenddolau's 'druid' in a pagan enclave around the head of the Solway Firth. Robin Crichton, for example, sees Gwenddolau's stronghold as 'a last bastion of the old pagan religion where earlier attempts at Christian conversion had actually been reversed in favour of a return to the traditional ways. By the second half of the 6th century Merlin was the Chief Druid'.[33]

If we are to imagine Myrddin, or rather the Merlin-archetype, as a sixth-century druid we must accept that the ancient druidical 'order' survived to some extent in northern Britain long after the end of Roman rule. Nikolai Tolstoy proposed that this was indeed the case, and that Myrddin/Merlin fits the mould of a Dark Age druid. He noted that the druids of pre-Christian times were said by contemporary Roman writers to dwell in the deepest parts of remote forests. In such places, he suggested, they may have felt safe from Roman hostility, just as Myrddin sought a woodland refuge after his traumatic experience at Arfderydd.[34] Tolstoy likewise identified Myrddin's prophetic powers and other supernatural talents as druidic abilities. He wondered if they reflected 'authentic tradition' about the historical Merlin-archetype who, he suggested, may have been a leading figure among the surviving remnants of British druidism: 'Possibly in name and certainly in function he was the Chief Druid, who presided over rituals necessary to preserve the harmony of the natural order [. . .]'.[35] Tolstoy believed that Myrddin's Pictish contemporary Broichan was likewise a druid, accepting this as the correct interpretation of *magus*. He was, however, also aware of alternative meanings such as 'wizard'.[36] He saw Broichan's encounter with St Columba as evidence for the survival of druidism in Dark Age Britain. Moreover, tenth-century Welsh poetry supplied what Tolstoy regarded as supportive data: 'The poem Armes Prydein alternates the authority for its prophecy between Myrddin and the druids, and may it not fairly be asked whether Merlin himself was a surviving druid? What has been conjectured of his refuge in the Caledonian Forest certainly accords with druidic practice.'[37]

Ean Begg and Deike Rich, in the introduction to their 1991 book *On the Trail of Merlin*, echoed Tolstoy in their assessment of the historical Merlin-archetype: 'He undoubtedly continued and embodied the spirit of druidism, and may even have been the last great druid of the Strathclyde Britons.'[38] They, too, saw the Columba-Broichan story as proof of druidism's survival in the Old North. In their opinion, the historical Merlin was 'chief druid to King Gwenddolau'. Accepting present-day popular notions about Celtic Christianity and its supposed affinity with paganism and Nature, they regarded the early Celtic saints themselves as 'Christianized druids'. Needless to say, this view of the men and women who founded the first churches in Britain and Ireland has

little basis in historical fact.[39] It reflects a common misconception that originated in modern times. The so-called 'Celtic Church' of the Dark Ages was not,
as some people appear to believe, an institution separated from – still less
opposed to – the contemporary mainstream of Roman Catholicism. Nor was
its clergy overly populated by nature-loving ascetics who, in defiance of Rome,
held an ambivalent view towards pagan practices. Prominent Celtic saints such
as Columba, Brigid, Patrick and Kentigern would have been horrified to see
themselves cast as mavericks or pagan sympathisers. While it is certainly true
that stories about the old gods and the Celtic Otherworld were documented by
Christian writers and preserved in the monasteries of Britain and Ireland, these
were regarded as works of historical or literary value rather than as sacred texts.
This is not to say that the coming of Christianity swept all vestiges of Celtic
paganism away. The names of the old gods were long remembered and, in a few
cases, continued to be venerated.[40] Deities traditionally associated with healing
and protection, for example, were invoked in time of need, even by Christian
converts. But the key point is that the organisational infrastructures of paganism were unlikely to have survived the onslaught of the new religion. The two
institutions could not exist side-by-side. Wherever Christianity came, the old
beliefs died out within a couple of generations. Christian missionaries in the
Celtic lands were not, as is sometimes imagined, willing to turn a blind eye to
pagan worship. They were determined to eradicate it. In such a climate of non-
tolerance it is very unlikely that druidism, in whatever form, was able to survive.

In the Old North, in what is now southern Scotland, archaeological evidence
shows that the aristocratic, landowning elite proudly displayed their Christian
credentials on memorial stones. This custom was well under way by c.500.
Christian inscriptions occur all over the region, from the Clyde to the Solway
and from the Forth to the Tweed.[41] If the noble families were embracing
Christianity with such enthusiasm then the kings to whom they answered were
surely doing the same. It seems incredible that we should be asked to imagine
that one of these kings, ruling a domain at the eastern end of the Solway Firth,
resisted this trend or felt that it was in his interest to do so. What political advantage could he hope to gain from it? Nor should we seek analogies further south,
in Anglo-Saxon England, where some heathen kings such as Penda (died 655)
kept faith with the old gods while others embraced Christ. Anglo-Saxon paganism, confronted by Christianity from c.600, disappeared within a few generations. Christianity had taken root among the North Britons more than 200 years
earlier and is not likely to have made slower progress. Faced with this scenario we
should envisage Gwenddolau as a Christian king like Rhydderch and Urien, like

The former Powsail Burn (now Drumelzier Burn) running towards the River Tweed
[© Freyja Appleyard-Keeling]

The present-day confluence of Tweed and Powsail [© Freyja Appleyard-Keeling]

Merlin's Grave. This thorn-tree beside the Powsail Burn is a popular destination for modern visitors [© Freyja Appleyard-Keeling]

Local tradition places the original site of Merlin's Grave in this field near the old course of the Powsail [© Freyja Appleyard-Keeling]

Drumelzier Kirk [© Freyja Appleyard-Keeling]

Tinnis Castle: probable site of Dunmeller, the fortress of King Meldred [© Freyja Appleyard-Keeling]

The Altar Stane, partially hidden in undergrowth on the roadside near Altarstone Farm
[© Freyja Appleyard-Keeling]

Stobo Kirk [© Freyja Appleyard-Keeling]

Above. St Kentigern
and the wild man
Myrddin depicted in a
window at Stobo Kirk
[© Freyja Appleyard-
Keeling]

Left. Stobo Kirk: an
alternative 'Altar Stone'
in the north aisle
[© Freyja Appleyard-
Keeling]

Upper Tweeddale from the road between Stobo and Dreva, looking south-west towards Drumelzier [© Freyja Appleyard-Keeling]

Alt Clut, Dumbarton Rock, ancient stronghold of the Clyde Britons [© Barbara Keeling]

The Clochoderick Stone. According to legend, this marks the grave of Rhydderch Hael, king of Dumbarton [© Derek Alexander]

Old churchyard at Hoddom, Dumfriesshire, on the site of a monastery said to have been founded by St Kentigern [© Barbara Keeling]

Above. Aerial view of Liddel Strength, one of the candidates for Caer Gwenddolau [© Cumbria County Council. Reproduced with permission.]

Right. Hartfell Spa, suggested by Nikolai Tolstoy as the site of Merlin's cave [© Fliss Hawksworth]

the unnamed rulers of Galloway and Lothian whose territories were dotted with stone memorials bearing Christian inscriptions. He is unlikely to have tolerated druids, or any other kind of pagan priests, within the bounds of his kingdom, still less in his royal court at Arfderydd. Even if he did allow pagan worship, or openly practised it himself, would it have prompted his Christian contemporaries to invade his lands? There is no evidence that British kings in this period engaged in religious warfare or that they were motivated by the kind of crusading zeal imagined by Skene and others.[42] All of this should make us extremely wary of seeing Myrddin as a druid. His retreat to the wild forest, his subsequent befriending of woodland beasts and his prophetic talents are not exclusively druidical traits. Even Nikolai Tolstoy, while considering it 'intrinsically likely' that druidism survived in northern Britain in the fifth and sixth centuries, freely acknowledged that Myrddin might not have been a druid, regardless of the possibility that 'his inspiration was very much in the druidic tradition'.[43]

Gwenddolau: hero, villain or pagan?

In the triad of the Three Fortunate Assassinations, the man-eating birds frequently seen as alluding to Gwenddolau's paganism might merely reflect a hostile attitude towards him in later Welsh tradition.[44] This can be contrasted with a more favourable attitude in a triad which praises his warband as one of the Three Faithful Warbands of the Island of Britain because its soldiers 'continued the struggle at Arfderydd for a fortnight and a month after their lord was slain'. In each of these triads we are undoubtedly seeing a different perspective on the battle of Arfderydd during the period when stories about it were circulating in Wales. Although most of these stories have not survived, the triad of the Faithful Warbands suggests that at least one tale placed Gwenddolau and his soldiers in a positive light. Another must have depicted him in a less positive way as the keeper of ravenous birds who devoured his fellow-Britons. Both the heroism of his warriors and the savagery of his birds can be interpreted as storytelling motifs designed to elicit different responses from an audience. There is no reason to assume that the birds were meant to indicate his religious affiliations, or that a Welsh audience would necessarily associate such creatures with paganism. Their purpose was more likely to have been to highlight his transformation from a historical figure into a legendary one with supernatural attributes.[45]

Myrddin the Christian

In the Myrddin poetry, the lines supposedly alluding to Myrddin's paganism can be contrasted with others in which he expresses Christian beliefs. In *Yr Afallennau*, for example, he laments his role in the death of his nephew with the words: 'Alas, Jesus! that my death came not before there came by my hand the death of Gwenddydd's son.' Later in the same poem he says of his woodland exile: 'After suffering sickness and sadness around Celyddon Wood, may I become a blessed servant to the Lord of Hosts.' This is a common theme in Christian writings: the prayer of the penitent sinner who endures the hardship of an ascetic lifestyle in the hope of purification and salvation. In the third stanza of *Yr Oianau*, Myrddin's Christian beliefs are stated even more unambiguously:

> 'May I get from Jesus the support
> of the kings of the heavens, highest lineage.
> Not fortunately born is one of the children of Adam
> who will not believe in God on the Last Day.'[46]

Christian sentiments are likewise expressed in the *Cyfoesi* and *Peirian Vaban*. In the *Cyfoesi*, Gwenddydd urges Myrddin to 'take communion before death'. All of these references imply that Welsh tradition regarded Myrddin not as a pagan but as a Christian. The alternative idea, that he belonged to a pagan enclave, appears to be a modern development based largely on Skene's interpretations. Skene placed a lot of emphasis on Gwenddolau's possession of a 'sacred fire' and magical birds but rather less on the Christian allusions in the Myrddin poetry. Nowhere in the poems are Myrddin or Gwenddolau depicted as anything other than members of the same Christian elite to which Rhydderch and Urien belonged. While it could be argued that Welsh storytellers might have put a Christian 'spin' on the older North British sources – the Arfderydd folklore and the Lailoken tales – there is no reason to assume that this was at the expense of pagan references. Indeed, the supposed hints of non-Christian beliefs in the poems might themselves be Welsh additions to original material from the North.

Lailoken the Christian

The Myrddin of Welsh tradition is depicted as more of a Christian than a pagan. There is little to be gained by pretending otherwise. His religious affiliations, in so far as they are expressed at all, are consistent with those held by the northern wild man Lailoken in the Scottish tales. Lailoken's beliefs are made clear in the tale of his encounter with Kentigern when he says 'I am a Christian' and 'a Christian believer of the Catholic faith'. He constantly pleads to be given the sacrament, not because he has never had it but because it is now a distant memory. As Kentigern tells his monks, the madman has spent 'many years of his life as one possessed among the wild creatures of the woods, and not known Christian communion'. Lailoken regards himself as a penitent sinner, weighed down by a burden of guilt. He dwells alone among the wild creatures 'since I am unworthy to perform my penance among men'.[47] During the battle which he claims to have caused, a voice from the heavens threatens him with being handed over to 'the minions of Satan', but at no point in the tale of his meeting with Kentigern does he indicate that he has ever renounced his Christian beliefs. Although God temporarily abandons him until his penance in the wilderness is complete, he himself remains faithful to God. In the account of his dealings with King Meldred, the theme of religion is less prominent but the final sentence of the prose narrative, before the short verse on Merlin's triple death, states that Lailoken's grave is in the cemetery at Dunmeller. This must refer to burial as a Christian and is a further indication that he was not regarded as a pagan. As with the Welsh material, it could perhaps be argued that the original story acquired a layer of Christianity during its evolution in the North, at the hands of either the Strathclyde Britons or their Scottish successors, and that an older stratum of pagan references was then removed. However, there is no reason to assume that this is what happened. While it cannot be denied that Lailoken was drawn into the Kentigern hagiography at some point and given a role in promoting the saint's reputation as a holy man *par excellence*, we have no warrant for seeing him as a pagan character whom the hagiographers converted into a Christian one. In the final analysis, we seem to be faced with a choice between two scenarios for the Merlin-archetype. In one, he was a pagan who survived a sixth-century battle in which Christian forces triumphed. In the other, he was a Christian like the victors and remained so until the end of his days. According to the first of these scenarios, the original story was sprinkled with Christian allusions by later writers and all explicit references to paganism were expunged. According to the second, there was no pagan narrative from the outset. Readers of this book will make up their own minds after weighing the various pieces of evidence.

Church and grave: Stobo and Drumelzier

A little to the south of their castle on the haughland of Drumelzier, the Tweedie family built a chapel where the parish church stands today. The churchyard

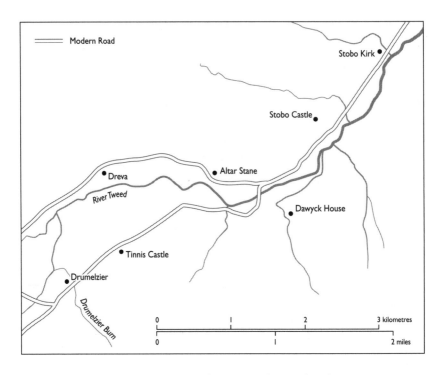

Map 5 Upper Tweeddale: Drumelzier and Stobo

stands on elevated ground which falls steeply on the north-west side towards the Drumelzier Burn, a stream formerly known as the Powsail. This kind of topographical setting was attractive to the founders of churches in the Dark Ages and is sometimes a good indicator of antiquity. At Drumelzier, it is possible that the remains of an ancient church lie beneath today's post-medieval structure. Such a site would have been a place of worship for Christian Britons in the sixth and seventh centuries, and perhaps later for Anglo-Saxon settlers moving westward from Bernicia. It would have preceded by five hundred years the medieval chapel of the Tweedies. Beneath the modern churchyard there might yet lie traces of a burial-ground established in Early Christian times, a place perhaps used as a family cemetery by the lords of the hillfort at Tinnis Castle. When the tale *Lailoken and Meldred* mentions the wild man's grave in a Christian cemetery at Dunmeller, it may even be referring to the hallowed earth around Drumelzier's parish church. Popular tradition, however, identifies an alternative site for the grave, taking more literally a prophecy attributed to the fourteenth-century Scottish seer Thomas the Rhymer:

> When Tweed and Pausayl meet at Merlin's grave,
> Scotland and England shall one monarch have.

More will be said of this prophecy in Chapter 8. For the present, we may note that it records a medieval tradition on the whereabouts of Merlin's grave. Pausayl is an older spelling of Powsail, the former name of the Drumelzier Burn which meets the Tweed at the edge of farmland below the church mound. Modern visitors reach this confluence on foot, by following a rough track alongside the burn from the northern end of a road-bridge in the centre of the village. After a while, the burn takes a sharp bend to the left, pointing towards its junction with the river. Most visitors here turn aside from the track to follow the burn to where it passes the last fence before the water-meeting. There they find a thorn tree standing in a small enclosure. In modern popular tradition, this marks Merlin's final resting-place, for the seer is believed to have been buried beneath a thorn. The setting certainly has an aura of timeless tranquillity: a quiet corner of river-meadow beside a little beach of pebbles, with the clear waters of Tweed flowing slowly by. However, notwithstanding the peacefulness of the spot and the fact that Tweed and Powsail do indeed meet here, most visitors are probably unaware that this is not the place mentioned in the prophecy. The land has changed since Thomas the Rhymer's time. When visitors turn aside from the track to follow the burn after its sharp westward bend, they are not following the original water-course but an artificial channel dating from the early nineteenth century. The burn originally ran straight across the fields, reaching the Tweed further down-stream from the present-day confluence. Its course was perhaps altered in order to reclaim additional farmland.[48] Nevertheless, the old alignment is still traced by the track itself, which at one time ran down to the river. Nowadays this ends at a gate, beyond which the farmland is separated from the Tweed by a margin of tangled undergrowth. Such is the thickness of the vegetation that the place where river and burn originally joined is hidden from view. Thorn-trees stand here and there, some quite old and gnarled. Perhaps they are descended from the tree that supposedly marked the grave of Merlin? Old maps mark the wizard's grave in an adjoining field running alongside the track but the exact location is difficult to identify. Most visitors instead make for the thorn-tree near the realigned confluence which, despite being further away from the original site, is at least easier to pinpoint. Photographs of this tree can be found in many places online, each image a testament to the enduring popularity of the Merlin legend. The strength of local tradition can also be sensed in the place-name Merlindale, borne by a small settlement on the opposite bank of the Tweed.

Some four miles north-east of Drumelzier, the Tweed passes through Stobo, a village of houses and farm-buildings scattered along the main road to Peebles. The local community here has its own church, the Stobo Kirk, nestling on a hillside near the river. As at Drumelzier, the church is sited close to the confluence of the Tweed with one of its many tributaries, in this case the Easton Burn. However, at Stobo Kirk the structural fabric is very old indeed, much of it medieval in date. The oldest stonework goes back to the twelfth century, perhaps as early as c.1120, and survives in the tower, nave and chancel.[49] According to local tradition, the church was built on the site of an earlier one founded by St Kentigern in the sixth century. A legend of the district asserts that the saint converted Merlin from paganism to Christianity in a baptismal ceremony at an 'altar stone' within the bounds of Stobo parish. This is derived from *Lailoken and Kentigern* which tells of the wild madman's heckling of the saint and his desperate pleading for communion. Kentigern eventually places the sacrament on a stone altar but the setting is Glasgow rather than Tweeddale. In any case, Lailoken was already a Christian and had no need to undergo the ritual of baptism a second time. The Stobo legend is plainly a local variant of the Glasgow communion story. Its antiquity is unknown but its roots may lie in the Middle Ages, when Stobo Kirk had a close connection with Glasgow Cathedral. The bishops of Glasgow owned substantial estates in the neighbourhood and, from the 1200s, a palatial country residence. Their presence accounts for an old saying which asserted that Stobo belonged to 'God, St Kentigern and the bishop of Glasgow'.[50] Stories about Lailoken may, however, have been circulating in local folkore long before the bishops arrived, reflecting ancient traditions connected to nearby Drumelzier. The hagiographical link between Kentigern and Lailoken was no doubt similarly well-established before c.1100 but it was surely the arrival of the bishops that brought Stobo into the saga. Local folklore then borrowed the communion episode and transferred it to a suitable 'altar'. It may have been much later, perhaps under the influence of Skene's suggestion that Myrddin Wyllt was a pagan, that this was turned into a tale of Christian conversion. The ceremony is said to have taken place at the Altar Stane, a large boulder on a minor road above the north bank of the Tweed, roughly midway between Stobo and Drumelzier. We may note in passing that baptismal ceremonies are more usually associated with a font, not an altar. One tradition asserts that the Altar Stane was formerly a venue for ancient pagan rites but this may have arisen from the name, which was surely borrowed from the Lailoken-Kentigern story. An alternative 'altar' is built into the wall of the north aisle of Stobo Kirk but its date and provenance are unknown. Also in the north aisle is a window of stained glass depicting 'Kentigern and Myrddin', the latter a bearded figure kneeling to receive the saint's blessing.

There is no evidence that Kentigern founded the first church at Stobo, or that he ever preached in the area. The notion that he performed a baptism at a nearby 'altar stone' is almost certainly fictional and can be traced back to the arrival of the bishops of Glasgow and to the revived cult of the cathedral's patron saint. Indeed, the pictorial window at Stobo Kirk is simply a modern addition to the hagiography surrounding Kentigern. The real Lailoken is unlikely to have met him, either at Stobo or at Glasgow or anywhere else. Further up the valley, at Drumelzier, we can feel slightly more trusting of local tradition. While there is certainly no proof that a chapel and graveyard existed there in the Dark Ages, or that the seer was buried in the fields below the church, none of this folklore can be dismissed outright. There is nothing particularly implausible or outlandish about any of it. In fact, none of the Drumelzier locations can be conclusively ruled out of the original or 'true' story of Merlin on the basis of current archaeological or historical knowledge. Local tradition from as far back as the twelfth century and probably earlier asserts that this part of Upper Tweeddale is where the Merlin legend began. Drumelzier lay within the Forest of Calidon, the great wilderness where Welsh poetry showed Myrddin dwelling in exile. We have seen that there is no compelling evidence to support the notion that either he or Lailoken should be regarded as pagans. Nevertheless, if both represent the historical Merlin-archetype, this enigmatic figure might indeed have roamed the riverlands between Stobo and Drumelzier at the end of the sixth century.

A Christian tale?

The survival of the Lailoken legend is undoubtedly due to its inclusion in the Kentigern hagiography, where the theme of a guilt-ridden outcast could be used to highlight the saint's role as an intermediary between merciful God and penitent sinner. The hagiographers turned it into a typical story of 'saintly resolution' in which the outcast comes at last to salvation through contact with a saint. This was a popular theme in hagiographical writing and can be traced back to the earliest phases of Christianity, finding echoes far from the Celtic world in tales of wild hermits who wandered the deserts of Egypt.[51] Such figures endured the rigours of an ascetic life so that their souls might eventually be purified and their sins absolved. Lailoken's legend must have seemed an easy fit with this kind of topic and became a useful religious sermon. In its surviving form, as an integral part of the Kentigern hagiography, it leaves little room for speculation that Lailoken was originally depicted as a pagan. There are no tangible hints that the oldest version of his legend portrayed him as anything other than Christian. Neither his prophetic ability nor his closeness to Nature is incompatible with Christian beliefs or more accommodating of pagan ones. Moreover, even if dwelling in the wilderness with animal companions qualifies as an alternative lifestyle it is not necessarily a sign of Nature-worship. Similar remarks can be applied to Myrddin. Setting the religious arguments aside, what we are actually seeing in both the Scottish and Welsh traditions is not so much a pagan druid as a 'wild man of the woods', a lonely fugitive from the terrors of Dark Age warfare. As we shall see in the next chapter, this type of character has a special literary significance of his own.

6

WILD MAN AND SEER

The central character of Geoffrey of Monmouth's *Vita Merlini* was stricken by madness after witnessing the deaths of warriors in battle. Distressed by the carnage and grieving for those whom he knew, he fled the battlefield to seek solitary refuge in the Forest of Calidon. There he became a wild man of the woods, living among the trees like a furtive animal. From his sylvan refuge he uttered prophecies and had dealings with various characters. Geoffrey's Merlin was based on the forest-dwelling madman Myrddin Wyllt, famed in Welsh poetry, who went insane at the battle of Arfderydd or Arthuret. Myrddin, in turn, was an adaptation of Lailoken, the North British wild man overcome by madness during a bloody battle fought 'in a field between Liddel and Carwinley' on the boundary of Arthuret parish. After Geoffrey's time, the wild aspect of Merlin became less prominent in medieval literature, but did not entirely vanish. It can be glimpsed in the later French romances where Merlin is described as a shaggy-haired *homme sauvage*.[1] The theme of the wilderness fugitive is thus an important part of the Merlin legend, a common element linking older and later versions. It is a key aspect of the central character in his various guises, from Lailoken and Myrddin Wyllt through to Geoffrey's Merlin. To what extent it goes back to the very beginning of the story is an interesting question. Might there have been a real, sixth-century wild man at the legend's historical roots?

In this chapter, we consider the wider significance of the Wild Man figure as a motif in medieval European literature before narrowing our focus to his portrayal in Celtic tradition. This brings us to the legend of Suibhne Geilt, a well-known Wild Man story from Ireland. As we shall see, Suibhne has much in common with his British counterparts in the Merlin legend. Like them, he is not only a wilderness-dweller but also a seer who foretells the future. Like theirs, his story includes a reference to Threefold Death. These connections are discussed below, after a brief survey of the Wild Man theme itself.

Wild Men

The figure of the 'wild man' is of great antiquity, having been a popular storytelling motif for several thousand years. He represents the primitive, uncivilised, bestial nature of humankind. At his most extreme he is a symbol of chaos and violence, a creature utterly bereft of decency or morality. He epitomises the depths to which any of us can sink if we abandon the normal rules of behaviour and self-restraint. Moreover, he represents our childlike desire to act recklessly or on impulse, to be 'as free as the beasts'.[2] This urge is usually suppressed in adulthood but still lurks beneath the surface, perhaps explaining the enduring popularity of characters such as Tarzan who live a carefree existence outside the boundaries of civilisation. The earliest wild man known to literature appears in the legend of Gilgamesh, an epic poem from Mesopotamia composed c.2100 BC.[3] This tells of an eponymous hero, king of the desert city of Uruk, who supposedly lived some 500 years earlier. One of the main characters is Enkidu, a wild man who dwelt as a beast of the desert. Covered in hair, he ate grass and drank water alongside the animals. Arriving at Uruk, he encountered Gilgamesh and the two men engaged in a wrestling contest. Gilgamesh won but he and Enkidu became firm friends and embarked on an adventure together. Also from the ancient Near East comes the story of King Nebuchadnezzar, ruler of Babylon in the sixth century BC. According to the Old Testament, Nebuchadnezzar's reign was interrupted by a seven-year bout of madness during which he lived like a creature of the wilderness. Wandering naked and surviving on a diet of grass, his hair became shaggy, like the feathers of a bird, and his fingers turned into claws.[4] His transformation into a half-human madman was God's punishment for an over-inflated pride and was bestowed upon him by a voice speaking from Heaven.

Later, in the Early Christian era, the Bible story of Nebuchadnezzar was still the most familiar account of a wild man, but Christian writers soon developed their own variants on the theme. In the early centuries AD, a number of hagiographical *vitae* began to appear, telling the stories of holy men and women who lived a solitary, ascetic existence as hermits ('anchorites') in the wilderness. Among the earliest of these works was the Life of St Anthony, written by Athanasius of Alexandria in the fourth century. Anthony was a model of ascetic virtue who, as a young man, spent fifteen years in the Egyptian desert (c.270–85). Although not a true wild man in the conventional sense – he was neither mad nor covered in hair – he nevertheless provided inspiration for later authors. The oldest example of a 'hairy anchorite' story comes from another fourth-century *vita*, the Life of Paul of Thebes (also known as Paul the Hermit) by St Jerome.

Paul, like Anthony, lived as a recluse in the desert. He dwelt on a mountainside, in a cave next to a spring, using the leaves of a nearby tree for clothing and subsisting on wild fruit. The account of his spartan existence contains themes and motifs that reappear in the Merlin legend.[5] We are reminded, in particular, of the woodland spring in *Vita Merlini* and the apple-tree in the Myrddin poems.

A more typical wild man in the mould of Nebuchadnezzar and Enkidu emerged as a common motif in the literature of medieval Europe, usually as a wanderer lurking in the woods. He became a popular figure in tales, to the extent that his image was widely represented in manuscript illustrations, wood-carving and heraldry. A savage but pitiable figure, his wildness was usually due to insanity, hardship or some other circumstance not of his own making.[6] Having not been born among the beasts, he was capable of returning to the human fold to resume a normal existence among other people. Without such rehabilitation, his madness would continue to drag his thoughts down deviant paths. From a Christian perspective, this meant that the wild man might become so mentally disturbed that he no longer recognised God's presence. Such a handicap was horrifying to the medieval European mind and probably explains why stories often depicted the wild man in a negative light, as more bestial than human, until he at last found redemption. His only positive traits were various supernatural powers, these being acquired through his physical and psychological separation from normal human experience.[7] We may also note that the medieval European wild man was more than a character of literature. He existed in reality, being represented by unfortunate persons so mentally deranged that they became social outcasts who – by choice or coercion – withdrew to remote places far from other people.[8] Wildness and madness were thus synonymous in the real world as well as in works of the imagination. It goes without saying that medieval society would have included wild mad women with wild mad men, for mental illness is not gender-selective. In literature, such women were represented by the forest-dwelling wild man's female counterparts, one of whom was the 'wood damsel', a hairy maiden pursued by demonic hunters.[9]

In the Celtic regions of the British Isles, the insane wild man was represented in literature by the Welsh *gwyllt* (later *wyllt*) and the Irish *geilt*. These represent the earliest manifestations of the European 'Wild Man of the Woods', combining elements of both the beast-like savage and the desert-dwelling Christian hermit.[10] One group constituted a specifically Celtic sub-type: the penitent sinner afflicted by madness and weighed down by an overwhelming burden of guilt. This character's insanity was due to his having taken part in a ferocious battle in which he witnessed scenes of slaughter. Fear, horror and guilt compelled him to withdraw from the field of combat. With his mind utterly overthrown, he fled in panic and eventually vanished into a nearby forest where he lived among wild animals. He acquired powers of prophecy and became a seer. In spite of his madness he was aware of the cause of it, accepting it as a form of penance handed down by God. His wilderness existence can thus be described as 'purposeful ascetism'.[11] At some point during this penitential period he foresaw a triple or 'threefold' death which was eventually suffered by himself or by another. Five examples of the penitent Celtic wild man are known: Merlin, Myrddin, Lailoken, Alladhan and Suibhne Geilt. The first four are British, in the sense that they are identifiable as native Britons. The fifth is Irish or, perhaps less plausibly, a Scot from Argyll. The British ones have already been discussed in previous chapters of this book. Our attention now shifts to their Irish counterpart.

Suibhne Geilt

The old Irish tale *Buile Shuibhne*, 'The Frenzy of Suibhne', was mentioned in Chapter 3. There we noted that the wild madman Suibhne Geilt, 'Wild Sweeney', is said to have travelled to Britain where he met an individual similarly afflicted by insanity. The British madman called himself Alladhan but was known to other folk as 'Man of the Wood'. Also in Chapter 3 we considered the possibility that the Gaelic name *Alladhan* might be an Irish rendering of *Lailoken* or *Llallogan*. We also observed that Suibhne and Lailoken have a number of elements in common, such as prophetic powers and a madness induced by battle. The parallels between the two traditions will be seen more clearly below.

Buile Shuibhne had probably developed into the version known today before the end of the ninth century, although it survives only in a manuscript of the twelfth.[12] It is one of a trio of tales relating to a historical war between the Ulster king Congal Cláen ('Half-Blind') and Domnall mac Áeda, the high king of Ireland. The first tale, *Fled Dúin na nGéd* ('The Feast of Dun na nGéd'), attributes much of Congal's hostility to an incident at a banquet hosted by Domnall. During the meal, a goose egg on a silver dish was set out in front of Congal. To his anger and dismay, it changed suddenly into a hen's egg on a wooden dish. War eventually broke out and the two sides met in battle at Mag Rath, near the present-day village of Moira in County Down.[13] Each king was accompanied by vassals and allies, with Congal being assisted by an army of Scots from Dál Riata. This famous clash of arms, recorded in contemporary chronicles, took place in 637. It is the main theme of the second of the three tales, *Cath Maige Rátha* ('The Battle of Moira'), which tells of Congal's defeat and death. The same tale identifies Suibhne as a prince who ruled an Ulster sept as one of Congal's vassals. He survived the battle but was overcome by madness and vanished into the woods. An account of his subsequent life as a wild man is told in *Buile Shuibhne*, which also gives a more detailed explanation of why he went insane during the battle. He had previously encountered an Irish saint called Ronan and, during a disagreement over land, Suibhne had thrown Ronan's book of psalms into a lake. He later murdered a monk and hurled a spear at Ronan himself. In great wrath, the saint placed a curse on Suibhne, condemning him to madness and nakedness and foretelling that he would be slain by a spear. Sure enough, when the great battle of Mag Rath was raging around him, Suibhne heard warriors on both sides yelling three loud cries which reverberated in the sky above. The noise completely unnerved him, affecting him so deeply that he lost control of mind and body. All of this was due to the saint's curse that had been laid upon him: 'His fingers were palsied, his feet trembled, his heart beat quick, his senses were overcome, his sight was distorted, his weapons fell naked from his hands, so that through Ronan's curse he went, like any bird of the air, into madness and imbecility.'[14]

The bird analogy was more than a metaphor. As his madness took hold, Suibhne rose up into the air and literally flew away from the battlefield, eventually landing in a yew tree in a forest. Fleeing thereafter into the wilderness, he lived as a wandering madman for a number of years. He was tormented by his experience in the battle, feeling a mixture of horror, grief and personal guilt. It was during this period that he visited northern Britain, travelling first to the Hebrides before coming to 'the land of the Britons', passing *dunadh righ Bretan* 'the fort of the king of the Britons' at Dumbarton Rock.[15] He eventually reached a great forest where he met the wild man Alladhan. These two then spent a whole year together, until each foresaw that his own death was drawing near. Suibhne returned to Ireland to continue his wandering, eventually making his way to a monastery where St Moling was in charge as abbot. Moling welcomed him but foretold that the monastery would be the place of his death and burial. Suibhne dwelt there for a whole year, subsisting on milk provided by a woman called Muirghil. The milk was not served in a bowl but in a small hole in the ground, shaped by Muirghil's heel. Each day, Suibhne crept furtively to drink the milk, lapping it up like an animal. A tragedy eventually unfolded when another woman taunted Muirghil for being visited each day by the madman. The taunt was overheard by Muirghil's sister-in-law, who in turn relayed it to Muirghil's husband, Mungan. In a fit of jealousy, believing that his wife was having an affair, Mungan stabbed Suibhne with a spear, inflicting a fatal wound. When St Moling arrived on the scene, he gave holy communion to the dying fugitive whose soul was thus reconciled to God.

The obvious similarities between the legend of Suibhne and those of Myrddin and Lailoken show that all three are closely related to one another. This could mean that they represent two separate traditions – one Irish, the other British – each arising independently from a common Celtic stock of wild man motifs. Yet the storylines are not so much similar as virtually identical, suggesting that what we are seeing are the British and Irish versions of a single legend.[16] On the British side, there can be little doubt that Myrddin Wyllt and Lailoken are essentially one and the same – a northern wild man who fought at the battle of Arfderydd in 573. Throughout this book, we have suggested that he really existed. In Chapter 3, we considered the possibility that Irish story-telling borrowed elements of his story and attached them to Suibhne, a character who was already developing in Irish folklore. Here, we may note an alternative scenario in which the Irish legend is the source of the original story of a warrior who goes insane during a battle.[17] It sees Suibhne as the template for the wild madman, with his British counterparts as copies. However, this seems less likely than the idea of a borrowing in the opposite direction, not least because it is not supported by chronology. Lailoken/Myrddin, the North British wild man, went mad in the carnage of Arfderydd in 573. Suibhne went mad on the battlefield of Moira sixty years later. Lailoken was linked with St Kentigern, whose death is noted in the Welsh Annals under the year 614. The saint in Suibhne's story was Moling who died in 697. The Irish context is therefore a generation or more later than the British. This suggests that the original version of the story was older than Suibhne's and of North British provenance. It influenced the Irish legend rather than the other way around. Also relevant here is the role of Alladhan in *Buile Shuibhne*. Regardless of any linguistic relationship between their names, it is almost certain that Alladhan and Lailoken represent one character.[18] Lailoken's appearance in the Irish legend, albeit with the Gaelic name Alladhan, can be contrasted with Suibhne's total absence from the Lailoken tales and the Myrddin poems. Moreover, while Suibhne travels to Britain, neither Lailoken nor Myrddin, nor indeed the Merlin of *Vita Merlini*, makes a reciprocal visit to Ireland – nor even to Gaelic-speaking Dál Riata. The balance of probability, then, seems to favour the belief that the story of Suibhne Geilt borrowed its wild man narrative from North British tradition. This may have happened as far back as the eighth century.[19] Although the real Suibhne may have originally been known to Irish storytellers as a seventh-century warrior who fought on the losing side in the great battle of Moira, his tale seems to have been embellished with aspects of the wild madman of sixth-century northern Britain. Lailoken was a soldier traumatised by the horror of war, a tragic figure whose legend became attached to the hagiography surrounding St Kentigern. Suibhne was easily transformed into Lailoken's Gaelic counterpart and was allocated a benevolent saint of his own. His epithet *geilt* is probably not a term of native Irish origin but a borrowing from the North British legend, a Gaelic rendering of a Cumbric word similar to Welsh *gwyllt* or *wyllt*.[20]

The wild man story is likely to have travelled to Ireland via Dál Riata, the most obvious intermediary in cultural exchange between northern Britain and the Gaelic world. This was the main territory of the Scots throughout much of the early medieval period, until their merger with the Picts in the ninth century. Dál Riata encompassed Argyll and the southern Hebrides and, prior to the battle of Moira in 637, a portion of north-east Ireland. As a Gaelic-speaking community in mainland Britain, the Scots provided a conduit for the movement of tales across the Irish Sea. Their Irish connections probably made them familiar with the legend of Suibhne. There is even a possibility that his legend originated in Dál Riata and that Suibhne himself was a member of the Scottish contingent at Moira.[21] His conventional identification as an Ulster prince might therefore be incorrect.

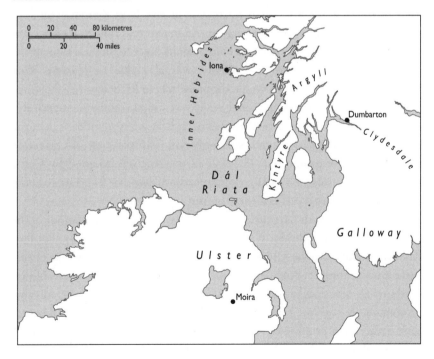

Map 6 The legend of Suibhne Geilt

Prophecy

Merlin's ability to predict future events has always been a major theme in his legend. He possesses it through every stage of his evolution, from North British wild man to Arthurian wizard. In Geoffrey of Monmouth's *Historia Regum Britanniae*, Merlin appears to possess prophetic powers from birth. Thus, we see the boy Merlin Ambrosius, having been brought from Carmarthen to Vortigern's fortress, demonstrating his ability. This episode can be contrasted with the North British tradition represented by the Lailoken tales and the Myrddin poems, in which the power of prophecy was not inherent but was acquired later in life as a consequence of battle-madness.[22]

Some supporters of the idea that the original Merlin was a sixth-century pagan draw attention to his prophetic talent. They see it as an attribute associated with non-Christian beliefs such as druidism. To bolster their case, they cite Roman references to the prophecies uttered by Gaulish druids in pre-Christian times.[23] Prophesying does indeed appear to have been associated with the ancient druids but it was by no means exclusive to them. According to the writers of hagiographical *vitae*, Christian priests were just as likely to gaze into the future. Jocelin of Furness described a prophecy uttered by St Kentigern on dealings between the Britons and the English. Adomnán told how St Columba in 574 accurately predicted the deeds of King Áedán's descendants and foresaw the sequence of their succession.[24] Columba was also able to reassure King Rhydderch of Alt Clut that he would die peacefully in his bed rather than on a battlefield. Whether such prophesying really was undertaken by Kentigern and Columba or merely invented by their hagiographers is less significant than the fact that it was not regarded as an exclusively non-Christian trait. We therefore have no reason to assume that the craft of the seer was adopted by Celtic Christian priests from their pagan counterparts, still less that its presence in the Middle Ages was a legacy of ancient druidism.

Prophesying seems to have little connection with religious affiliation. In the cases of Lailoken and Myrddin Wyllt, the ability manifested itself only after they went mad and fled into the wilderness. Prior to losing their wits, they were unable to gaze into the future.[25] Prophecy was part of a package of supernatural abilities linked to their new status as deranged wild men. Myrddin, for example, was able to communicate with the forest animals. Suibhne – who mainly uttered nature poems rather than prophecies – acquired the power of flight or levitation. A more general observation is that the majority of prophecies connected with the Merlin legend concern political events. These are often retrospective, in the sense that the prophet foresees events that had already happened when the text was written. One example is the sequence of Welsh kings foretold by Myrddin in the *Cyfoesi*, where the list of names stretches from the sixth century to the thirteenth. Other prophecies are not retrospective but instead reflect wishful thinking on the part of the writer. Thus, in the tenth-century poem *Armes Prydein Vawr*, Myrddin's soothsaying becomes a useful conduit for contemporary Welsh hopes of a decisive victory over the English. The 'great prophecy' of the title sprang from a literary tradition reaching back 500 years to the earliest conflicts between native Britons and incoming Anglo-Saxons. Faced with what must have seemed an inexorable struggle, the Britons of the sixth century looked ahead to a glorious future era when their descendants would finally expel the invaders. Writing in the 540s, the British monk Gildas referred to a prophecy in which the Anglo-Saxon occupation was limited to a span of 300 years.[26] This hope of future victory evolved into a Welsh tradition of political prophecy that continued throughout the Middle Ages.[27] It spawned the allegorical tale of red and white dragons in the ninth-century *Historia Brittonum* as well as Myrddin's vision of a grand anti-English alliance in *Armes Prydein*. It envisaged the saviours of Britain as Cynan and Cadwaladr, two legendary heroes who would return from death to lead the last campaign against the hated 'Saxons'. Myrddin mentions both of them in his prophecies and they also feature in Geoffrey of Monmouth's *Vita Merlini*.

As a literary theme, prophecy is obviously a useful tool for a writer seeking to promote a particular ideology. It has been employed for this purpose since ancient times and in many parts of the world. Its universality provides another argument against the idea that Merlin's soothsaying indicates an adherence to druidism or to some other form of Celtic paganism. In his wild man guise he lurked beyond the frontiers of normal human society, living as a crazed loner whose closest companions were untamed beasts. Regardless of whether we believe he was real or not, his acquisition of supernatural powers in stories told about him is hardly a remarkable or surprising development. He was a stereotypical outsider, almost an Otherworld figure, whose very strangeness gave him an aura of mystery. Such figures inevitably attract a supernatural aspect as their legends evolve.

We come now to the question of whether the Merlin-archetype, the sixth-century wild man, was regarded as a seer in his own lifetime. There may be grounds for thinking that he was. Individuals claiming to foretell the future would have been as common in Dark Age Britain as in our own time. People in the twenty-first century still consult fortune tellers and psychics who claim to possess special knowledge of what is to come. Fifteen hundred years ago, in an age when superstition was regarded as normal and rational, those who were believed to possess powers of prophecy would have been viewed with awe. Some would have been dismissed as charlatans, then as now, while others were no doubt presumed to be authentic. A solitary eccentric, living in the darkest depths of a forest, was as likely as anyone to be thought of as possessing strange talents. The Merlin-archetype, lurking alone in the Forest of Calidon, would have been a prime candidate. If he really did utter dire foretellings of the future, his words might have been taken seriously by contemporaries. There are examples of this kind of credulity in a later age, in twelfth-century Wales, where people known as *awenyddion* or 'inspired ones' spoke garbled prophecies that were eagerly listened to. The *awenydd* was regarded as a genuine soothsayer to whom folk could turn for guidance and reassurance. When asked a question, the *awenydd* became as if possessed by a spirit, yelling incoherent streams of words, amid which the assembled listeners might discern something that appeared to make sense. Eventually, the trembling seer would be roused from this strange trance or 'ecstasy'. Gerald of Wales, a contemporary witness, was struck by the resemblance to Merlin, whom he describes as prophesying in a similarly 'frantic' state of mind.[28] If Gerald is to be believed, the *awenyddion* really did exist in twelfth-century Wales. Such individuals might have been around in earlier periods too. If they were present in sixth-century northern Britain, it is feasible that the Merlin-archetype was one of them. The unintelligible prophecies of Lailoken, heard by St Kentigern at Glasgow, are consistent with Gerald's description of the behaviour of the *awenyddion*. Of course, the reality of Lailoken's situation may have been rather more tragic: a troubled survivor of old wars, living as a social outcast in a superstitious age. While it may be unlikely that he claimed to be a prophet, we can perhaps imagine him muttering strange words of doom to any traveller who passed by – these pronouncements then being mocked as gibberish by some listeners but perceived by others as meaningful insights into the future.

The name *awenydd* derives from *awen* or 'inspiration' through which the gift of prophesying was bestowed. An alternative translation of *awen* is 'muse' which was perhaps the intended meaning of the author of *Historia Brittonum* when he used an older form *aguen* in reference to a sixth-century bard: *tunc talhaern tat aguen in poemate claret* ('Talhaearn the father of the muse was then renowned in poetry'). In neo-druidism, a modern form of paganism in which nature is especially venerated, *awen* provides both inspiration and truth. This does not mean that the *awenyddion* of medieval Wales were druids or pagans. Indeed, Gerald observed that they invoked 'the true and living God, and the Holy Trinity' when uttering their prophecies. They were Christians who were believed to have the gift of foretelling. The same can perhaps be said of the Merlin-archetype in the sixth century.

Awenyddion

Concerning the soothsayers of this nation, and persons as it were possessed.

There are certain persons in Wales, whom you will find nowhere else, called *awenyddion*, or people inspired; when consulted upon any doubtful event, they roar out violently, are rendered beside themselves, and become, as it were, possessed by a spirit. They do not deliver the answer to what is required in a connected manner; but the person who skilfully observes them, will find, after many preambles, and many nugatory and incoherent, though ornamented speeches, the desired explanation conveyed in some turn of a word: they are then roused from their ecstasy, as from a deep sleep, and, as it were, by violence compelled to return to their proper senses. After having answered the questions, they do not recover till violently shaken by other people; nor can they remember the replies they have given. If consulted a second or third time upon the same point, they will make use of expressions totally different; perhaps they speak by the means of fanatic and ignorant spirits. These gifts are usually conferred upon them in dreams: some seem to have sweet milk or honey poured on their lips; others fancy that a written schedule is applied to their mouths and on awaking they publicly declare that they have received this gift.[29]

Threefold Death

The demise of a character by triple or threefold death is not exclusive to the Merlin legend, nor is it found only in Celtic literature. It is, however, often connected with prophecy. A typical form of the story tells of a seer who foresees that a certain individual will suffer three separate deaths, in the sense of dying by three causes or methods. This is frequently dismissed as nonsense by onlookers, who are then proved wrong when the prophecy comes true. Tales of this sort have timeless appeal and the Threefold Death has been a popular storytelling motif for many hundreds of years. It was well-known across medieval Europe, from the British Isles to the Baltic lands, with numerous variations on the basic theme being found in literature and folklore.[30] Its oldest known occurrence comes from northern Britain at the end of the seventh century, when Adomnán described St Columba's prophecy about an evil man who would die in three different ways: a spear-thrust in the neck, a fall from a tree and, lastly, drowning in water.[31]

Threefold death seems to have entered the Merlin legend at an early stage. It was almost certainly present in the North British version glimpsed behind the two Lailoken tales, each of which contains a scene where Lailoken foretells his own triple demise. Neither Kentigern in the first tale, nor King Meldred's wife in the second, believe that anyone can be slain more than once, so they dismiss the prophecy as false. Lailoken is then proved a true seer when he has his fateful encounter with the shepherds, who chase him over a cliff so that he falls onto a sharp stake in the River Tweed and drowns. His threefold death is clearly a major narrative theme. It does not, however, appear in the Welsh version of the story – the Myrddin poems – alongside the battle of Arfderydd and other northern material. Perhaps it was deliberately left out when the poems were being composed? However, it was retained in the Irish version, in a somewhat altered form, as the episode in which Suibhne Geilt is stabbed by a spear while stooping to drink from a puddle of milk. A note adds that some people say Suibhne was pierced not by a spear but by a deer's horn concealed in the ground where he drank. We may be seeing the remnants of a triple-death episode that had once been present in Suibhne's legend, having been borrowed from the original North British story.[32] The same motif reappears in *Vita Merlini*, although not in relation to Merlin's own demise. In *VM*, Merlin merely foretells that another person will die a threefold death. However, when later Scottish tradition deduced that Lailoken and Merlin were one and the same, this unusual fate was transferred to Merlin himself. Hence we encounter the lines at the end of *Lailoken and Meldred*: 'Pierced by a stake, suffering by stone and water, Merlin is said to have met a triple death.'[33]

There is no need to imagine that the historical Merlin-archetype behind the Lailoken tales really did endure a threefold death. It was simply a storytelling motif, to show that he was a true seer whose prophecies – even the most far-fetched ones – came true. Dying in such a convoluted way provided him with a suitably dramatic demise. This is not to say that the motif itself did not have historical roots. Actual instances of ritual sacrifice involving three modes of execution, perhaps in imitation or veneration of gods or other mythological characters, were reported among the Gauls in Roman times. In Iron Age Britain, similar rites may be represented archaeologically by the 'bog body' known as Lindow Man, the corpse of an individual who was strangled, struck on the head and had his throat cut, perhaps in a religious ceremony.[34] Savage rituals of this kind were no doubt prohibited when Christianity replaced paganism, but were not wholly forgotten, hence their reappearance in Christian writings as a literary theme. An example appears in Adomnán's Life of St Columba, which reports a miracle-story in which Columba foretold that Áed the Black, a man with a violent past, would suffer a threefold death. The prophecy was duly fulfilled when Áed died from a spear-thrust, a fall from a boat and drowning in water.[35] However, the survival of the Threefold Death as a literary motif should not be taken as evidence for its continued use as a ceremonial rite. There is no evidence that human sacrifice was practised anywhere in the British Isles in the Dark Ages. We therefore have no need to imagine storytellers giving the Merlin-archetype a triple death because they believed him to have been a Dark Age pagan. Still less should we be tempted to suggest that this was how he actually died.[36]

Shamanism

Thirty years ago, in his fascinating study of the Merlin legend, Count Nikolai Tolstoy suggested that the figure at the legend's North British roots may have been a sixth-century shaman. This was, he proposed, an appropriate label for the druid-like seer whom he envisaged as the original, pagan Merlin of the earliest traditions. He identified this figure's abode as Hartfell Spa, a spring on Hart Fell above the town of Moffat in Dumfriesshire. The location does indeed look plausible, given that it sits roughly twenty-five miles north of the Arfderydd battlefield and fifteen miles south of the alleged grave-site at Drumelzier. Tolstoy noted a number of similarities between the Myrddin-Lailoken narratives and the documented practices of shamanism, such as a trance-like state, mental derangement and retreat into the wilderness.[37] The similarities are hard to deny, but do they make 'shaman' an accurate label for a sixth-century British seer? Perhaps they do. It would be going too far, however, to link them exclusively with paganism. Analogies from other parts of Europe, most notably the *benandanti* or 'good walkers' of sixteenth-century Italy, indicate that shamanistic practices are not incompatible with Christian beliefs.[38] The wild man at the heart of the Merlin legend might indeed be accurately labelled a Celtic shaman, but we could also argue that he was a Christian one too.

7

ARTHURIANA

Modern representations of Merlin frequently depict him as a mentor, friend and counsellor of the fabled King Arthur. Merlin is shown as a key figure at the royal court, deploying his sorcery in the king's best interests. However, this close connection is not reflected in older versions of their respective legends. Arthur is a remote figure in the Welsh traditions of Myrddin, being wholly absent from the poems. In the North British tales of Lailoken he makes no appearance at all. Myrddin is likewise absent from the oldest, pre-Galfridian versions of the Arthurian legend. How, then, did these two characters end up in the same story? The answer lies in the twelfth century, in the writings of Geoffrey of Monmouth, who takes most of the credit for bringing Merlin and Arthur together. Indeed, it is mainly due to Geoffrey that the Arthurian sage is now the most recognisable Merlin, while the northern wild man at the root of the legend is all but forgotten. Geoffrey's King Arthur, the mighty ruler of Camelot, is likewise the most familiar Arthur to modern eyes. He is traditionally associated with places such as Tintagel in Cornwall and Glastonbury in Somerset, yet it is possible that his legend – like Merlin's – began in Scotland. Indeed, although the primary geographical setting for both characters is often assumed to be Wales or south-west England, their true origins may lie in the Old North. In Merlin's case, the argument for North British origin has already been presented in this book, with the weight of evidence suggesting that his legend arose in the Dark Age kingdom of Strathclyde. In this chapter we examine a parallel argument for Arthur's origins, even if it requires a brief digression from our main topic. The detour can be justified because Merlin has become so entangled with Arthuriana that it is difficult to study him in isolation. Moreover, both he and Arthur are independently linked to an area that includes Strathclyde and other parts of southern Scotland as well as a few districts in northern England. The possibility that both legends originated not only in northern Britain but in the same part of it seems a good enough reason to discuss Arthur in a book about Merlin.

Geoffrey's Merlin and Arthur

Geoffrey of Monmouth's influence on the development of the Merlin legend cannot be overstated. This is due not so much to *Vita Merlini* as to the slightly earlier and far more popular *Historia Regum Britanniae*. In *VM*, King Arthur is a shadowy figure whose reign is already over when Merlin and Taliesin refer to him in conversation. Taliesin tells Merlin about the Fortunate Isle, a place of healing where the shape-shifter Morgen dwells with her eight sisters. 'It was there,' he adds, 'that we took Arthur after the battle of Camlan, where he had been wounded.'[1] Taliesin then wonders if the time has come for Arthur to be summoned to lead the Britons against the invading Saxons 'if he has recovered', but Merlin foresees that the war of liberation will be led instead by Conan of Brittany and Cadwaladr of Wales. It is interesting to note that here, as in *HRB*, Arthur is not yet the mighty 'future deliverer' of the Britons, the saviour who will return one day to drive their enemies into the sea.[2] This particular mantle was bestowed upon him by later writers and evolved into the idea that he sleeps in a hidden place until called upon to rescue his people. Some fifty lines of *VM* are given over to an account of Arthur's reign, a sequence of events in which Merlin – the narrator – apparently played no part.[3] The narration ends with a reference to the great battle of Camlan in which Arthur fought his treacherous nephew Modred. Merlin says that the king received a mortal wound in the battle and 'left the kingdom', not to die but to seek healing on the Fortunate Isle in 'the palace of the nymphs'. Elsewhere in *VM* we hear of a figure known as 'The Cornish Boar' whose great-nephews wrought havoc with their violent rivalry. This is usually assumed to be Arthur, whose Cornish connection had already been established in *HRB* by the placing of his court at Celliwig.[4] In *HRB*, Geoffrey gives a detailed account of Arthur's life and assigns to Merlin an active role at the start of it. In the seventh book of *HRB* – the *Prophetiae Merlini*, originally a separate work in its own right – Merlin had prophesied Arthur's reign. He subsequently plays a role in Arthur's conception, becoming involved when King Uther Pendragon desires to sleep with Igerna, the wife of Duke Gorlois of Cornwall. At a banquet, Uther's clumsy advances towards the lady are rebuffed. She informs her husband who immediately takes her back home to Cornwall, but their hasty exit enrages Uther and he responds by invading their land. Gorlois then sends Igerna to the great stronghold of Tintagel, thinking she will be safe there, but Uther gains access through a deception devised by Merlin. The latter's potions enable the king to take on the likeness of Gorlois and, in this cunning disguise, he enters Igerna's bedchamber to satisfy his lust. The child of this union is Arthur. Years later, after Uther's death, Arthur becomes king at the tender age of fifteen. By then, Merlin is already dead. In Geoffrey's account, the king and the wizard are not true contemporaries. It was left to later writers to develop the notion of Merlin being present throughout Arthur's reign. One of these was Robert de Boron, writing in the early 1200s, who invented the now-famous episode in which Merlin encourages the teenage king to pull a magical sword from a block of stone, thus proving his right to rule. Other writers built on Robert's work by extending Merlin's role as Arthur's mentor further into the reign, eventually establishing the wizard as a constant companion of the king.[5]

The pre-Galfridian Arthur

Modern depictions of Arthur in literature, film and other media usually portray him as a heroic king ruling from his great castle of Camelot. In most cases, the visual setting recalls the High Middle Ages of the twelfth to fourteenth centuries. Arthur and his henchmen typically appear as medieval knights in plate armour and chainmail, with shields bearing heraldic devices. They engage in jousting tournaments and go to war against the king's enemies. Some knights, such as Lancelot and Gawain, undertake perilous adventures like the quest for the Holy Grail. Others, such as the treacherous Modred (Mordred), turn against Arthur and attempt to destroy him. Much of this context can be traced back to the writers of the French romances, who clothed and equipped their characters as if they were people of their own era. Geoffrey of Monmouth, the real architect of the Arthurian legend, was nevertheless clear that the story took place in the post-Roman period (c. AD 400 to c. AD 550). This was the chronological context depicted in his Welsh source-material, a body of traditional lore in which Arthur featured as a mighty figure of the remote past. Outside Wales, Arthur was virtually unknown until the twelfth century when Geoffrey brought him to the attention of a wider audience. In the old Welsh tales, Arthur usually appears as a warrior of renown, sometimes as a semi-supernatural figure who fights magical creatures. In some stories his adventures are set in the Otherworld, while in others he visits real places. The oldest Welsh Arthurian material, whether in verse or prose, often survives only in manuscripts written long after Geoffrey's time. Specialist scholars have nevertheless scrutinised these texts, identifying material that can be described as 'pre-Galfridian' (i.e. composed before c.1130) in collections such as the Black Book of Carmarthen, the Red Book of Hergest and the White Book of Rhydderch. From the Red Book (written c.1400) comes a complete version of the prose tale *Culhwch and Olwen*. This may be the oldest known Arthurian story, attaining its present form in the late tenth or early eleventh century.[6] It tells of Culhwch, King Arthur's young cousin, who loved Olwen, the daughter of a giant. To win the girl's hand in marriage, Culhwch must undertake a series of difficult tasks set down by her father. Culhwch goes to Arthur's court to ask for help and is eventually assigned a seven-strong band of warriors led by Cei, Bedwyr and Gwalchmai (Kay, Bedevere and Gawain in post-Galfridian literature). After one of the tasks is accomplished, Arthur himself joins the quest and effectively takes over. He leads the hunt of Twrch Trwyth, a fearsome magical boar, chasing the creature across many lands. He secures the release from prison of Mabon, son of Modron, a representation of the ancient British god Maponus whose cult was active in Roman times. The story depicts Arthur as a great king whose court was attended by a 200-strong entourage of warriors and servants. It associates him with Wales and Cornwall but implies that his authority was recognised over a much wider area. This is already the heroic Arthur whom a modern audience will instantly recognise. For a rather different portrayal we turn to another pre-Galfridian text from Wales, a 'Life' of Saint Cadoc of Llancarfan. This was written in the late eleventh century, more than 500 years after Cadoc is presumed to have lived, and casts Arthur in a somewhat unsympathetic light. It tells of the slaying of three of Arthur's warriors by a man who subsequently receives sanctuary from Cadoc at the monastery of Llancarfan. When Arthur comes there, seeking vengeance upon the killer, Cadoc offers him a herd of cattle in compensation for the three deaths. This is accepted by Arthur but he is made to look foolish when the beasts are later transformed into ferns.[7] Arthur also appears in a number of Welsh triads that apparently pre-date Geoffrey of Monmouth. Like the tale of Culhwch and Olwen, these suggest that Welsh story-tellers in the eleventh century saw Arthur as a great king, even if some contemporary hagiographers did not. Looking further back, to the early ninth century, Arthur's royal status is entirely absent. Twelve victories are attributed to him in a controversial passage in *Historia Brittonum* (written in Wales c.830) but he is not described there as a king. In fact, the author of *HB* draws a distinction between Arthur and the kings of the Britons, calling him a *dux* ('leader') who joins them in their wars against the Anglo-Saxons.[8] The passage in question is one of the most famous pieces of Arthurian lore:

> Then Arthur together with the British kings fought against them in those days, but he was their leader in battle. The first battle was at the mouth of the river which is called Glein. The second, third, fourth, and fifth battles were above another river called Dubglas which is in the region of Linnuis. The sixth battle was above the river which is called Bassas. The seventh battle was in the forest of Celidon, that is *Cat Coit Celidon*. The eighth battle was at Fort Guinnion, in which Arthur carried the image of Holy

Mary ever-virgin on his shoulders; and the pagans were put to flight on that day. And through the power of our Lord Jesus Christ and through the power of the Blessed Virgin Mary, His mother, there was great slaughter among them. The ninth battle was fought in the City of the Legion. The tenth battle was fought on the banks of a river which is called Tribruit. The eleventh battle was fought on the mountain which is called Agned. The twelfth battle was on Mount Badon in which there fell in one day 960 men from a single charge by Arthur; and no one struck them down except Arthur himself, and in all the wars he emerged as victor.[9]

Only a couple of these battles are mentioned elsewhere. According to the Welsh Annals, compiled in the mid tenth century, the battle of Badon (Latin: *bellum badonis*) was fought in 516. The original entry probably gave only the date and the place, but a later annalist added that the fighting went on for three days and three nights until the Britons were victorious. Also added was the claim that Arthur carried the Holy Cross on his shoulders, a curious detail that might refer to a shield emblazoned with a Christian device. In the *HB* battle-list, a shield painted with the image of the Virgin might similarly be intended in the reference to Arthur's 'shoulders' at Fort Guinnion. Like the author of *HB*, the Welsh annalists may have believed that Arthur's foes at Badon were Anglo-Saxons. Twenty-one years later, in an entry for 537, the same annals record the battle of Camlan. This is the event described by Geoffrey of Monmouth in both *Historia Regum Britanniae* and *Vita Merlini* as the scene of Arthur's fateful clash with Modred. Again, the original entry in the annals probably gave only the year and the location. To this, a later scribe added the words 'in which Arthur and Medraut (Modred) fell'.[10] Such additions and alterations were commonplace in annal-writing, not only in Wales but elsewhere in the British Isles and further afield. They are often difficult to identify and therefore hard to date. In the case of the Welsh Annals, we have previously encountered one addition that can be confidently dated to the mid-twelfth century or later. This comes in the entry for 573, the battle of Arfderydd, to which was added the obviously post-Galfridian information 'Merlin went mad'. By then, of course, Merlin's connection with Arthur was already well-established as a literary theme. The two were regarded as contemporaries, or near-contemporaries, in Geoffrey of Monmouth's reworking of Welsh Arthurian lore, in spite of a sixty-six-year gap between Camlan and Arfderydd in the annals.

The oldest reference to Arthur in Welsh literature is often assumed to be a line of poetry in *The Gododdin*. This collection of verses commemorating warriors from a North British kingdom in Lothian is supposedly the work of the sixth-century bard Aneirin. Arthur appears in a verse about Gwawrddur, a warrior who 'fed black ravens on the rampart of the fortress, though he was no Arthur'.[11] The implication is that Arthur was regarded by the people of Gododdin as a great hero of the past, a figure whose achievements not even the mighty Gwawrddur could match. Neither this verse nor any other in the collection mentions Arthur again. There is certainly no hint that he came from Gododdin or that he was associated with this kingdom in a direct way. We cannot even be sure that the line in question was part of the original text and not a later interpolation. Indeed, one of the most troubling aspects of *The Gododdin* is that none of its verses can be identified as having been composed before the ninth century. There is likewise no proof that any part of any verse was created by a northern poet rather than a Welsh one. This uncertainty means that the brief reference to Arthur might have no connection with the period in which he allegedly lived. It may belong to a much later period, such as the ninth or tenth century, when his legend was already well-known in Wales.[12] It also means that *The Gododdin* cannot qualify as the oldest surviving source of the Arthurian legend. As we saw in Chapter 2, the same point can be made in relation to the legend of Merlin, who appears (as Myrddin) in another verse of the same text.

The Arthur of history

According to the Welsh Annals, Arthur was active as a war-leader in the early sixth century. This is consistent with his chronological setting in *HB*, where his twelve victories appear between St Patrick, who died in the second half of the fifth century, and the Bernician king Ida who supposedly died in 547. Taking both sources at face value, we are seemingly presented with the deeds of a genuine historical figure, a renowned military leader of the post-Roman period. Large numbers of people accept the annal entries and the battle-list as good evidence for a 'real' Arthur and see no reason to doubt his existence. Others believe that the doubts are too great to be ignored, and that the case for Arthur's historical existence is actually quite weak.[13] The whole topic warrants a closer look, for it has much in common with the parallel debate over whether or not Merlin was 'real'. In each case, the most recognisable figure today is a character best-known from legendary tales written in the twelfth century or later: Arthur, the chivalric medieval king; and Merlin, his trusted wizard and counsellor. Both are often assumed to be based on individuals who lived in the Dark Ages. This book argues that Merlin can indeed be traced back to a historical figure of the sixth century. What, then, of the similar claim for Arthur?

Some historians propose that the evidence for a real Arthur is good enough to warrant his inclusion in serious academic studies of post-Roman Britain. They see

him as an important player in the conflict between native Britons and incoming
Anglo-Saxons, a renowned warlord operating on a national scale. They attempt to
locate his battles, not only his twelve victories but also his final encounter at
Camlan. The proposed locations are then used to reconstruct the geography of his
career. Other historians are more sceptical, questioning the validity of the Welsh
sources and wondering why the two most reliable accounts of the period – written
respectively by Gildas and Bede – make no mention of Arthur. Gildas was a British
cleric who wrote in the 530s or 540s. His major work *On the Ruin and Conquest of
Britain* looked back at the wars between native Britons and incoming Anglo-
Saxons in the previous century.[14] He noted that the Britons had been led by
Ambrosius Aurelianus, a competent commander whose victories had briefly stalled
the Anglo-Saxon advance. Ambrosius was described by Gildas as 'almost the last of
the Romans' which probably meant that he was a native Briton from the Romanised
landowning class. Gildas referred to a great victory at Mount Badon, undoubtedly
the *bellum badonis* dated to 516 in the Welsh Annals, but did not name the British
commander. He added that the battle occurred in the year of his own birth, which
is thought to have been around 500. This is somewhat earlier than the date given by
the Welsh annalists and is actually regarded as the more authoritative. Gildas noted
that the British victory was followed by a long period of peace which endured at the
time of writing. At no point in this entire sequence of events did he mention
Arthur. Two hundred years later, his account formed the basis of a summary in
Bede's *Ecclesiastical History*, published in 731.[15] Bede referred to both Ambrosius
and Badon but, like Gildas, made no mention of Arthur. Proponents of the idea
that Arthur played a key role in the history of post-Roman Britain are therefore
confronted by a difficult question: If he was so important, why was he ignored by
Gildas and Bede? The simplest and most obvious answer is that he did not exist. If
this seems overly sceptical, two alternative possibilities can still be considered by
supporters of a 'real' Arthur. The first is that a warrior of this name was indeed
present at Badon and other sixth-century battles, but in a role too insignificant to
be worthy of mention. His later fame would then be due to exaggeration by Welsh
storytellers. The second possibility is that he was a successful general like Ambrosius,
but in a different theatre of war from the one reported by Gildas. In this scenario,
Ambrosius campaigned in southern Britain – the area with which Gildas was
chiefly concerned – while Arthur fought primarily in the North. Gildas seems to
have been relatively unconcerned with northern affairs so it is quite feasible that he
would not have mentioned a North British Arthur. The possibility has led to a
belief in some quarters that the roots of the Arthurian legend should be sought in
Scotland.

Scottish Arthurs

The idea that Arthur originated in early Scottish history has a long pedigree. It can be traced back to medieval times, when the popularity of the Arthurian romances prompted many places in Britain to claim a connection with the great hero. In Scotland, local folklore from as far back as the 1400s associated him with Arthur's Seat, a hill overlooking the city of Edinburgh, while a document from 1339 shows that a well near Crawford in South Lanarkshire was known as 'Arthur's Fountain' two hundred years after the publication of *Historia Regum Britanniae*. Later in the fourteenth century, the mighty stone castle on the site of Rhydderch Hael's fortress at Dumbarton was referred to as 'Arthur's Castle'. Queen Guinevere was said to be buried beneath a mound in the Perthshire village of Meigle where a Pictish monument carved in the ninth century was regarded as her gravestone.[16] Most famous of all was a dome-shaped Roman building that once stood near the River Carron near Falkirk. From at least the mid thirteenth century, this unique monument was known as Arthur's O'on ('Oven'), right up until 1743 when it was demolished to provide stone for an industrial dam.[17] In the post-medieval period, when the oldest Welsh traditions about Arthur began to receive attention from historians, the battle-list in *Historia Brittonum* revealed *Cat Coit Celidon* (Welsh: 'Battle of Celidon Wood') as a likely Scottish location. Its identification with the Forest of Calidon or Celyddon, the ancient woodlands of southern Scotland, is undoubtedly correct and raises the possibility that other places in *HB*'s list might also be found north of the Border. Nineteenth-century historians such as W.F. Skene pored over maps to look for Scottish places with names that sounded vaguely like names in the list. One such site was Bowden Hill, near Linlithgow, identified by Skene as Mount Badon. Less plausibly, Bassas was identified as the isolated Bass Rock in the Firth of Forth by one of Skene's contemporaries and as Dunipace near Falkirk by another.[18] Scottish candidates have inevitably been found for the river Dubglas ('black stream') via its modern equivalent Douglas, but obscure names such as Guinnion and Tribruit pose more of a challenge. Arthur's last battle at Camlan was placed by Skene at Camelon, the site of a Roman fort near Falkirk, simply on the basis that the two names sound alike. Skene felt confident that this battle must have been fought in Scotland because Modred or Medraut, traditionally seen as Arthur's principal foe at Camlan, was identified by Geoffrey of Monmouth as a prince of Lothian. To what extent the technique of 'sounds-like' etymology furthers our knowledge of Dark Age history is debatable. With the exception of *Coit Celidon*, none of the Scottish candidates for Arthur's battles can be placed north of the Border with much confidence. Few carry greater weight than various English and Welsh candidates that have been put forward with just as much enthusiasm. A place known as 'City of the Legion', for example, should surely be identified as one of the three legionary fortresses of Roman Britain: Chester, Caerleon or York, none of which is in Scotland. The stark truth is that eleven of the twelve battles continue to defy identification. This has not deterred people from wrestling with the list in *HB* but, in spite of their continuing efforts, little consensus has so far emerged. Some supporters of a historical Scottish Arthur have therefore turned to other sources, to records from northern Britain that appear to mention such a figure. These texts refer to Artúr of Dál Riata, a prince of the Scots and namesake of the legendary king. Artúr's historical existence is not in doubt: he was one of several sons of Áedán mac Gabráin, king of Kintyre, who himself appears as a minor character in later Welsh lore. Little is known of Prince Artúr beyond a brief mention in Adomnán's Life of Columba where his untimely death is noted. Columba had previously foreseen that neither Artúr nor two other sons of Áedán would succeed to the kingship, a prophecy fulfilled when all three were slain in battle.[19] Much has been written in support of the idea that Artúr mac Áedain is the 'real' Arthur and it remains a popular theory today.[20] However, its flaws were highlighted by Rachel Bromwich who deemed it 'unacceptable on many counts'. Professor Bromwich pointed out that the conventional chronology for Arthur, based on the Welsh Annals, assigns him to a period before 540, whereas Artúr mac Áedain is unlikely to have been born by then. She also observed that Artúr's father had a negative image in Welsh tradition, being known as 'Áedán the Treacherous':

> And it seems to me quite incredible that a Scottish prince, and one moreover who was the son of that Aedan whose name passed into Welsh tradition with the epithet *Bradawg* ('The Treacherous' or 'The Wily') should eventually come to fill the role of epic hero of the Britons, and the centre of a cycle of tales in all Brittonic-speaking lands.[21]

An alternative theory sees Artúr mac Áedain not as the figure behind the legendary King Arthur but merely as someone named after him. It imagines Arthur as a famous (and real) hero who was commemorated within a generation or so of his death by people who bestowed his name on their sons. In addition to Artúr of Dál Riata, three other namesakes are sometimes cited in this context. One who certainly had a Scottish connection was Artuir 'son of Bicoir the Briton' who killed an Irish prince in Kintyre c.625. Nothing more is known of him but his father arguably came from Alt Clut, the British kingdom closest to Dál Riata. Equally sparse is our knowledge of an 'Artuir' whose grandson, a cleric called Feradach, attended an Irish synod in 697. Feradach's name is Gaelic, which could mean that he hailed from Ireland or Dál Riata, but there is no further mention of him or of his grandfather. The final namesake is Arthur, son of Pedr, a Welsh prince from Dyfed born probably in the late sixth century. Like the other three, he is an obscure figure of whom little more can be said. The possibility nevertheless remains that all four were named after a hero of the recent past, a famous warlord transformed by later legend into a mighty king.[22] We may note that Rachel Bromwich regarded this as yet another unconvincing scenario: 'If these four were all named after "the historical Arthur", it would be a type of commemoration for which Celtic tradition offers no parallel, as far as I know.'[23]

The oldest Welsh traditions about Arthur show him leading the native Britons against their enemies in the late fifth and early sixth centuries. Many adherents of the belief that he was 'real' assume that he, too, must necessarily have been a Briton. Those who suggest that his story originated in southern Scotland rather than in Dál Riata see him as a North British hero like the warriors commemorated in *The Gododdin*. They propose that a corpus of stories about him developed in the North before travelling to Wales in the eighth or ninth century. In Wales, this material was then altered and embellished until the northern Arthur became a pan-British hero who fought against Saxons in the South as well as in the North. The theory benefits from the fact that transfers of northern lore to Wales certainly did occur. Indeed, without this kind of literary migration the North British material might not have survived in the quantity we know today. It could have been diminished or erased by the Scottish conquerors of Strathclyde, last kingdom of the northern Britons, when they imposed their own culture upon its people. If this had happened, we would now probably know little of Rhydderch Hael, Urien Rheged or the battle of Arfderydd, for the main repository of these traditions was surely the folklore of Clydesdale. This is probably where remnants of the literature of vanished kingdoms like Rheged and Gododdin were preserved, in written text and human memory, before eventually migrating to Wales. Supporters of the idea that the original Arthur was a sixth-century North Briton believe that he, too, was long remembered by the people of the Clyde. Some suggest that he himself may have been a native of the area, perhaps a great warrior who served the kings of Alt Clut. Attempts have been made to match his twelve victories to places within striking distance of Dumbarton, the most recent being a detailed philological study by Andrew Breeze.[24] Of the various 'Scottish Arthur' theories, the idea of him being a Cumbric-speaking Clydesider does seem more credible than the notion that he hailed from Gaelic Dál Riata. It fits better with his portrayal in old Welsh tradition as a British hero, a compatriot of the Welsh themselves. It nevertheless assumes that he originated as a figure of history rather than of legend and, at present, there is not enough evidence to confirm or deny the belief.

Locating Arthur's battles

Many attempts have been made to place Arthur's battles in Scotland or in the Anglo-Scottish borderlands. Some of the proposed locations are shown below. These are followed by a selection of alternatives from further south, in England and Wales. For further discussion, see Breeze 2015.

River Glein	River Glen (Northumberland)
River Dubglas	Douglas Water (South Lanarkshire)
River Bassas	Dunipace (Falkirk), Bass Rock (East Lothian) or a misprint for Tarras (Tarras Water in Dumfriesshire or Carstairs in South Lanarkshire)
Coit Celidon	Forest of Calidon in southern Scotland
Fort Guinnion	Kirkgunzeon (Dumfriesshire) or Carwinning (North Ayrshire)
City of the Legion	Castle Lyon (Falkirk)
Tribruit	Dreva (Borders)
Mount Agned or Breguoin	Edinburgh or *Bremenium* (High Rochester, Northumberland)
Mount Badon	Bowden Hill (West Lothian)
Camlan	Camelon (Falkirk) or *Camboglanna* (Castlesteads, Cumbria)

Dubglas – a river somewhere in Lincolnshire (if *Linnuis* is the district of Lindsey)

Bassas – Baschurch (Shropshire)

Fort Guinnion – *Vinovia* (Binchester in County Durham)

City of the Legion – Chester, Caerleon or York

Badon – Badbury Rings (Dorset), *Baddanbyrig* (Luddington Castle in Wiltshire) or Braydon (Wiltshire)

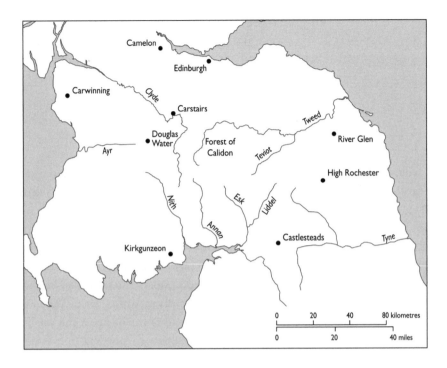

Map 7 The search for Arthur's battles: some Scottish locations

The connection between Merlin and Arthur is a literary device of the twelfth century and has no ancient warrant. It is fiction rather than history. The 'real' Merlin or Merlin-archetype was unlikely to have been born before 537, the date traditionally assigned to the battle of Camlan where Arthur is said to have died. Even if Arthur was a historical figure – a point of continuing uncertainty – he and the Merlin-archetype would not have been contemporaries. Nothing in the earliest Welsh Arthurian material of the ninth century drew a line of connection between them, nor did the Myrddin poetry, which was probably starting to take shape around the same time. If there really was any ancient link between Arthur and Merlin, it perhaps lay not in history but in storytelling, and specifically in the folklore of Strathclyde where their respective legends may have formed.

8

SCOTTISH MERLINS

It seems undeniable that the roots of the Merlin legend lie in Scotland. They seem to begin with Lailoken, the wild man of Strathclyde, whom we can identify as the Merlin-archetype – the historical figure behind the Arthurian wizard. This is neither a new theory nor a particularly radical one, being based on information in medieval texts that are well-known among historians. Indeed, the case for an original 'Scottish Merlin' has been made many times before, not only by modern writers but also by medieval predecessors. The idea that Merlin's primary geographical context is southern Scotland rather than Wales or Cornwall is almost as old as the first appearance of his name in the twelfth century. Its evolution is examined in this penultimate chapter, via an overview of the literature and by highlighting a selection of 'Scottish Merlins'. These figures are drawn from a wide range of texts and from a broad chronological span, ranging from poems, stories and political propaganda of the Middle Ages to historical studies written in modern times.

Merlin Caledonius

We begin with Geoffrey of Monmouth and with his great work *Historia Regum Britanniae*. It is immediately obvious that the Merlin of *HRB* has no connection with Scotland. His portrayal owes almost nothing to Lailoken or to Myrddin Wyllt, being a different figure altogether. He is Merlin Ambrosius, the Welsh seer and sorcerer who moved Stonehenge from Ireland to Britain. Geoffrey did, however, draw on the Myrddin poems for the central character of *Vita Merlini*, thus introducing his readers to a figure who had Scottish as well as Welsh connections. This was not the Merlin of *HRB*, even if Geoffrey envisaged the two as one individual. We may note that the Merlin of *VM* is only 'Scottish' by relocation, having originally been a king of Dyfed in South Wales. After a battle against King Guennolous of Scotland at an unnamed northern location, *VM*'s Merlin sought refuge and solace in the Forest of Calidon. There he was visited by his sister Ganieda, wife of King Rodarch of Cumbria (i.e, Strathclyde).

VM makes no reference to Merlin's death, so the reader is left to wonder if the poem's central character ended his days in Scotland or back home in Wales.

Geoffrey probably had no first-hand knowledge of any region north of Chester.[1] His first-hand experience of places outside Wales and southern England appears to have been quite limited, although it is likely that he made visits to France and Brittany. He almost certainly had no knowledge of the precise location of Calidon, beyond a vague idea that it lay somewhere in Scotland. On the other hand, it is possible that he correctly associated King Rodarch of the 'Cumbrians' with the former kingdom of Strathclyde rather than with the English county of Cumberland. The county was still in its infancy, or had yet to come into being when *VM* was published.[2] At that time, the term 'Cumbria' straddled both sides of the Anglo-Scottish border and still applied to large swathes of territory formerly ruled by the kings of Strathclyde. Geoffrey may have had in mind the Scottish, most northerly portion of this region when he called Rodarch's kingdom Cumbria. Whether he had any precise notion of the geography of Clydesdale seems rather more doubtful.

How far Geoffrey's Scottish or North British Merlin was influenced by Lailoken directly, rather than through the intermediary of Myrddin Wyllt, is an interesting question. Although Lailoken is not mentioned in *VM*, there is reason to believe that Geoffrey was aware of his legend and that he took information directly from it. *VM*'s description of Rodarch's court seems to have been taken from Lailoken's inprisonment in Meldred's fortress at Drumelzier.[3] The episode has no parallel in the Myrddin poetry and may have come to Geoffrey in a form similar to the Scottish version preserved in the Lailoken tales. Since its arrival in Wales in the ninth century or thereabouts, the Lailoken/Arfderydd material had been thoroughly reworked into a framework for the Myrddin poems. The episode at Meldred's fortress did not survive this process and seems to have been discarded from Welsh tradition, so where would Geoffrey obtain his knowledge of it?

The answer surely lies in his connections with Glasgow Cathedral and with the lore surrounding St Kentigern to which the Lailoken legend had become attached. Geoffrey, as we have already observed, probably never visited Scotland, so any link with Glasgow can only have been distant and indirect. The link was probably made when he was appointed to St Asaph, a fairly new episcopal see in North Wales to which he was formally consecrated as bishop in 1152. St Asaph's principal church stood beside the River Elwy, a little under thirty miles west of Chester at a place called in Welsh 'Llanelwy'. Curiously, Geoffrey might never have visited the place in person.[4] Asaph himself is a rather obscure figure, but the traditional story portrays him as a young man who assisted Kentigern during the latter's supposed exile in Wales. Kentigern is said to have founded the first church at Llanelwy as a base for his own missionary activities, leaving Asaph in charge when he eventually returned to northern Britain. Needless to say, the reliability of this tale is debatable, not only because so little is known about Asaph but also because Kentigern's exile in Wales is probably fictional. A fragmentary *vita* of Asaph apparently once existed in a medieval manuscript but this is no longer extant.[5] In fact, our earliest account of him comes from the Life of Kentigern by Jocelin of Furness. Interestingly, Jocelin's source may have been none other than Geoffrey of Monmouth who, after his appointment as bishop, perhaps invented the link between Asaph and Kentigern.[6] The wider context here is a complex picture of twelfth-century ecclesiastical rivalry, primarily between the archbishops of Canterbury and York, but also involving the Welsh sees of St David's and Llandaff and the bishops of Glasgow as well.[7] A propagandist motive in the conventional foundation-tale of St Asaph therefore seems likely, with Kentigern's alleged exile in Wales being invented for the same reason. The supposed connection between the two saints might reflect friendship or shared interests between St Asaph and Glasgow Cathedral, the former being promoted as a foundation of the latter's patron saint. Detailed information on Kentigern can only have come to Wales via the custodians of his hagiography at Glasgow. If the material included a version of *Lailoken and Kentigern*, this could explain how Lailoken came to the notice of Geoffrey of Monmouth, who then gave his readers a glimpse of the northern wild man in *Vita Merlini*.

Although the Merlin of *VM* can be called Scottish or North British, his namesake in *Historia Regum Britanniae* certainly cannot. Nevertheless, the fame of *HRB* eventually brought its personification of Merlin northward to the Border and beyond. In Scotland, his obvious similarities with Lailoken were noticed and the two were identified as the same individual. Thus, in *Lailoken and Kentigern*, a scribe has added that 'some say he was Merlin, who was an extraordinary prophet of the British; but this is not certain'. Likewise, in *Lailoken and Meldred* the narrative ends with a two-line verse: 'Pierced by a stake, suffering by a stone and by water, Merlin is said to have met a triple death.' Nowhere in his writings does Geoffrey actually refer to Merlin as 'Caledonius', this epithet being devised by his contemporary and fellow-countryman Gerald of Wales. Gerald deduced that Merlin Ambrosius in *HRB* could not be the same person as *VM*'s Merlin so he distinguished the latter by the epithets *Silvestris* ('of the Wood') and *Caledonius* ('of Scotland').[8]

Thomas the Rhymer

The references to Merlin in the Lailoken tales bring Geoffrey's Arthurian wizard back to his Scottish roots. The verse at the end of the Lailoken-Meldred story connects him specifically with Drumelzier in Tweeddale, where Lailoken is said to have suffered a triple death. Merlin is again linked to this place in a prophecy attributed to Thomas the Rhymer, a Scottish seer who lived in the century after Geoffrey.[9] Thomas, otherwise known as Sir Thomas of Erceldoune, was a real person but also the hero in a fantastical tale composed in the early fifteenth century. It tells of his abduction by the Queen of Elfland, from whom he subsequently obtained his prophetic power. The tale survives as a verse romance in a number of medieval manuscripts as well as in a later ballad published by Sir Walter Scott in his *Minstrelsy of the Scottish Border* at the beginning of the nineteenth century. Prophecies attributed to Thomas were quoted by Scottish historians from the fifteenth century onwards, appearing in such works as Walter Bower's *Scotichronicon*. Many of the prophecies dealt with political topics such as the volatile relationship between the Scottish and English crowns. One of the most famous refers to Merlin's grave at Drumelzier:

> When Tweed and Pausayl meet at Merlin's grave,
> Scotland and England shall one monarch have.

This was published in the early eighteenth century in Alexander Pennycuik's historical and geographical survey of Tweeddale.[10] It presumably appeared in earlier texts but, if so, none of these has survived. Its ultimate source is a prophecy uttered by Lailoken in the presence of King Meldred: 'When the confluence of the two rivers comes up to my tomb, the marshal of the British race will defeat the foreign race.' Thomas the Rhymer's 'Pausayl' is the Powsail or Drumelzier Burn. The monarch who will one day unify Scotland and England is most likely meant to be King Arthur, the legendary sovereign of the whole of Britain. This reflects a popular theme of Arthurian lore in which the king is not dead but merely awaiting the call to save his people or, as in this case, to reunite the two halves of Britain. A different interpretation of the prophecy claims that it was actually fulfilled in 1603 when the Tweed overflowed its banks to flood the adjacent fields. The river and the Powsail Burn then merged for a brief time and, in the same year, James VI of Scotland succeeded to the English throne as king of all Britain.

Another link between Thomas the Rhymer and Merlin is the legend of Canonbie Dick, an old Scottish folktale about a horse-dealer from Canonbie in the Border country.[11] One of Dick's journeys brought him to the Eildon Hills near Melrose where he encountered a strange figure dressed in antique clothes. The stranger wanted to buy two horses, which Dick duly sold. Further meetings were arranged, and more horses were purchased by the stranger. Eventually, Dick suggested a visit to the stranger's abode, which turned out to be a huge cave delved in the hillside. Inside lay a band of sleeping knights beside their steeds, and also a table with a horn and sword placed upon it. The stranger then revealed himself to be none other than Thomas the Rhymer. He told Dick of a prophecy that the person who drew the sword and blew the horn would become the king of all Britain. Dick then sounded a blast on the horn, waking the knights from their slumber, but a great tumult arose and blew him out of the cave. So ends the tale. It incorporates the motif of the Sleeping King, a storytelling theme in which a hero of legend lies in a secret underground chamber with his soldiers, waiting for a time when he will be summoned to fight the forces of evil. The same theme appears in an English story about Alderley Edge in Cheshire, where the strange figure is identified as Merlin and the sleepers are Arthur and his knights.[12] In Scotland, another version of the Canonbie Dick tale shifts the location to a cave beneath Arthur's Seat near Edinburgh and specifically names the guardian as Merlin. Indeed, it is likely that the Eildon story originally had Merlin in this role before later replacing him with Thomas the Rhymer. This would be consistent with the popularity of the legend of Thomas in the Middle Ages and with a growing belief that he – rather than Merlin – was Scotland's premier seer. Canonbie Dick's mysterious stranger perhaps began as a Scottish representation of Geoffrey of Monmouth's Arthurian wizard. His namesake in Thomas the Rhymer's prophecy is, however, connected with Drumelzier and probably closer to the roots of the Merlin legend.

The Nouquetran

In the early thirteenth century, a writer called Guillaume le Clerc ('William the Clerk') produced *Le Roman de Fergus*, an Arthurian romance in which the story takes place almost entirely in Scotland.[13] The Fergus of the title was based loosely on a historical figure of this name, a twelfth-century nobleman who founded the powerful lordship of Galloway. His descendants ruled what was essentially a semi-independent territory within the medieval kingdom of Scotland until its formal absorption in the mid-1200s. Although its language is French, Guillaume's *Fergus* was probably commissioned by a member of the Scottish nobility, perhaps a high-ranking individual at the royal court. It is unlikely to have been commissioned in Galloway, for its tone is rather disparaging to the region's ruling dynasty. The eponymous hero is a young peasant who wants to become a knight at King Arthur's court in Carlisle. To prove his worth, he is given a task by Sir Kay: he must retrieve a horn and wimple from the Black Mountain which is guarded by the fearsome Black Knight. Kay tells Fergus that the mountain is also known as The Nouquetran 'where Merlin dwelt many years'. The name Nouquetran appears nowhere else in medieval literature, nor does it resemble any place-name associated with Merlin in other texts.[14] The mountain itself remains unlocated and was probably never meant to be a real place anyway. It is described in almost fantastical terms as being immeasurably high and steep-sided, accessible only by a perilous path made by a giant. Rather than being an actual location, it seems to represent the common literary motif of an insurmountable obstacle standing in the way of a hero's progress. In this sense it contrasts with Guillaume's earlier geographical descriptions, which are given in a rather more realistic way. The overall impression is that he or his source possessed an accurate knowledge of parts of the Anglo-Scottish borderland.[15] When Fergus sets out on his quest, he begins at Carlisle and rides to the castle of Liddel. This was not Liddel Strength at Arthuret/Arfderydd but another Norman motte-and-bailey stronghold in Liddesdale on the Scottish side of the Border. The journey to the Nouquetran nevertheless begins in the area where the Merlin-archetype fought in the great battle of 573. Starting from Arthur's royal court at Carlisle, Fergus would have travelled through the parish of Arthuret, perhaps on the same route taken by Gwenddolau's enemies as they approached the battlefield.[16] This is a real landscape that can still be traced on a modern map. It eventually gives way to an imaginary one when Fergus reaches the Nouquetran, a stereotypical 'dark mountain' serving a specific role in the narrative. This clear separation between real and fictional geography has not, however, deterred several modern attempts to locate the mountain. These usually speculate on the possible meaning of its name or treat the *Roman de Fergus* as a reliable guide. Nikolai Tolstoy, for example, noted that the mountain seems to be an echo of the lofty height in the Forest of Calidon upon whose summit the wild prophet of *Vita Merlini* made his abode. Tolstoy proposed that the brooding bulk of Hart Fell, 'a ponderous mass of mountain skirted by the Moffat and the Annan, rising ever higher, shoulder upon shoulder', fitted Guillaume's description of the Nouquetran.[17] Needless to say, similar claims could be made for other large hills in southern Scotland – if we choose to believe that the Black Mountain is real rather than imaginary. Taking a more sceptical stance, we should disregard the Nouquetran in our search for the origins of the

Merlin legend, for Guillaume le Clerc's Merlin is none other than his namesake from *Historia Regum Britanniae* in a Scottish setting. This is Geoffrey of Monmouth's creation who sheds little light on either Lailoken or Myrddin Wyllt, still less on the archetype lurking behind them. The connection between the *Roman de Fergus* and the landscape of the battle of Arfderydd is no more than a coincidence arising from Guillaume's placement of Arthur's court at Carlisle. The Scottish Merlin who 'dwelt many years' at the Nouquetran is not the historical figure behind the legend.

Merlin, Arthur and Anglo-Scottish relations

From the fourteenth century onwards, the Merlin of Arthuriana began to appear as a character in Scottish pseudo-histories. These blended real history with myth to present an imaginative version of the story of Scotland. They usually depicted Arthur in his familiar guise as a mighty king, with Merlin cast as a prophet and sorcerer at the royal court. Both characters were often treated unfavourably, chiefly because of the political implications of Merlin's prophecies. In Geoffrey of Monmouth's *Historia Regum Britanniae*, Merlin prophesied that Arthur would one day return to regain his authority over the whole of Britain. To many Scots in the Middle Ages, this was a profoundly unsettling prospect.[18] They did not welcome the idea of being conquered – or reconquered – by an ambitious southern king, whether legendary or otherwise. Moreover, *HRB* had not only shown Arthur as conquering Scotland but had also depicted his treacherous nephew Modred as a Scottish king. This, too, made Arthur seem like an enemy of the Scots. His negative image north of the Border was strengthened by the attitudes of contemporary English writers, many of whom saw Arthur as a model for their own kings. Arthur's supposed domination of Britain provided a template for English territorial ambitions in the 1300s and 1400s, with Merlin duly portrayed as the prophet of England's future greatness. Moreover, Merlin's prophecy about Arthur's triumphal return to resume the overkingship of Britain appeared to legitimise English claims of sovereignty over the Scots.[19] Scottish writers responded by promoting Modred, not Arthur, as the legitimate overlord of ancient Britain. Modred's Scottishness was well-established in *HRB* so he was an obvious choice. Merlin could then be dismissed as a charlatan, a false prophet, or used as a mouthpiece for Scottish political prophecy. In the fourteenth century, John of Fordun's *Chronicles of the Scottish People* included the following lines of verse, which had supposedly been uttered by the British cleric Gildas in the sixth century:

Scotia shall mourn her famous kings of old –
Her kings so just, rich, bountiful, and bold.
For an unkingly king – so Merlin sings –
Shall wield the sceptre of victorious kings.[20]

Fordun does not say who this 'unkingly' monarch is but presumably had a candidate in mind. It hardly needs stating that the prophecy has no real connection with Gildas and is nothing more than medieval invention. It is nevertheless interesting for its reference to Merlin's prophetic 'song' about Scottish kings. Another curious item comes from the fifteenth century when Walter Bower reported a tradition that the eagles of Loch Lomond were able to foresee the future. The tradition itself is obscure and otherwise unknown but Bower credited Merlin as the source.[21] Other Scottish writers were reluctant to say anything positive about Merlin, regarding him as tainted by association with Arthur whose legendary subjugation of Scotland was strongly resented. Hector Boece, writing in the sixteenth century, rejected the romanticised account of Arthur's conception in *HRB*, seeing Uther's trickery of Igerna as an evil deed facilitated by the 'necromancy of Merlyne'. Boece asserted that Arthur ('gottin in adultery') had not conquered Scotland – as the English claimed – but had been slain by the Scottish king Lothus.[22] This type of ill-feeling towards Arthur and Merlin was a characteristic of Scottish historical writing in the late medieval period and continued through the arguments over political union during the sixteenth century. At its heart was a broader opposition to the perceived 'Englishness' of Arthur and to the idea of a single, pan-British kingdom ruled by a southern monarch. Its clearest expression came as the medieval era was drawing to a close, in *The Complaynt of Scotland*, a document examined below.

Merlin and the Union of the Crowns

In the sixteenth century, the English king Henry VIII sought a dynastic marriage between his son Edward and Mary, Queen of Scots. Mary was only a baby at the time, having succeeded to the Scottish throne on the death of her father James V in December 1542. The effective ruler of Scotland during her infancy was the Earl of Arran who held the role of regent. Scottish resentment at the prospect of this marriage led to the plan being rejected by the country's parliament, whose members saw it as another lever for English political ambitions. Henry responded by declaring war on the Scots. Known in later times as 'The Rough

Wooing', the conflict lasted from 1543 to 1551. Hostilities on the battlefield were accompanied by propaganda campaigns, with both sides producing printed works for mass distribution. One pamphlet vigorously opposed the view that the two countries should be united under a single monarch. Written anonymously, but perhaps by the Dundee minister Robert Wedderburn, it appeared in 1549 under the title *The Complaynt of Scotland*. It denounced a number of English propagandist texts and saw Merlin's prophecies as giving the English an excuse for making war:

> *the prophesies of Merlyne, to the quhilk the Inglishmen giffis more confidens nor thai gif to the evangel, by cause that there ald prophane prophesis sais, that Ingland and Scotland sal be baitht undir ane prince, on this misteous prophesis, thai have intendit weyris contrar Scotland.*

('The prophecies of Merlin, to which the Englishmen give more confidence than they give to the Gospel, because an old profane prophecy says that England and Scotland shall be both under one prince. On this obscure prophecy, they have intended wars against Scotland.')[23]

This was a response to the way in which contemporary English writers – and some Scottish ones – employed Merlin as an advocate for the union of the crowns. It illustrates the extent to which attitudes towards Merlin had hardened among those Scots who strongly opposed the union. The *Complaynt* was specifically aimed at those Scottish writers who had used Merlin as a conduit for pro-unionist prophecies. It not only dismissed these prophecies as nonsense but countered them with a bold prediction that England would one day be conquered by the Scots.[24] An even more disparaging assessement of Merlin appeared in George Buchanan's *Rerum Scoticarum Historia*, published in 1582. Buchanan pulled no punches, describing Merlin as 'audacious and wicked' and as 'an egregious imposter, and cunning pretender, rather than a prophet'.[25] The pro-unionist side were eventually able to claim victory when, in 1603, James VI of Scotland succeeded the childless Elizabeth I on the English throne. Merlin, whose prophecies had supposedly foretold the event, could thus be seen as vindicated. The path was now clear for his rehabilitation north of the Border.[26] He was even promoted by Scottish writers such as Thomas Craig and Thomas Dempster as a true native of Scotland.[27] It is a strange irony that the wheel had thus come full circle, bringing the wizard of Arthurian romance back to the land where his legend had started a thousand years earlier.

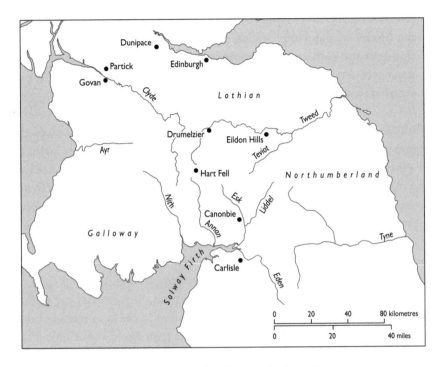

Map 8 Scotland and the Merlin legend

Modern Scottish Merlins

In the post-medieval era, Scottish writers continued to highlight Merlin's connection with their country. Antiquarians of the eighteenth and early nineteenth centuries, with a keen interest in relics of the ancient past, reported snippets of folklore from places associated with Merlin. George Chalmers, in the first volume of his *Caledonia* (1807), was familiar with the Welsh poems attributed to Myrddin Wyllt, deducing from these that Merlin's homeland was 'Caledonia, the land of the Picts'.[28] Later in the same volume he followed a description of prehistoric burial mounds in Peeblesshire with the words 'But, what are the barrows of the warriors to the grave of Merlin!' For, although he believed that a historical figure of the sixth century lay behind the Merlin legend, he seems to have been less trusting of the folklore surrounding the alleged grave-site at Drumelzier. He dismissed any notion that the prophecy attributed to Thomas the Rhymer was genuine, still less that it had been fulfilled by the union of the crowns in 1603. He observed that Drumelzier did not lie close to the heartland of the kingdom of Strathclyde, which is where he placed the Merlin legend's origins:

It is, indeed, curious to remark, that the Merddin of the Cambro-British, the Merlin of the Scoto-Saxons, who was undoubtedly a Strathclyde Briton of the sixth century, should have been buried, according to the popular tradition, in the remotest part of the Strathclyde kingdom, at the junction of the Tweed and Powsail.[29]

Chalmers was not only sceptical of the Drumelzier tradition but also of the notion that the battle of Arfderydd had been fought near the Solway Firth. As we noted in Chapter 4, he suggested Airdrie in Clydesdale as a better location. The matter was eventually settled later in the nineteenth century, in Skene's perceptive exploration of the history behind the Merlin legend. His famous paper on Arfderydd finally pinpointed the place where both Lailoken and Myrddin were said to have gone mad. In the same paper, Skene suggested that the battle was a contest between pagan and Christian forces, the former being led by Merlin and his patron Gwenddolau. To support this idea, Skene drew on his extensive knowledge of ancient Welsh literature, in particular the poems, genealogies and triads relating to the Old North. Crucially, in reference to a triad relating to Arfderydd, his translation of the term *mygedorth* as 'sacred fire' rather than as 'battle fog' formed a key plank of his belief that the real Merlin was a pagan sorcerer or druid. In Chapter 5 we saw how this became an influential theory that has coloured subsequent discussion of Merlin's origins.

Skene was familiar with the Myrddin poetry but apparently saw its Christian allusions as forming no great obstacle to his theory. He seems to have regarded the poems as originally having a pagan aspect that was hidden beneath a later Christian overlay during a long process of composition and transmission in Wales. Skene's reputation as a major scholar of ancient Celtic literature undoubtedly helped his theory to become widely known and accepted. Its repetition by later writers kept it alive into the twentieth century, ensuring that its popularity remained undimmed long after he himself had passed away. Today, at the beginning of the third millennium, the idea that the Merlin legend originated among sixth-century North British paganism continues to hold a special allure. However, as we have already seen, it relies on little more than a single inference deduced from an erroneous translation of one line of Welsh poetry.

Skene's theory was substantially expanded more than a hundred years later by Nikolai Tolstoy, in *The Quest for Merlin*. Published in 1985, Tolstoy's book remains the most detailed study of the North British or 'Scottish' Merlin to date. Although some of its ideas have not been widely accepted, the book has had a major influence on how the roots of the Merlin legend are presented to the general reader. Tolstoy's Merlin is a composite figure, a blend of wild man, poet, sorcerer, druid and shaman. The Scottishness of this multi-faceted individual is made clear when Tolstoy equates him with both Lailoken and the Arfderydd fugitive Myrddin. Like Chalmers, Tolstoy is sceptical of the Drumelzier burial tradition. He wonders if the summit of Hart Fell might be a more likely grave-site, but believes that the actual location remains unidentified.[30]

The pagan North British druid envisaged by Skene and Tolstoy reappears in Adam Ardrey's *Finding Merlin* in which the figure behind the legend is described as 'a druid of the old way'.[31] Ardrey offers a number of original ideas, such as a suggestion that the historical Merlin dwelt not in the remote forests of the Clyde–Tweed watershed but closer to Glasgow and the heartlands of King Rhydderch. He proposes that Rhydderch's wife Languoreth, whom he sees as the figure behind Gwenddydd/Ganieda, was someone whose historical significance has been underestimated. Like Tolstoy, Ardrey places Merlin's origins against a backdrop of religious conflict between paganism and Christianity. However, whereas Tolstoy imagines a straightforward contest between two very different ideologies, Ardrey sees a more nuanced struggle in which the Christian side was also divided into two opposing camps led respectively by St Mungo (Kentigern) and his hostile companion Telleyr, one of two brothers with whom the saint dwelt at Glasgow. Although Telleyr is a very obscure figure, known only from a single chapter in Jocelin's Life of Kentigern, Ardrey sees him as the leader of a group of Christians whose tolerant attitude towards paganism placed them at odds with Kentigern/Mungo.[32] In this scenario, the 'Telleyr Christians' were eventually pushed aside by the fanatical 'Mungo Christians' whose victory ensured that a more rigid version of Christianity held sway among the Clyde Britons. Ardrey is here alluding to a real ecclesiastical conflict that impacted upon the churches of Britain and Ireland in the sixth century, reaching an inevitable climax in the seventh. It is often characterised as a struggle between native 'Celtic' Christianity and an authoritarian 'Roman' counterpart that sought to dominate it. Much is often made of the differences between the two sides as if they represented rival branches of Christianity akin to the opposing sides in the Reformation. In reality, the Celtic and Roman factions were not separate institutions at all. Their main bone of contention was disagreement over the method used annually for calculating the date of Easter Sunday. Many British and Irish clerics preferred to use a calculation regarded as obsolete by a majority of their peers in other parts of western Christendom. Nevertheless, even the most stubborn advocates of 'Celtic' practices remained loyal and deferential to the Pope.

Contemporary writers on both sides of the Irish Sea reported on the long-running debate until its key issues were finally settled.[33] At the heart of the debate lay the so-called 'Easter Controversy' which exercised the minds and consciences of clergyfolk in many parts of the British Isles. Unfortunately, we know very little about how it affected the people of the Clyde. This is a gap that Ardrey attempts to fill, by imagining Kentigern as a champion of the Roman side and Telleyr as his chief 'Celtic' opponent whose ally was Merlin the pagan. In the wake of Kentigern's triumph, Merlin then retires from public life to become 'a pensioner of the king', a situation that protects him from being murdered by the victorious 'Mungo Christians'. The latter instead resort to character-assassination, denigrating Merlin as insane and treating him as a joke figure. This forces him to leave the royal estate at Partick where he has been living peacefully. His sister, Queen Languoreth, in the role assigned to Ganieda in *Vita Merlini*, later comes to live with him in his observatory. According to Ardrey, this lay close to Partick rather than in the Border hills further south. This reimagining of the conventional geography of *Vita Merlini* and the Myrddin poems is one of the key differences between Ardrey and Tolstoy. Moreover, Ardrey challenges centuries of Tweeddale folklore by shifting Merlin's grave to a hill near Drumelzier Farm at Dunipace, three miles north-west of Falkirk. This is a bold theory, not least because there is no parallel tradition to support it. Ardrey suggests that Dunipace did not stake any claim to Merlin because it lay in a region that has always played an important role in Scottish history. Being in the spotlight and hence under the watchful eye of the Christian 'establishment', local people would have been forbidden from venerating the grave of a famous pagan. Not so the folk of remote and isolated Upper Tweeddale who, in Ardrey's opinion, were so 'off the beaten track', that they were able to create and nurture their own traditions about the location of Merlin's grave.

Some of Tolstoy's theories reappear in Robin Crichton's *Merlin: the Hidden History*, a privately printed booklet from 2015. Crichton draws on the legends of Lailoken and Myrddin Wyllt to tell 'the story of the clash between Christianity and traditional belief – a duel between St Mungo the priest and Merlin the pagan'. Like Ardrey, Crichton depicts Kentigern as a religious zealot driven by a desire to stamp out the last vestige of paganism among the North Britons. Early sections of Crichton's study give interesting overviews of political geography, social organisation and religious beliefs in sixth-century northern Britain. He identifies Rhydderch Hael of Alt Clut as a key protagonist at the battle of Arfderydd and sees Merlin entering the fray in its final stages after previously observing from the sidelines.[34] While Ardrey locates Merlin's wilderness refuge in the lower Clyde valley, around Partick, Crichton follows Tolstoy's suggestion of Hart Fell. Tolstoy has little to say about Drumelzier and Stobo but Crichton stays closer to the Lailoken legend by bringing both places into his narrative. He identifies the hillfort at Tinnis Castle as the stronghold of King Meldred and suggests that the latter is commemorated in the name Drumelzier. He sees these places as lying within 'the chiefdom of *Goddeu* (the Land of Trees)', which may have been a forested district in the upper reaches of Clydesdale or Tweeddale.[35] This geographical context makes Crichton's narrative a fairly close match with the one presented here. Indeed, his Merlin is much nearer than either Tolstoy's or Ardrey's to the original figure behind the Lailoken tales and, in that sense, may be more authentic historically.

An even more recent 'Scottish Merlin' is the main character in a graphic novel by Pete Renshaw and T. S. Beall, produced in conjunction with an artist-led heritage project called Govan's Hidden Histories.[36] The story is written in a light-hearted style, being intended primarily for young readers. Nevertheless, its purpose is not only to amuse and entertain but also to raise awareness of the town's rich history. It depicts Merlin as the custodian of the 'Thirteen Treasures of Govan', ostensibly a collection of ancient magical items now concealed as architectural, sculptural and historical landmarks in the area. The inspiration comes from the fabled Thirteen Treasures of the Island of Britain, a list of objects described in Welsh texts of the late medieval period.[37] Most of the items in the original Welsh lists are associated with the Old North and with familiar figures from the poems and triads. Examples include the sword of Rhydderch Hael, with its fiery blade, and the halter of Clydno Eiddin which summoned any horse that its owner wished for. Although none of the original Thirteen Treasures of Britain is directly linked to Merlin in any of his guises, he seems a logical choice for the role assigned to him in the graphic novel, in which he embarks on a journey to reveal the long-hidden treasures of Govan. The narrative is essentially a tour of local heritage sites, with Merlin inviting the reader to assist in the quest.[38] An accompanying map shows where the Thirteen Treasures can be found. Thus, the Cauldron of Dyrnwch the Giant, an item on the original Welsh list, turns out to be cunningly concealed as a piece of Victorian street architecture – the dome-shaped canopy of the Aitken Memorial Fountain. Another original item, a magical whetstone belonging to Tudwal Tudclyd (father of Rhydderch Hael), is identified as one of five tenth-century hogback gravestones in the old parish church. At one point in the story, Merlin says that his former name was Lailoken and that he used to dwell in the woods. Kentigern is also mentioned – under his alternative name Mungo – and so is Rhydderch's wife in her role as Merlin's sister. These references connect the Merlin of the novel with the wild man of Scottish folklore and Welsh poetry. They also highlight the link between Lailoken and this part of Clydesdale, for Govan lies across the river from Partick where – according to Jocelin of Furness – 'Laloecen' dwelt at Rhydderch's court. The site of Partick Castle, where the ancient royal residence probably lay, is only a stone's throw from the Riverside Museum which houses four of the Thirteen Treasures.

To end this selective survey of Scottish Merlins we turn briefly to the world of modern politics and to a speech delivered by Scotland's former First Minister Alex Salmond at a conference of the Scottish National Party (SNP) in November 2014. Praising the economic policy of the country's SNP-led government, Salmond described Finance Secretary John Swinney as a 'financial magician, Scotland's Merlin'. The speech was widely reported in the Scottish media, momentarily reconnecting the name of the legendary seer with the land where his legend began.

SCOTLAND'S MERLIN: FACT OR FICTION?

The various threads of history, literature and folklore can now be drawn together. They weave a many-coloured tapestry of people, places and events – the legend of Merlin. The oldest part of this tapestry represents the beginning of the legend and offers a portrait of the original figure behind it, an individual whom we have here labelled the 'Merlin-archetype'. The evidence suggests that he actually existed, that he was a real person and that his story was first told in Scotland. This story is presented in the following reconstruction. It is a tale in two sections, reflecting Merlin's dual aspect as a figure inhabiting both a real and an imaginary world. The story begins in the Dark Ages, in one of the long-vanished kingdoms of northern Britain.

The real Merlin

Sometime around the middle of the sixth century AD, perhaps around the year 540, a boy was born in the lands around the head of the Solway Firth. His family were native Britons of high status, members of the landowning aristocracy. They lived on a substantial estate worked by tenant farmers upon whose toil their lifestyle depended. The newborn child was known as Llallawg, or affectionately as Llallogan ('Little Llallawg'), these names being given from birth or bestowed later as nicknames. Llallogan's family owed allegiance to a local king whose core domain lay near the confluence of the rivers Esk and Liddel. The area around the confluence was called Arfderydd, taking its name from a stream flowing into the Esk just below the river-junction. In later times, Arfderydd gave its name to the medieval parish of Arthuret, while the stream became known as the Carwinley Burn.

Like most high-born young men of the kingdom, Llallogan entered military service in his late teens as a soldier in the royal army. Mounted on a horse, carrying a spear and shield and wearing a tunic of chainmail, he fought for the king in raids and battles. His loyalty and prowess were rewarded with gifts from the royal treasury: jewellery, fine clothing and other trappings of wealth. By c.570, when he was around thirty years of age, he was recognised as a trusted companion of the king and received a position of rank at the royal court. The king at that time was Gwenddolau, son of Ceidio. In common with most other British kings in this period, Gwenddolau considered himself a Christian. So did the majority of his people, including his loyal henchman Llallogan.

In 573, the kingdom was invaded by enemies from beyond the border. An alliance of rivals, led by the brothers Gwrgi and Peredur, attacked Gwenddolau's heartland. In a ferocious battle at Arfderydd, the invaders were victorious and Gwenddolau was slain. His outnumbered warriors were slaughtered around him. Only a few survivors escaped to tell the tale and one of these was Llallogan. Although alive and unhurt, he was deeply traumatised by the terrible carnage that he had witnessed and in which he had played a part. Weighed down by grief and horror, he fled to the great forest of Calidon, which lay beyond the northern edge of the kingdom. There he hid himself away, living as a fugitive or hermit, subsisting on whatever food he could find among the trees and undergrowth. Battle-trauma had completely overthrown his mind, cutting him off from reality. To the few travellers who chanced upon him on their journeys through the forest he appeared insane – a crazed wild man of the woods. He babbled constantly, often inchoherently, though when his words were intelligible he seemed to utter doom-laden predictions about the future. People began to wonder if his madness had awoken some strange power of prophecy within him. A rumour grew that he was indeed a true seer. This news reached the ears of Meldred, king of a small realm in the upper valley of the River Tweed on the fringes of the forest. Meldred, like Llallogan, was a Briton. His chief residence was a fortress on a cone-shaped hill overlooking the Tweed. In the Cumbric language of the North Britons this was the *din* or 'fort' of Meldred. Centuries later, when Cumbric was displaced by the Gaelic speech of the Scots, *din* became *dun* and the name of the fortress was recorded as *Dunmeller*. The place is now Tinnis Castle near the village of Drumelzier.

Meldred was eager to learn if Llallogan really did possess the gift of prophecy, so he ordered him to be captured and brought to the fortress. There, in the king's hall on the lofty height, the madman became a figure of curiosity and amusement. At some point he was released from captivity and tried to resume his solitary life in the forest, but a group of local men hunted him down and brutally killed him. King Meldred heard of the murder and ensured that the victim received a Christian burial in consecrated ground. Not far from the hilltop fortress stood a church under his protection and patronage. Its small cemetery looked out over the confluence of the Tweed and a stream known in later times as Powsail. Here, in a grave marked by a stone incised with a simple cross, the wild man of the woods finally found peace.

The early legend

Stories about Llallogan continued to be told long after his death. In some, his involvement with the famous battle of Arfderydd was the main theme. These became attached to a larger body of lore surrounding the battle and its participants, among whom the most famous were Gwenddolau and his principal enemies Gwrgi and Peredur. The Arfderydd tales began to take shape in the last quarter of the sixth century and became popular throughout the British kingdoms of the North. By c.670, however, all but one of these realms had fallen to the Anglo-Saxons of Northumbria. The sole survivor was the kingdom of Alt Clut, the ancient land of the Clyde Britons, ruled from a royal citadel on Dumbarton Rock. Here, the old lore surrounding the battle of Arfderydd was preserved and nurtured. Among this material were several stories about Llallogan, depicting him as a fugitive from the great battle, who went mad and became a forest-dwelling prophet.

Eventually, the similarities between Llallogan and the ascetic hermits of ancient Christian tradition led to his tale being turned into a parable on penance and redemption. He was then assimilated into the hagiography of St Kentigern or Mungo, the national saint of the North Britons whose tomb lay at Glasgow on the Clyde. This attachment of the wild man's story to the ecclesiastical legend of Glasgow's patron saint was probably complete by c.900. It was easy for the hagiographers to bring Kentigern and Llallogan together, not least because they were roughly contemporary with one another. Moreover, they shared a common geographical link with places within or around the Forest of Calidon, such as Clydesdale, Tweeddale, Eskdale, Annandale and Lothian. It was only a small step to put them together in a single narrative. For the hagiographers, the troubled wild man became a useful vehicle for showcasing Kentigern's compassion. In reality, the two individuals probably never met. How many Llallogan stories appeared in the earliest Kentigern hagiography is unknown. There may have been quite a few but only two are identifiable today. In one, the wild man is at Glasgow, begging the saint for communion. In another, the setting is King Meldred's fortress in Tweeddale and there is no mention of Kentigern, although the underlying message is a Christian one. This tale also gives a prominent role to Meldred's queen, whose name is not recorded.

The lore of the Old North was kept alive by the Clyde Britons, in both oral and written forms. Of the Arfderydd material, some was probably rendered into heroic verse while the rest continued to circulate as prose saga. The Llallogan stories were still embedded in these traditions but were now also part of the legend of Kentigern. Being a well-known character in both religious and secular folklore, Llallogan inevitably came to the attention of storytellers in lands beyond the borders of Alt Clut. His fame spread westward to Dál Riata, the territory of the Scots, and thence to Ireland where it influenced the legend of Suibhne, a historical figure of the seventh century. Irish storytellers transformed Suibhne into a Gaelic version of Llallogan by depicting him as a warrior who went insane during a battle before fleeing into the wilderness. They even brought the two madmen together in an episode where Suibhne meets his British counterpart 'Alladhan' in Clydesdale.

The kingdom of Alt Clut was destroyed by Vikings in 870. It was succeeded by the kingdom of Strathclyde in which the lore and legend of the Britons continued to be maintained. However, after the Scottish conquest of Strathclyde in the eleventh century, most of this ancient literature was discarded. The surviving remnants were those deemed worthy of preservation by the new masters. Amongst the latter were the bishops of Glasgow, who rose to prominence in the 1100s. Kentigern's hagiography survived, not least because the Scots regarded it as useful for their own propaganda. As the premier saint of the conquered Britons, Kentigern became a key figure in a clever rewriting of history that gave legitimacy to the Scottish takeover. The traditions surrounding him were edited and repackaged, or simply rejected and discarded. A new version of his legend was compiled, with much of the older British hagiography retained in suitably amended form. One survivor of this process was the tale of Kentigern's encounter with Llallogan at Glasgow. Another was the account of Llallogan's dealings with King Meldred in Tweeddale. Both were deemed worthy of inclusion in a new *vita* or 'Life' of Kentigern commissioned by Bishop Herbert of Glasgow in the mid-twelfth century. An alternative version of the Meldred story, in which the king was replaced by Kentigern's royal patron Rhydderch Hael, appeared in a later *vita* commissioned by Bishop Jocelin and written by his namesake Jocelin of Furness. In these twelfth-century texts, the wild man's name was given as Lailoken or Laloecen.

The later legend

From the eighth century onwards, the ancient literature of the North Britons became popular among the Britons of Wales. Heroic tales of long-dead northern kings and faraway battlefields entered the repertoire of Welsh poetry and storytelling. Among these was the material relating to the battle of Arfderydd, with the story of Llallogan attached. In Wales, the wild seer of the Forest of Calidon gained a new audience but underwent a change of identity. He was merged with Myrddin, the legendary founder of Carmarthen, whose own story had not yet been fully developed. Myrddin assumed Llallogan's identity and took over his role. A new, composite figure was created, a sixth-century prophet whose story spanned both Wales and northern Britain. His wildness and obscure prophecies were presented to Welsh audiences in a series of newly-composed poems that came to be regarded as his own works. This character's original name was almost forgotten, surviving only in a few lines of poetry as a pet-name for Myrddin.

By c.900, Myrddin had been elevated to the rank of Welsh national prophet. He became a mouthpiece for political prophecy relating to the ongoing struggle against English domination. The poetry associated with him was amended accordingly, to show him foretelling a great Welsh victory which would drive the hated 'Saxons' into the sea. His political role was well-established when he came to the attention of Geoffrey of Monmouth in the twelfth century. Geoffrey borrowed Myrddin and turned him into Merlin, a new character incorporating some elements of the old. Just as Myrddin had taken over the identity of Llallogan, so Geoffrey's Merlin took over certain characteristics of Ambrosius or Emrys, a boy-prophet long famed in Welsh folklore. Geoffrey included Merlin in his *Historia Regum Britanniae* of c.1139, portraying him not only as a seer but as a sorcerer. By giving Merlin a supporting role in an elaborate retelling of the old Welsh legends of Arthur, Geoffrey invented a figure whose image endures to the present day. Some years later, Geoffrey depicted a rather different Merlin in a long poem called *Vita Merlini*, creating a character much closer to the wild madman of older Welsh and North British tradition. Indeed, Geoffrey seems to have consulted the Myrddin poetry and the Kentigern hagiography directly, drawing information from both sources. The old and new Merlins were sufficiently dissimilar to prompt a belief in some quarters that they were not one and the same, in spite of their creator's insistence that they were.

Multiple copies of Geoffrey's works were made and distributed. Some came to Scotland where the similarities between Merlin and Lailoken were soon recognised. Scottish writers deemed the two figures to be identical and annotated Lailoken's story to reflect this. However, Merlin did not completely supplant Lailoken, perhaps because of his association with the controversial King Arthur whom many Scots regarded as the legendary oppressor of their country. Nevertheless, the people of Upper Tweeddale began to nurture a tradition that Merlin had once walked in their lands and that he had met St Kentigern at Stobo Kirk. They believed that the wizard's grave lay at Drumelzier in Tweeddale, in the very place where his original legend was probably formed.

History and myth

So ends the reconstruction of Merlin's story. Some readers of this book may find it convincing. Others will not. It has presented a case for believing that the original Merlin or Merlin-archetype was a real person who died in southern Scotland in the latter years of the sixth century. Not everyone is prepared to accept this scenario. Some see Merlin as a wholly mythical character with no place in genuine history. Others are less sceptical and see the Merlin-archetype as real but not northern, preferring to place him in Wales or Cornwall or Brittany, or envisaging him in a pan-Celtic context. Even those who assign to him a North British origin are not in unanimous agreement on his identity. Some, for instance, are happy to accept him as the historical figure behind Lailoken but wonder if his real name might have been 'Merdin' or something similar. They propose that this name might already have become attached to the Merlin-archetype in the northern material before the latter arrived in Wales. In such a scenario, the alleged Carmarthen origin of Merdin/Myrddin becomes a red herring and 'Llallogan' is not a given name but simply a nickname. One important issue, then, is not whether a historical archetype really existed in the Old North but what to call him. Here, at the end of this book, it is suggested that his name was indeed Llallogan (or a Cumbric variant of it). It is further proposed that he was a warrior who fought at the battle of Arfderydd in 573, in which he became afflicted with what would today be diagnosed as post-traumatic stress disorder. It is highly likely that his story was first told in the kingdom of Strathclyde. This means that Scotland can confidently claim as her own an important part of the Merlin legend – not the Arthurian material created by Geoffrey of Monmouth and the writers of the later romances, but the original tale at the legend's deepest roots.

APPENDIX 1

LAILOKEN

Jocelin of Furness, *Life of Kentigern*
(English translation in A.P. Forbes' edition of 1874)

Of the prophecy of a certain man, and of the burial of the saints in Glasgow
In the same year that St Kentigern, set free from earthly things, migrated to the heavens, King Rederech, who has been often mentioned before, remained much longer than usual in the royal town, which was called Partick. In his court there lived a fool called Laloecen, who was in the habit of receiving the necessaries of food and clothing from the munificence of the king; for the chiefs of the earth, the sons of the kingdom, given to vanity, are used to having such persons about them, that by their foolish words and gestures they may excite to jokes and loud laughter the lords themselves and their servants. This man, after the death of St Kentigern, gave himself up to the most extreme grief, and would receive no consolation from anyone.

When they asked him why he mourned so inconsolably, he answered that his lord, King Rederech, and another of the chiefs of the land, by name Morthec, would not live long after the death of the holy bishop, but would die within the year. That the saying of the fool was uttered not foolishly but prophetically, was clearly proved by the fact of the death of both in the same year. Nor is it much to be marvelled at that the Creator of all things should allow to be announced through the mouth of a fool what was determined, when even Balaam the soothsayer, by his inspiration seeing beforehand many important events, with foreboding mind declared them; and when Caiaphas prophesied that the redemption of the people was to come from the death of Christ; when by the mouth of a she-ass the madness of a prophet was rebuked; when the destruction of Jerusalem was foretold by a madman, as Josephus writes. Therefore in the same year in which the holy Bishop Kentigern died, the king and prince afore-said died and were buried in Glasgow.

Lailoken and Kentigern (from *Vita Merlini Silvestris*)

One day, in the time when St Kentigern was living in the wilderness, he was praying in the forest when a naked, hairy madman, an utterly wretched creature, ran towards him in a frenzy. His name was Lailoken. Some folk say that he was Merlin, a famous prophet of the Britons, but this is not certain.

Legend tells that when St Kentigern saw the wild man he greeted him with these words: 'I implore you by the Father, Son and Holy Spirit to speak to me, whatever kind of creature you are. Are you on God's side? Do you believe in God? Who are you? Why do you wander alone in this wilderness, with only the beasts of the forest as your companions?'

The madman immediately stopped in his tracks and replied: 'I am a Christian, although not worthy of such a great name. I endure much torment in the lonely wilderness, for it is my destiny to live among the wild creatures, being unworthy to endure my penance among mankind. For it was I who caused the deaths of all those who were slain in the battle – well known to everyone in this country – which was fought on the field between Liddel and Carwannok [Carwanolow]. During that battle the sky opened high above my head, and I heard a voice like thunder, speaking to me from heaven: "Lailoken, Lailoken, because you alone are guilty of the blood of all the slain, you alone must suffer for all their sins. You will be handed over to Satan's angels and, from now until you die, your companions shall be the beasts of the forest." I turned my gaze towards the voice but my eyes saw a light too dazzling for any man to endure. I also saw countless battalions of a celestial army, like flashes of lightning, with burning lances and shining spears in their hands. Fiercely they brandished their weapons at me. As I turned away, an evil spirit seized me and brought me here to dwell among the wild woodland creatures, as you yourself can see.'

With these words he dashed away into a secret part of the forest known only to beasts and birds. St Kentigern felt great pity for the poor wretch and lay face-down on the ground, saying: 'Lord Jesus, this man is the most miserable of all unhappy men, living in this filthy wilderness, like a beast among beasts, naked and exiled, eating nothing except grass. Wild animals are naturally covered in bristles and hair, and it is right that they eat grass, roots and leaves. But this man is our brother. In his nakedness he has our shape, our flesh and blood, our frailty, yet he lacks everything that human nature requires, except only the free air we all breathe. How does he survive among the wild creatures of the forest, facing hunger and cold and deprivation?'

The holy bishop Kentigern was so moved by pity that the tears flowed down his cheeks. Then, for the love of God, he resumed his strict penance of solitude in the woods. Praying earnestly, he beseeched the Lord to help the wild man, so wretched and filthy, a creature possessed by a demon, in the hope that sorrow and misfortune might eventually bring salvation for his soul in the afterlife.

Legend says that the madman afterwards ventured forth from the wilderness on many occasions, to sit on a certain steep crag that rises above the Molendinar Burn near Glasgow, to the north of the church. His loud shouting and wailing often disturbed St Kentigern and his monks while they were gathered in divine contemplation. Like a prophet, the wild man sat there and foretold the future. But nobody believed him, because his prophecies were obscure and garbled, and because he never repeated them. A few worthless words were, however, remembered and written down by those who heard him.

One day, when the madman was due to depart from the misery of the world, he arrived as usual at the crag, while St Kentigern was celebrating the morning mass. He was wailing and shouting and demanding in a loud voice that he should be deemed worthy of receiving the body and blood of Christ before he departed from the world. St Kentigern could not endure this irreverent yelling, so he sent a monk to order him to be quiet. The wretched man replied with mild, kind words: 'Please, good sir, go back to holy Kentigern and ask him for the sake of charity to condescend to fortify me with the divine sacrament, since today I shall with his help pass happily from this wicked world.'

When the blessed bishop heard this from the mouth of his cleric, he smiled in a pious way and spoke to those who were standing near, for they were urgently pleading on behalf of the possessed and loudly-shouting fellow. And Kentigern said: 'Is this not the same miserable wretch who has often tried to lead ourselves and others astray with his words? Is he not the one who has lived for many years among the wild forest creatures, possessed by a demon, without the benefit of Christian communion? Therefore I do not think it fitting to give him the sacrament.' But then he said to one of his clerics: 'Go and ask him what manner of death he will suffer, and if he really is going to die today.'

So the cleric went and spoke to the madman, just as the bishop had requested. The madman answered: 'Today I shall be beaten to death by stones and clubs.'

The cleric returned to the bishop and told him what he had heard from the madman's lips. Then the bishop told the cleric to go back, because he did not believe that the wild man was speaking truthfully about the manner of his death: 'Let him speak more truly about when and by what means he will die.' The bishop said this to see if there was any chance of the wretched man speaking the truth and being consistent in his words. 'If so, then perhaps this is indeed the last day of his life, but keep in mind that he never says the same thing twice and always tells things differently from what he has said before.'

So the cleric again asked the madman, who answered: 'Today my body will be pierced by a sharp wooden stake, and thus will I die.'

Returning to the bishop, the cleric reported what he had heard from the madman. So the bishop called all his clerics together and said, 'Now you have heard for yourselves why I am reluctant to grant his request. There is no consistency in what he says.' The clergy said, 'Reverent lord and father, do not be angry with us if we beseech you once more on his behalf, asking for help. Let him be questioned a third time, to see if he is capable of speaking the truth in something that he says.'

So the bishop sent a cleric for the third time, to ask the poor, blessed wretch how he would meet death. The madman replied thus: 'Today I shall end my life in water.' The cleric was most indignant at this response and said, 'Brother, you are behaving stupidly. You are a foolish, deceitful liar. Yet you ask a holy and truthful man to fortify you with the spiritual food that should only be given to those who are truthful and righteous.'

The deranged wretch was suddenly restored to his senses by the Lord and became a happy man. He immediately began to weep again and said: 'Alas for me, miserable as I am! Lord Jesus, how long must I endure this awful fate? How long must I suffer these torments? Why am I rejected even by your faithful ones, when I was guided here by you? Behold, they do not believe my words, despite my having spoken only what you inspired me to foretell.' Turning to the cleric, he said, 'I urgently beg that the bishop himself comes to me, for today I have been entrusted by the Lord to his protection. Let him bring with him the holy sacrament that I have requested for my final journey, and then he shall hear what God has deigned to reveal to him through me.'

And so the bishop came, after giving in to the pleadings of his monks, carrying the bread and the communion wine. As he drew near, the blessed wretch came down from the crag and lay face-down at the bishop's feet, before speaking these words: 'Greetings, holy father, chosen warrior of the most high king! I am that same harmless wretch whom you once encountered in the wilderness, when I was still in the hands of Satan's angels, destined to wander alone. You implored me, through the true and eternal God and in the name of the Trinity, to explain the cause of my suffering. You may remember that you were touched with pity for my anguish and torment, and poured out tearful prayers to the Lord, that he would turn to everlasting joy all the distress and misfortune endured by my body in this world. You gave new meaning to the words of the Apostle, who said that the sufferings of this age cannot compare to the future glory that will be revealed to God's chosen. The Lord listened to your prayers and took pity on me, for today he has restored me to my senses and to God the almighty father, as befits a Christian believer of the catholic faith. Also, after giving me instructions through these signs, he has sent me specially to you, in the sight of these other chosen ones, so that you will send me to him today after I have received his most sacred body and blood.'

When the holy bishop Kentigern heard that this was the same fellow whom he had previously encountered in the wilderness, and heard from him many other things that are not included in this little book, his doubt changed to certainty. Overcome with pity, with tears running down his cheeks, he then spoke kindly to the poor weeping wretch, who was urgently begging for the grace of God: 'Behold, this is the body and the blood of our Lord Jesus Christ, who is the true and eternal salvation of the living who believe in him, and the everlasting glory of those who receive him worthily. Whoever receives this sacrament worthily will live forever and will not die, but whoever receives it unworthily will die the death and will not live. Therefore if you consider yourself worthy of such a great gift, here it is upon the altar of Christ. Approach it in the fear of God and with humility, so that Christ himself might condescend to receive you, for I dare not give it to you or withhold it from you.'

The blessed wretch quickly washed in water, then faithfully confessed his belief in the one God and in the Trinity. He humbly approached the altar with complete faith and in true devotion and took the sacrament of everlasting protection. After taking it, he raised his hands to heaven and said: 'I give you thanks, Lord Jesus, for I have now received the most holy sacrament that I desired.' Turning to St Kentigern, he said: 'Lord, if my earthly life ends today, as you have heard from me, then the most eminent king of Britain, and the holiest of bishops, and the most noble of lords shall follow me within this year.'

The bishop replied: 'Brother, do you still persist in your foolishness? Have you not cast aside the irreverent spirit? But go in peace, and may the Lord be with you.'

Having received the bishop's blessing, Lailoken dashed away, like a wild goat freed from the hunter's snare, and happily sought refuge in the undergrowth. But since things ordained by the Lord must come to pass, it happened that on the same day he was stoned and beaten to death by some shepherds of King Meldred. At the very moment of death he fell down the steep bank of the River Tweed near the fortress of Dunmeller, onto a sharp stake that was sticking up in a fish-trap. He was impaled through the middle of his body and his head bent forward into the water. And thus, exactly as he had foretold, he gave up his soul to the Lord. When St Kentigern and his clerics learned that these things had happened to the madman in the way he had prophesied, they believed him. Fearing that the rest of his prophecies would undoubtedly come to pass, they began to tremble and weep. They praised the name of the Lord, who is always wonderful and blessed through his saints, for ever and ever. Amen.

Lailoken and Meldred (from *Vita Merlini Silvestris*)

It is said that Lailoken was imprisoned as a bound captive in the fortress of Dunmeller, on the orders of King Meldred who wanted him to utter a new prophecy. Lailoken refused to eat or drink for three days, speaking no word to any of the many people who approached him. On the third day, as the king sat on his high throne, his wife gracefully entered the hall. On her head, caught in her wimple, was a leaf from a tree. When the king saw the leaf, he pulled it off and tore it into little pieces. Lailoken saw this and began to laugh loudly. King Meldred, seeing that the madman was in a cheerful mood, spoke to him in a flattering and charming way: 'Lailoken, my good friend. Tell me, I beg, what is the cause of your laughter, the sound of which is ringing in our ears? If you answer my question, I will set you free to go wherever you wish.'

Lailoken immediately replied: 'You captured me and ordered me to be bound with thongs, because you were eager to hear a new prophecy. Therefore I shall pose a new riddle on a new topic. From poison comes sweetness and from sweet honey comes bitterness. But neither is so, though both remain true. There, I have posed the question. Tell me the solution if you can, and then let me go free.'

The king replied: 'This is a difficult and perplexing riddle, and I do not know how to unravel it. So give me one that is easier to understand, and with the same conditions.'

Lailoken put forward a second riddle much like the first. 'Wickedness returned good with evil, and goodness sent it back the same way. But neither is so, though both remain true.'

The king said: 'Do not speak any more riddles. Tell me plainly why you laughed, and the solutions to these two riddles, and then you will be freed from captivity.'

Lailoken answered: 'If I speak plainly, my words will bring sadness to you and death-bearing sorrow to me.' But the king replied: 'Even if it turns out like that, I still want to hear it.' So Lailoken addressed the king with these words: 'Since you are a wise judge, give your judgement on the following matter, and then I will obey your commands.'

The king answered: 'Tell me quickly and you will hear my judgement.' So Lailoken said: 'A certain person bestows the highest honour on an enemy and the worst punishment on a friend, but what do these two really deserve?'

The king replied: 'Punishment for the first. Reward for the second.' To this Lailoken said: 'You have judged correctly. Therefore your wife deserves a crown while you deserve the worst kind of death. But it is not so, for you each remain the same.'

The king began to grow impatient. 'Everything you do is shrouded in obscurity,' he said. 'Please explain these riddles and I will give you whatever you ask for, if your request is reasonable.'

Then Lailoken said: 'I desire one thing that you can easily grant, in addition to letting me go free. I wish my body to be buried in the churchyard on the east side of this fortress, in a grave suitable for a believer, not far from the green place where the Pausayl Burn joins the River Tweed. For it will happen in a few days that I shall suffer a threefold death. But when the meeting of the waters comes close to my grave, the marshal of the British race will defeat the foreign race.' By this he indicated the defeat and division of the Britons and their eventual reunification. After he had spoken on these and on other matters that the king, queen and courtiers wanted to know about, his request for burial was granted. They all swore an oath to release him, free and unharmed, so that he could go wherever he wished.

When his bonds were untied and he was ready to leave, Lailoken stood upright and said: 'What is more bitter than a woman's spite, which was infected with the serpent's venom from the beginning? And what is more sweet than the judgement of law which protects the meek and humble from the spite of the wicked? This woman, your wife, has today bestowed the highest honour on her enemy, while you tore a faithful friend to pieces. But neither is really so, because you thought you were doing the right thing, and she was completely unaware that she was bestowing honour on her enemy. The second riddle is similar to the first. Wickedness did good in the very moment when this wicked woman honoured her betrayer. Goodness performed a wicked deed when the just man killed his faithful friend. But neither is really so, because both people were unaware of what had been done. A short time ago, while the queen was committing adultery in the king's garden, the leaf of a tree fell on her head, to betray her by revealing her adultery to the king. And this leaf, caught up in her wimple, was honoured by the queen when she came into the hall, flaunting it in the presence of everyone. The king noticed the leaf and pulled it off, breaking it into tiny pieces with his fingers. This is how the woman bestowed honour on an enemy who was about to betray her crime, and how the king did harm to a friend who wanted to alert him to the crime so that it might not be repeated.'

With these words Lailoken went off into the pathless wilderness of the woods. Nobody pursued him, for all the people were struck by awe and wonder. The adulteress, pretending to be upset, began to try and soothe the king with sweet words: 'My noble lord and king, do not believe what this madman said. His sole purpose in devising those riddles was to get himself released and sent away. My lord, I stand here ready to prove my innocence of the charge laid against me. You yourself heard, as we all did, what that wicked fraud said about his death. He claimed he will die three times, which is simply not possible. When someone dies, they stay dead. Death cannot be repeated, so his claims are obviously false. And besides, if he was really a true prophet and seer, he would never have allowed himself to be captured and bound, just so that he could later beg for his freedom. Therefore, if you don't pursue him now, you will seem to be approving the insult he has done to me and the wrong that has been done to your kingdom. You are a king who cherishes justice, so you should not let such an offence go unpunished, for the honour of the kingdom will be lost if you spare him.'

The king answered: 'Most foolish of women, if I do decide to take your advice, you will be proved the foulest of adulteresses, while he will be proved a true seer. For he said that if I do now as you advise, the outcome will be a sad one for me and the beginning of fatal sorrow for him. My sadness is already obvious, but for him the sorrow is hidden while he still lives.'

These words sent the woman into a flood of tears, because she could not get her own way. So she began in secret to plot Lailoken's death. After some years, on the day when he had been fortified with the holy sacrament, he happened to be crossing the fields near the fortress of Dunmeller at sunset. There he was attacked by certain shepherds whom the wicked woman had sent against him. Just as he had foretold, he met his death in the manner described above. It is said that the king handed over his body for burial in the place he himself had chosen when he was alive. The fortress is roughly thirty miles from the city of Glasgow. Lailoken lies buried in its cemetery.

Pierced by a stake, having suffered stoning and drowning,
Merlin is said to have met a triple death.

APPENDIX 2

ALLADHAN

Buile Shuibhne (English translation in O'Keeffe's edition of 1913)

Suibhne then left Carraig Alastair and went over the wide-mouthed, storm-swept sea until he reached the land of the Britons. He left the fortress of the king of the Britons on his right hand and came on a great wood. As he passed along the wood he heard lamenting and wailing, a great moan of anguish and feeble sighing. It was another madman who was wandering through the wood. Suibhne went up to him.

'Who are you, my man?' said Suibhne.

'I am a madman,' said he.

'If you are a madman,' said Suibhne, 'come hither so that we may be friends, for I too am a madman.'

'I would,' said the other, 'were it not for fear of the king's house or household seizing me, and I do not know that you are not one of them.'

'I am not indeed,' said Suibhne, 'and since I am not, tell me your family name.'

'Fer Caille ("Man of the Wood") is my name,' said the madman, whereupon Suibhne uttered this stave and Fer Caille answered him as follows:

> Suibhne:
> 'O Fer Caille, what has befallen you?
> sad is your voice;
> tell me what has marred you
> in sense or form.'

> Fer Caille:
> 'I would tell you my story,
> likewise my deeds,
> were it not for fear of the proud host
> of the king's household.
> Alladhan am I

who used to go to many combats,
I am known to all
as the leading madman of the glens.'

Suibhne:
'Suibhne son of Colman am I
from the pleasant Bush;
the easier for us is converse
here, O man.'

After that, each confided in the other and they asked tidings of each other. Said Suibhne to the madman: 'Give an account of yourself.'

'I am the son of a landholder,' said the madman of Britain, 'and I am a native of this country in which we are, and Alladhan is my name.'

'Tell me,' said Suibhne, 'what caused your madness.'

'Not difficult to say. Once upon a time two kings were contending for the sovereignty of this country, viz. [namely], Eochaid Aincheas, son of Guaire Mathra, and Cugua, son of Guaire. Of the people of Eochaid am I,' said he, ' for he was the better of the two. There was then convened a great assembly to give battle to each other concerning the country. I put *geasa* [Irish: 'taboos', 'curses'] on each one of my lord's people that none of them should come to the battle except they were clothed in silk, so that they might be conspicuous beyond all for pomp and pride. The hosts gave three shouts of malediction on me, which sent me wandering and fleeing as you see.'

In the same way he asked Suibhne what drove him to madness.

'The words of Ronan,' said Suibhne, 'for he cursed me in front of the battle of Magh Rath, so that I rose on high out of the battle, and I have been wandering and fleeing ever since.'

'O Suibhne,' said Alladhan, 'let each of us keep good watch over the other since we have placed trust in each other ; that is, he who shall soonest hear the cry of a heron from a blue-watered, green-watered lough or the clear note of a cormorant, or the flight of a woodcock from a branch, the whistle or sound of a plover on being woke from its sleep, or the sound of withered branches being broken, or shall see the shadow of a bird above the wood, let him who shall first hear warn and tell the other ; let there be the distance of two trees between us ; and if one of us should hear any of the before-mentioned things or anything resembling them, let us fly quickly away thereafter.'

They did so, and they were a whole year together.

At the end of the year Alladhan said to Suibhne: 'It is time that we part today, for the end of my life has come, and I must go to the place where it has been destined for me to die.'

'What death shall you die?' said Suibhne.

'Not difficult to say,' said Alladhan. 'I go now to Eas Dubhthaigh, and a blast of wind will get under me and cast me into the waterfall so that I shall be drowned, and I shall be buried afterwards in a churchyard of a saint, and I shall obtain Heaven ; and that is the end of my life. And, Suibhne,' said Alladhan, 'tell me what your own fate will be.'

Suibhne then told him as the story relates below. At that they parted and the Briton set out for Eas Dubhthaigh, and when he reached the waterfall he was drowned in it.

APPENDIX 3

MYRDDIN WYLLT

The following extracts from the poetry attributed to Myrddin refer to the battle of Arfderydd, Rhydderch Hael and Calidon/Celyddon. They represent the oldest Welsh traditions of Merlin and allude to the North British wild man of the Lailoken tales.

The English versions shown here are based on those published in Skene's *The Four Ancient Books of Wales* in 1868. Although not regarded as the best scholarly translations, they give the essential flavour of the Myrddin poetry. Alternative – and more accurate – translations can be found in Bollard 1990. A similar selection of extracts, translated by Professor Jarman, appears as an appendix in Tolstoy 1985.

From *Yr Afallennau* ('The Apple Trees')

Sweet appletree of luxuriant growth!
I used to find food at its foot,
when because of a maid,
I slept alone in the woods of Celyddon,
shield on shoulder, sword on thigh.
Hear, O little pig! listen to my words.
As sweet as birds that sing on Monday
when the sovereigns come across the sea,
blessed by the Cymry, because of their strength.

Sweet appletree in the glade,
trodden is the earth around its base.
The men of Rhydderch see me not,
Gwenddydd no longer loves nor greets me,
I am hated by Gwasawg, the supporter of Rhydderch.
I have despoiled both her son and daughter.
Death visits them all – why not me?

After Gwenddolau no one shall honour me,
no diversions attend me,
no fair women visit me.
Though at Arfderydd I wore a golden torc
the swan-white woman despises me now.

Sweet appletree, growing by the river,
who will thrive on its wondrous fruit?
When my reason was intact
I used to lie at its foot
with a fair wanton maid, of slender form.
Fifty years the plaything of lawless men
I have wandered in gloom among spirits.
After great wealth, and gregarious minstrels,
I have been here so long not even sprites
can lead me astray. I never sleep, but tremble at the thought
of my Lord Gwenddolau, and my own native people.
Long have I suffered unease and longing –
may I be given freedom in the end.

Sweet appletree, with delicate blossom,
growing concealed, in the wind!
As the tale was told to me
that my words had offended Gwasawg the minister,
not once, not twice, but thrice in a single day.
Christ! that my end had come
before the killing of Gwenddydd's son
was upon my hands!

Sweet appletree of crimson colour,
growing, concealed in the Wood of Celyddon.
Though men seek your fruit, their search is vain
until Cadwaladr comes [. . .]

From *Yr Oianau* ('The Greetings')

Listen, O little pig! happy little pig,
do not go rooting on top of the mountain,

but stay here, secluded in the wood,
hidden from the dogs of Rhydderch, defender of the Faith.
I will prophesy – it will be truth!
Listen, O little pig! we should hide
from the huntsmen of Mordei, if one dared,
lest we be pursued and discovered.
If we escape – I'll not complain of fatigue!
I shall predict, from the back of the ninth wave [. . .]
Listen, O little pig! I lack sleep,
such a tumult of grief is within me.
Fifty years of pain I have endured.
Evil is the joy which I have now.
May life be given me by Jesus, the most trustworthy
of the kings of heaven, of highest lineage!
It will not be well with the female descendants of Adam,
if they believe not in God, in the latter day.
Once I saw Gwenddolau, with the gift of princes,
garnering prey on every side.
Beneath the green sod is he not still!
He was the chief of the North, and the gentlest.

Listen, O little pig! go to Gwynedd.
Seek a mate when you rest.
While Rhydderch Hael feasts in his hall
he does not know what sleeplessness I bore.
Snow to my knees, owing to the wariness of the chief.
Ice in my hair, sad my fate!

Listen, O little pig! blessed little pig of the country!
Do not sleep in the morning, burrow not in the fertile region
lest Rydderch Hael and his cunning dogs should come,
and before thou couldst reach the wood, thy perspiration trickled down.

Listen, O little pig! thou blessed pig!
Hadst thou seen as much severe oppression as I have,
thou wouldst not sleep in the morning, nor burrow on the hill.
Listen, O little pig! is not the mountain green?
My cloak is thin; for me there is no repose.

Pale is my visage; Gwenddydd does not come to me.
Listen, O little pig! to me it is of no purpose
to hear the voice of water-birds, whose scream is tumultuous.
Thin is the hair of my head, my covering is not warm.
The dales are my barn, my corn is not plenteous,
my summer collection affords me no relief,
Before parting from God, incessant was my passion.
And I will predict, before the end of the world,
women without shame, and men without manliness.

Listen, O little pig! a trembling pig!
Thin is my covering, for me there is no repose.
Since the battle of Arfderydd it will not concern me,
though the sky were to fall, and the sea to overflow.

From *Ymddiddan Myrddin a Thaliesin* ('The Dialogue of Myrddin and Taliesin')

Myrddin:
How sad with me, how said,
Cedfyl and Cadfan are fallen!
The slaughter was terrible,
shields shattered and bloody.

Taliesin:
I saw Maelgwn battling –
the host acclaimed him.

Myrddin:
Before two men in battles they gather,
before Erith and Gwrith on pale horses.
Slender bay mounts will they bring.
Soon will come the host of Elgan.
Alas for his death, after a great joy!

Taliesin:
Gap-toothed Rhys, his shield a span –
to him came battle's blessing.

Cyndur has fallen, deplorable beyond measure.
Generous men have been slain –
three notable men, greatly esteemed by Elgan.

Myrddin:
Again and again, in great throngs they came,
there came Bran and Melgan to meet me.
At the last, they slew Dyel,
the son of Erbin, with all his men.

Taliesin:
Swiftly came Maelgwn's men,
warriors ready for battle, for slaughter armed.
For this battle, Arfderydd, they have made
a lifetime of preparation.

Myrddin:
A host of spears fly high, drawing blood.
From a host of vigorous warriors –
a host, fleeing; a host, wounded –
a host, bloody, retreating.

Taliesin:
The seven sons of Eliffer, seven heroes,
will fail to avoid seven spears in the battle.

Myrddin:
Seven fires, seven armies,
Cynfelyn in every seventh place.

Taliesin:
Seven spears, seven rivers of blood
from seven chieftains, fallen.

Myrddin:
Seven score heroes, maddened by battle,
to the forest of Celyddon they fled.
Since I, Myrddin, am second only to Taliesin,
let my words be heard as truth.

From *Cyfoesi Myrddin a Gwenddydd ei Chwaer*
('The Conversation of Myrddin and his Sister Gwenddydd')

Gwenddydd:
I have come hither to tell
of the jurisdiction I have in the North.
Every region's beauty is known to me.

Myrddin:
Since the action at Arfderydd and Erydon,
Gwenddydd, and all that happened to me,
dull of understanding I am.
Where shall I go for delight?

Gwenddydd:
I will speak to my Llallogan Myrddin,
wise man and diviner,
since he is used to making disclosures
when a girl goes to him.

Myrddin:
I shall become a simpleton's song,
ominous with the fears of the Cymry.
The wind tells me
Rhydderch Hael's standard cannot fall.

Gwenddydd:
Rhydderch Hael, while he is the enemy
of the bardic city in Clyd,
where will he come to the ford?

Myrddin:
I will tell the fair Gwenddydd
since she has asked so skilfully.
After tomorrow Rhydderch will cease to be.

Gwenddydd:
I ask my far-famed Llallawg,

intrepid battler,
who comes after Rhydderch?

Myrddin:
As Gwenddolau was slain at bloody Arfderydd,
and I have come from amid the furze –
Morgant the Great, son of Sadyrnin.

Gwenddydd:
I ask my far-famed Llallawg,
who fosters song amid the streams –
who will rule after Morgant?

Myrddin:
As Gwenddolau was slain at bloody Arfderydd,
and as I wonder why anyone should see me,
the country will call to Urien.

NOTES

Chapter 1

1 Clarke 1973, 26–35.
2 On Ambrosius Aurelianus, see Lacy 1996, 6–7; on Vortigern, see Chadwick 1959.
3 *Historia Brittonum* (*HB*), chs 40–2. Latin text and English translation in the edition by J. Morris (1980).
4 *Historia Regum Britanniae* (*HRB*). English translation by L. Thorpe (1966). See also Roberts 1991.
5 Jarman 1960, 9.
6 On Wace and Layamon, see Weiss 2002 and Loomis 1959 respectively.
7 Robert de Boron's *Merlin*: see the edition by Micha 1980 and translations in Brown 1990.
8 For an English translation of the Vulgate, see N.J. Lacy (ed.) *Lancelot–Grail: the Old French Arthurian Vulgate and Post-Vulgate in Translation*. 5 vols. (New York, 1992–6). The term Vulgate derives from Latin *vulgata* and simply means 'common' or 'popular' in the sense of 'generally accepted version'.
9 Goodrich 1990b, 130.
10 *Le Morte d'Arthur* survives in Caxton's text and in the formerly lost 'Winchester manuscript' rediscovered in 1934. The definitive scholarly edition is now P.J.C. Field (ed.) *Sir Thomas Malory: Le Morte Darthur* (Martlesham, 2013), based on the Winchester manuscript.
11 For detailed studies on the evolution of the Merlin legend in medieval European literature, see Ashe 2006 and the essays in Goodrich and Thompson (2003).
12 *VM*: Latin text and English translation in the edition by B. Clarke (1973). See also the edition and translation by Parry 1925. For commentary, see Tatlock 1943.
13 *Vita Columbae* (*VC*), Bk i, ch. 15. English translation by R. Sharpe (1995).

Chapter 2

1 Lloyd 1942; Roberts 1991, 98. For a broader study of Geoffrey of Monmouth, see Jankulak 2010.
2 Jarman 1991, 137–9. For an opposing view, see Tolstoy 1983, 20–1.
3 Jarman 1991, 138–9.
4 *Black Book of Carmarthen*: text and translation in Pennar (1989). The Black Book also contains the poem *Y Bedwenni* ('The Birch Tree'), an item excluded from the present study because it adds little to our knowledge of Myrddin's biography or 'back-story'. On this poem see Bollard 1990, 19.

5 English translation: Bollard 1990, 51.

6 English translation: Bollard 1990, 52.

7 Frykenberg 2006b, 1323.

8 Knight 2009, 10.

9 Jarman 1991, 137.

10 Bollard 1990, 13.

11 Tolstoy 1983, 14–15.

12 Tolstoy 1983, 16.

13 Jarman 1991, 136. Jarman noted that Carmarthen's famous 'Merlin's Oak', a tree supposedly planted by Merlin himself, might have been planted no earlier than 1659 (Jarman 1960, 28).

14 On Welsh political prophecy, see also Griffiths 1937.

15 *HB*, 31.

16 *Armes Prydein Vawr*. English translation by J. Bollard in M. Livingston (ed.) *The Battle of Brunanburh: a Casebook* (Exeter, 2011), 29.

17 Bollard and Haycock 2011, 253, 259. Since no such battle is known from Athelstan's dealings with the Welsh, the allusion is probably to his famous victory at Brunanburh (937) in which he defeated a combined force of Vikings, Scots and Britons. On the date and purpose of *Armes Prydein*, see Breeze 2011.

18 Bollard 1990, 14.

19 Triads can be thought of as 'mnemonic triple groupings of lore' (Bollard 1990, 53).

20 Bromwich 1961, 214.

21 Bollard 1990, 53.

22 Bromwich 1961, 214.

23 English translation: Bollard 1990, 19.

24 Bromwich 1961, 471.

25 Lloyd-Jones 1948, 4; Bromwich 1961, 471.

26 On the bard's role, see Alcock 2003, 405–7.

27 Bromwich 1961, 379.

28 The possibility has been acknowledged by a number of scholars, e.g. Tolstoy (1983, 12), Griffiths (1937, 74) and Lloyd-Jones (1948, 4).

29 Bromwich 1961, 380.

30 On these poems, see Rowland 1990, 75ff.

31 *HB*, 62.

32 English translations can be found in the Everyman edition of *The Mabinogion* by G. Jones and T. Jones (1993).

33 English translation based on Bollard 1990, 53. For the original text, see Tolstoy 1983.

34 Rhys 1888, 168.

35 Tolstoy 1983, 18.

36 As suggested by Tolstoy 1983, 18.

37 Koch 1997; Jarman 1988; Jackson 1969.

38 English translation: Jarman 1988, 30.

39 Williams 1938, 188.

40 English translation: Jackson 1969, 100. See also Koch 1997, 33.

41 Bromwich 1961, 469.

42 Jarman 1988, 106.

43 Jarman 1988; Jackson 1969, 133.

44 Bollard 1990, 14. Rachel Bromwich thought that the Myrddin reference 'may well be as old or older than the Armes Prydein' (1961, 469).

45 Pughe 1873, 267.

46 It has been suggested that the names Llallawg and Llallogan/Lailoken may derive from a place connected with the name Lollius borne by a Roman governor of Britain in the second century AD (Clarke 1973, 195). This theory has received little support (see Frykenberg 2006a, 1083).

Chapter 3

1 Clarkson 2014; Edmonds 2014; Edmonds 2015.

2 Broun 2004, 141

3 Clarkson 2014, 163.

4 Jackson 1958, 274.

5 Jackson 1958, 275. On the hagiography surrounding Teneu, see MacQueen 1955 and Durkan 2000.

6 Jackson 1958, 280.

7 C. Horstman (ed.) 1901 *Nova Legenda Anglie* (Oxford), 114–28.

8 Jackson 1958; Macquarrie 1997, 138–40; Frykenberg 2006a, 1082.

9 See Jackson 1958, 300–1 for discussion.

10 Jackson 1958, 307.

11 *HB*, 63.

12 Davies 2009, 86.

13 Jackson 1958, 318 n2; Davies 2009, 83–6.

14 Lowe 1999, 41–3; Lowe 2006.

15 Forsyth 2005.

16 The quote is from Jackson 1958, 321 n3.

17 On St Constantine, see Macquarrie 1997, 192–5.

18 Dalglish and Driscoll 2009, 35–6.

19 Cross 1952, 407.

20 Driscoll, O'Grady and Forsyth 2005, 148.

21 Jackson 1958, 327.

22 Jocelin of Furness, *Vita Sancti Kentigerni*, ch. 45. Latin text and English translation in the edition by A.P. Forbes (1874).

23 MacQueen and MacQueen 1989a.

24 Molendinar: *Mellodonor* in the manuscript. This is the stream (now culverted) between Glasgow Cathedral and the Necropolis.

25 Chadwick and Chadwick 1932, i, 109; Jackson 1958, 329; Clarke 1973, 194.

26 Bower, iii, 31. Text and translation in MacQueen and MacQueen 1989b, 83–7.

27 MacQueen and MacQueen 1989b, 229. See also Frykenberg 2006a, 1082.

28 Jarman 1991, 129. *Buile Shuibhne*: text and translation in O'Keeffe's edition of 1913.

29 Carney 1950, 101; Frykenberg 2006a, 1083.

30 Carney 1950, 101; Clarke 1973, 195; Jarman 1991, 130.

31 Jackson 1958, 335. Ward (1893, 512) suggested Lalocant as the original Cumbric form of Lailoken.

32 See, for example: Clarke 1973, 160; Galyon and Thundy 1990, 4; Knight 2009, 12–13.

Chapter 4

1 Translation by Jarman in Tolstoy 1985, 285.

2 Translation by Jarman in Tolstoy 1985, 287.

3 The manuscript is now preserved in the Harley collection at the British Library.

4 Translation by Jarman in Tolstoy 1985, 285.

5 Translation by Jarman in Tolstoy 1985, 286.

6 Bromwich 1961, 44.

7 Bromwich 1961, 30.

8 Bromwich 1961, 273. For the pedigrees, see Bartrum 1966, 73 and 89.

9 Chalmers 1807, i, 246; Watson 1926, 202.

10 Skene 1876.

11 Armstrong et al. 1950, 51–3.

12 The identification is accepted by philologists: see Armstrong et al. 1950, 51–3.

13 Graham 1913, 33; Phythian-Adams 1996, 35. I am grateful to Mark Brennand for permission to reproduce an aerial photograph of Liddel Strength.

14 Birley 1954.

15 Wilmott 1997.

16 Jackson 1963; Breeze 2006.

17 Clarkson 2014, 63–6.

18 Koch 2006b, 82. On the possible survival of local traditions about the battle, see Clarkson 1995.

19 On Arthuret church and parish, see Bulman and Frith 1935.

20 Breeze 2012, 5.

21 Mills 2011.

22 Breeze 2012, 6.

23 Clarkson 2010, 97.

24 This is a paraphrase of John Bellenden's sixteenth-century English translation of Boece's chronicle.

25 Clarke 1973, 171; Clarke 1969.

26 Lovecy 1991.

27 e.g. Morris 1973, 218.

28 Carey 2007, 246–7.

29 Clarkson 2010, 30–1.

30 Koch 1997, 205.

31 Miller 1975, 106–9.

32 Higham 1992.

33 Clarkson 2010, 99.

34 The English translations from *Yr Afallennau* and *Yr Oianau* (see below) are by Professor Jarman in Tolstoy 1985, 284–6.

35 The translation is from Bollard 1990, 52.

36 e.g. Lloyd 1911, 166–7; Parry 1955, 27.

37 The passage in question is translated in Bromwich 1961, 209.

38 Alcock and Alcock 1990.

39 Another Scottish tradition asserts that a large boulder known as Clochodrick has a name

meaning 'Stone of Rhydderch' and marks the king's burial-place (Watson 1926, 201), although an alternative derivation from the name 'Boderick' is possible (Alexander and McCrae 2012, 94).

40 Edmonds 2009, 56–7. Alex Woolf suggests that Maldred might represent the Gaelic name *Mael Doraid* (Woolf 2007, 250).

41 RCAHMS (1967) The Royal Commission on the Ancient and Historical Monuments of Scotland. *Peeblesshire: an Inventory of the Ancient Monuments.* 2 vols (Edinburgh).

42 Basil Clarke (1973, 203) wondered if the name Meldred might have some connection with Medraut, the older Welsh name behind Geoffrey of Monmouth's Modred, but the element *mel-* in early forms of the place-name Drumelzier seems to militate against original *med-*. Even the variant *Dunmedlar* of c.1200 contains intermediate 'l'.

43 Translation in Bollard 1990, 18.

44 Morris-Jones 1918, 47.

45 Isaac 1998; Padel 2013.

46 Clarkson 2010, 68–75.

47 Clarke 1973, 193.

48 Koch 2006b, 82; Frykenberg 2006d, 1791.

Chapter 5

1 English translation: Bromwich 1961, 206.

2 Chadwick 1976, 100.

3 Simpson 1938.

4 Simpson (1938) dated the mound's construction to c.1335.

5 Miller 1952, 117–19.

6 Watson 1926, 368. On Llywarch Hen, see Rowland 1990.

7 Gourlay 1931, 108.

8 *HB*, 63.

9 Chalmers 1807, i, 246.

10 Skene 1876, 92.

11 Bromwich 1961, 115.

12 Bromwich 1961, 11, citing Todd, *Cogad Gaedhel re Gallaibh* (London, 1867), 182.

13 Skene 1876, 95.

14 Skene 1876, 95.

15 Grant 1892, 324.

16 Gourlay 1931, 111.

17 Carruthers 1979, 146.

18 Carruthers 1979, 146.

19 Carruthers 1979, 147.

20 Tolstoy 1985, 71.

21 Tolstoy 1985, 72.

22 Tolstoy 1985, 79.

23 Tolstoy 1985, 71.

24 Tolstoy 1985, 72.

25 On ancient druidism, see Piggott 1968, Hutton 2007 and Hutton 2009.

26 Ross 1967, 52.

27 Sharpe 1995, 20.

28 Ross 1967, 53.

29 Tacitus, *Annals*, 4, 30.

30 Kelly 1988, 59–60.

31 Hutton 2009, 47.

32 *VC*, ii, 33. On translating *magus*, see Sharpe 1995, 334.

33 Crichton 2015, 5.

34 Tolstoy 1985, 110.

35 Tolstoy 1985, 124.

36 Tolstoy 1985, 315 n39. Tolstoy does not refer to Broichan by name.

37 Tolstoy 1985, 110.

38 Begg and Rich 1991, 19.

39 Clarkson 2012, 211–13; Fraser 2009, 80–1. On what 'Celtic' Christianity actually means, see Corning 2006.

40 Ross 1967, 5.

41 Thomas 1968; Smyth 1984, 34; Forsyth 2005. On the process of Christianisation in the fifth and sixth centuries, see Fraser 2009, 83–93.

42 Clarkson 2010, 96. Basil Clarke observed that the idea of a crusade led by Rhydderch against a pagan resistance led by Gwenddolau 'has no substance' (Clarke 1973, 161).

43 Tolstoy 1985, 110.

44 Jarman 1991, 121.

45 Bromwich 1961, 380.

46 English translation: Bollard 1990, 23.

47 English translation: Galyon and Thundy 1990, 5.

48 Crichton 2015, 28.

49 Seymour and Randall 1997.

50 Seymour and Randall 1997, 9.

51 Clarke 1973, 2; Galyon and Thundy 1990, 3.

Chapter 6

1 Tolstoy 1985, 219.

2 Bernheimer 1952, 3.

3 Sandars 1960.

4 Daniel 4: 31–3; Husband 1980, 9–10.

5 Frykenberg 2006d.

6 Bernheimer 1952, 8.

7 Bernheimer 1952, 9.

8 Bernheimer 1952, 12.

9 On wild women see Bernheimer 1952, 33ff, 128ff.

10 Bernheimer 1952, 13; Frykenberg 2006d, 1792. On the Celtic tradition, see also Thomas 2000 – I am grateful to Michelle Ziegler for drawing my attention to this article.

11 Frykenberg 2006d, 1792.

12 Knight 2009, 11; Jackson 1940, 536, n10, citing Murphy 1931, 102.

13 Anderson 1922, 162. See O'Donovan 1842 for text and translation of the Irish tales.

14 *Buile Shuibhne*, 15. Translation in Jarman 1991, 127. For discussion, see also Sailer 1998.

15 Jackson 1940, 547.

16 Frykenberg 2006c, 1633.

17 Jackson 1940, 550; see also Jackson 1951.

18 Jackson 1940, 548; Carney 1950, 101; Frykenberg 2006a, 1083.

19 Carney 1950, 100.

20 Frykenberg 2006c, 1633.

21 Jackson 1940, 550.

22 Jarman 1991, 124.

23 See, for example, Tolstoy 1985, 109.

24 Kentigern's prophecy: Jocelin, *Vita*, ch. 26; Columba's prophecy: *VC*, i, 9.

25 Jarman 1991, 124.

26 Gildas, *De Excidio Britanniae*, ch. 26. Latin text and English translation in the edition by M. Winterbottom (1980).

27 Jarman 1991, 136.

28 Tolstoy 1985, 167.

29 Gerald of Wales, *Description of Wales*, ch. 16. Latin text and English translation in the edition by L. Thorpe and B. Radice (1978).

30 Jackson 1940, 535; Jackson 1958, 393; Ó Cuív 1973.

31 *VC*, i, 36.

32 Frykenberg 2006d, 1799.

33 See also the discussion in Tolstoy 1985, 199–215.

34 Ross 1989.

35 *VC*, i, 29.

36 'As for Merlin himself, his fate was nothing less than a sacrifice in which he, as the god incarnate, underwent the Threefold Death of God Himself, symbolically or in reality'(Tolstoy 1985, 214).

37 Tolstoy 1985, 168–71.

38 Ginzburg 1983, 4.

Chapter 7

1 *VM*, line 930. Translation from Clarke 1973, 103.

2 Clarke 1973, 162.

3 *VM*, lines 1070–1124.

4 *VM*, line 586; Galyon and Thundy 1990, 57.

5 Brown 1990, 102.

6 Foster 1959; Loomis 1984.

7 Tatlock 1939.

8 Contrary to a widespread popular belief, Arthur is not explicitly referred to as *dux bellorum*, 'battle-leader', as if assigned a specific command in the manner of a Roman general (such as the *dux Britanniarum* based at York). The text of *HB* says simply *sed ipse dux bellorum erat*, 'but he was their leader in battle' without any implication of a formal rank or title.

9 *HB*, 56.

10 *Gueith camlann in qua Arthur et Medraut corruerunt.*

11 Translation in Jarman 1988, 64.

12 On the date and provenance of *The Gododdin*, see now the discussions in Woolf 2013.

13 On the 'Historical Arthur' debate, see Higham 2002, Green 2009 and Halsall 2013.

14 Text and translation in Winterbottom 1980.

15 Bede, *Historia Ecclesiastica.* English translation by J. McClure and R. Collins (1994).

16 Ritchie 1997.

17 Steer 1960.

18 Bowden Hill: Skene 1868, i, 57–8; *Bassas*: Glennie 1869, 55.

19 *VC*, i, 9.

20 Chadwick 1953, 165; Barber 1972, 311; Stirling 2012.

21 Bromwich 1976, 179.

22 Chadwick and Chadwick 1932, 161–2.

23 Bromwich 1976, 179.

24 Breeze 2015.

Chapter 8

1 Clarke 1973, 29 n1.

2 Clarkson 2014, 162.

3 Clarke 1973, 195.

4 Roberts 1991, 99. On St Asaph (the place) see Pearson 2000.

5 Thomas 1874.

6 Davies 2009, 86.

7 On the ecclesiastical politics, see Davies 2009 and Broun 2004.

8 Gerald of Wales, *Journey Through Wales*, Bk ii, ch. 8. Latin text and English translation in the edition by L. Thorpe and B. Radice (1978).

9 Murray 1875.

10 Pennycuik 1715, 26–7.

11 Grierson 1910.

12 The legend of Alderley Edge was popularised by Alan Garner in his 1960 novel *The Weirdstone of Brisingamen.*

13 Legge 1950; Wenthe 2012; Owen 1991.

14 Frescoln 1983, 253.

15 Wenthe 2012.

16 Tolstoy 1985, 83.

17 Tolstoy 1985, 86.

18 Tichelaar 2011, 86.

19 Tichelaar 2011, 86.

20 John of Fordun, *Chronica Gentis Scotorum*, ch. 23. Latin text and English translation in W.F. Skene's edition (1871).

21 Wood 2009, 107.

22 Allan 1997, 188. King Lothus or Loth is the same figure as Leodonus, the legendary maternal grandfather of St Kentigern.

23 *The Complaynt of Scotland*, text edited by A.M. Stewart (1979).

24 *Complaynt*, 67; Allan 1997, 191.

25 Buchanan, 236–7, 233; Allan 1997, 198.

26 Allan 1997, 201.

27 Allan 1997, 202.

28 Chalmers 1807, 234n.

29 Chalmers 1807, 907–8.

30 Tolstoy 1985, 215.

31 Ardrey 2007.

32 For a discussion of Telleyr's name, see Breeze 2008.

33 Corning 2006; Fraser 2009, 80–3.

34 Crichton 2015, 14.

35 Crichton 2015, 24. On the location of Goddeu, see Clarkson 2010, 35–8.

36 Renshaw 2016.

37 Bartrum 1963.

38 I am grateful to Tara S. Beall (t.s. Beall) for letting me see a draft of the graphic novel and to Tam McGarvey and Frazer Capie for discussing the Thirteen Treasures of Govan.

BIBLIOGRAPHY

Part 1: Primary Sources: Editions and Translations

Adomnán, *Vita Sancti Columbae*. R. Sharpe (ed.) *Adomnán of Iona: Life of Saint Columba* (London, 1995)

Armes Prydein Vawr. Edited and translated by J. Bollard in M. Livingston (ed.) *The Battle of Brunanburh: a Casebook* (Exeter, 2011), 28–36

Bede, *Historia Ecclesiastica Gentis Anglorum*. J. McClure and R. Collins (eds) *Bede: The Ecclesiastical History of the English People* (Oxford, 1994)

Black Book of Carmarthen. M. Pennar (trans.) *The Black Book of Carmarthen*. Welsh text edited by J. G. Evans (Felinfach, 1989)

Bower, Walter, *Scotichronicon*. Books 3 and 4. J. and W. MacQueen (eds) *Scotichronicon* (Aberdeen, 1989)

Buchanan, George, *Rerum Scoticarum Historia*. Latin edition by Robert Freebairn (Edinburgh, 1727)

Buile Shuibhne. J.G. O'Keeffe (ed. and trans.) *Buile Shuibhne* ('The Frenzy of Suibhne') (London, 1913)

The Complaynt of Scotland (c.1550). ed. A.M. Stewart. Scottish Texts Society, 4th series: 11 (Edinburgh, 1979)

John of Fordun, *Chronica Gentis Scotorum*. W.F. Skene (ed.) *John of Fordun's Chronicle of the Scottish Nation* (Edinburgh, 1871)

Gerald of Wales. L.Thorpe (trans.) and B. Radice (ed.) *The Journey Through Wales and The Description of Wales* (Harmondsworth, 1978)

Gildas, *De Excidio Britanniae*. M. Winterbottom (ed.) *Gildas: the Ruin of Britain and Other Works* (Chichester, 1980)

Y Gododdin. A.O.H. Jarman (ed.) *Aneirin: Y Gododdin* (Llandysul, 1988)

Guillaume le Clerc, *Le Roman de Fergus*. D.D.R. Owen (ed. and trans.) *Fergus of Galloway: Knight of King Arthur* (London, 1991)

HB Historia Brittonum. J. Morris (ed.) *Nennius: British History and the Welsh Annals* (Chichester, 1980)

HRB Geoffrey of Monmouth, *Historia Regum Britanniae*. L. Thorpe (trans.) *The History of the Kings of Britain* (Harmondsworth, 1966)

VK Jocelin of Furness, *Vita Sancti Kentigerni*. A.P. Forbes (ed.) *The Historians of Scotland: V – Lives of St Ninian and St Kentigern* (Edinburgh, 1874)

The Mabinogion. G. Jones and T. Jones (trans.) *The Mabinogion* (London, 1993)

Red Book of Hergest. English translations of many of the poems in this manuscript can be found in W.F. Skene's *The Four Ancient Books of Wales* (1868).

Robert de Boron, *Merlin*. A. Micha (ed.), *Etude sur le 'Merlin' de Robert de Boron* (Geneva, 1980). Selected English translations in Brown 1990.

VM Geoffrey of Monmouth, *Vita Merlini*. B. Clarke (ed. and trans.) *Life of Merlin* (Cardiff, 1973)

Vita Merlini Silvestris. W. MacQueen and J. MacQueen (eds) 'Vita Merlini Silvestris' *Scottish Studies* 29 (1989), 77–93

Part 2: Modern Scholarship

Alcock, L. (2003) *Kings and Warriors, Craftsmen and Priests in Northern Britain AD 550–850* (Edinburgh)

Alcock, L. and Alcock, E. (1990) 'Reconnaissance Excavations [. . .] 4: Excavations at Alt Clut, Clyde Rock, Strathclyde, 1974–5', *Proceedings of the Society of Antiquaries of Scotland* 120: 95–149

Alexander, D. and McCrae, G. (2012) *Renfrewshire: a Scottish County's Hidden Past* (Edinburgh)

Allan, D. (1997) 'Arthur Redivivus: Politics and Patriotism in Reformation Scotland', pp. 185–204 in J. Carley, J. and F. Riddy (eds.) *Arthurian Literature XV* (Woodbridge)

Anderson, A.O. (1922) *Early Sources of Scottish History, AD 500 to 1286*. Vol. 1 (Edinburgh)

Ardrey, A. (2007) *Finding Merlin: The Truth Behind the Legend* (Edinburgh)

Armstrong, A.M., Mawer, A., Stenton, F.M. and Dickins, B. (1950) *The Place-Names of Cumberland*, Parts 1 and 2 (Cambridge)

Ashe, G. (2006) *Merlin: the Prophet and his History* (Stroud)

Barber, R. (1972) *The Figure of Arthur* (Totowa)

Barber, R. (1986) *King Arthur: Hero and Legend* (New York)

Bartrum, P.C. (1963) 'Tri Thlws ar Ddeg Ynys Prydein', *Études Celtiques* 10: 434–77

Bartrum, P.C. (ed.) (1966) *Early Welsh Genealogical Tracts* (Cardiff)

Begg, E. and Rich, D. (1991) *On the Trail of Merlin: a Guide to the Celtic Mystery Tradition* (London)

Birley, E. (1954) 'The Roman Fort at Netherby', *Transactions of the Cumberland and Westmorland Antiquarian and Archaeological Society*, Second Series 53: 6–39

Bollard, J. (1990) 'Myrddin in Early Welsh Tradition', pp. 13–54 in P. Goodrich (ed.) *The Romance of Merlin: an Anthology* (New York)

Bollard, J. and Haycock, M. (2011) 'The Welsh Sources Pertaining to the Battle', pp. 245–68 in M. Livingston (ed.) *The Battle of Brunanburh: a Casebook* (Exeter)

Bernheimer, R. (1952) *Wild Men in the Middle Ages: a Study in Art, Sentiment and Demonology* (Cambridge, MA)

Breeze, A. (2006) 'Britons in the Barony of Gilsland, Cumbria', *Northern History* 43: 327–32

Breeze, A. (2008) 'Telleyr, Anguen, Gulath, and the Life of St Kentigern', *Scottish Language* 27: 71–9

Breeze, A. (2011) 'Durham, Caithness, and *Armes Prydein*', *Northern History* 48: 147–52

Breeze, A. (2012) 'The Name and Battle of Arfderydd, near Carlisle', *Journal of Literary Onomastics* 2: 1–9

Breeze, A. (2015) 'The Historical Arthur and Sixth-Century Scotland', *Northern History* 51: 158–81

Bromwich, R. (ed.) (1961) *Trioedd Ynys Prydein: the Welsh Triads* (Cardiff)

Bromwich, R. (1976) 'Concepts of Arthur', *Studia Celtica* 10–11: 163–81

Bromwich, R., Jarman, A.O.H. and Roberts, B.F. (eds) (1991) *The Arthur of the Welsh: the Arthurian Legend in Medieval Welsh Literature* (Cardiff)

Broun, D. (2004) 'The Welsh Identity of the Kingdom of Strathclyde, c.900–1200', *Innes Review* 55: 111–80

Brown, N.M. (1990) 'Robert de Boron and his Continuators', pp. 101–27 in *The Romance of Merlin: an Anthology* (New York)

Bulman, C. and Frith, R. (1935) *The Church and Parish of St Michael, Arthuret* (Carlisle)

Carey, J. (2007) *Ireland and the Grail* (Aberystwyth)

Carney, J. (1950) 'Suibne Geilt and the Children of Lir', *Éigse* 6: 83–110

Carruthers, F.J. (1979) *People Called Cumbri* (London)

Chadwick, H.M. (1959) 'Vortigern', pp. 21–33 in H.M. Chadwick, N.K. Chadwick, K. Jackson, R. Bromwich, P.H. Blair and O. Chadwick, *Studies in Early British History* (Cambridge)

Chadwick, H.M. and Chadwick, N.K. (1932) *The Growth of Literature. Vol. 1* (Cambridge)

Chadwick, N.K. (1953) 'The Lost Literature of Celtic Scotland: Caw of Pritdin and Arthur of Britain', *Scottish Gaelic Studies* 7: 115–83

Chadwick, N.K. (1958) 'Early Culture and Learning in North Wales', pp. 29–120 in N.K. Chadwick et al. *Studies in the Early British Church* (Cambridge)

Chadwick, N.K. (1976) *The British Heroic Age* (Cardiff)

Chalmers, G. (1807–24) *Caledonia* (London)

Clancy, T.O. (2006) 'Ystrad Clud', pp. 1818–20 in volume 5 of Koch 2006a

Clarke, B. (1969) 'Calidon and the Caledonian Forest', *Bulletin of the Board of Celtic Studies* 23: 191–5

Clarke, B. (ed.) (1973) *Life of Merlin* (Cardiff)

Clarkson, T. (1995) 'Local Folklore and the Battle of Arthuret', *Transactions of the Cumberland and Westmorland Antiquarian and Archaeological Society*, Second Series 95: 282–4

Clarkson, T. (2001) *Warfare in Early Historic Northern Britain.* Unpublished PhD thesis, University of Manchester

Clarkson, T. (2010) *The Men of the North: the Britons of Southern Scotland* (Edinburgh)

Clarkson, T. (2012) *Columba* (Edinburgh)

Clarkson, T. (2014) *Strathclyde and the Anglo-Saxons in the Viking Age* (Edinburgh)

Corning, C. (2006) *The Celtic and Roman Traditions: Conflict and Consensus in the Early Medieval Church* (London)

Crichton, R. (2015) *Merlin: the Hidden History* (Traquair)

Cross, T.P. (1952) *Motif-Index of Early Irish Literature* (Bloomington)

Dalglish, C. and Driscoll, S.T. (2009) *Historic Govan: Archaeology and Development* (Edinburgh)

Davies, J.R. (2009) 'Bishop Kentigern among the Britons', pp. 67–99 in S. Boardman, J.R. Davies and E. Williamson (eds) *Saints' Cults in the Celtic World* (Woodbridge)

Driscoll, S.T., O'Grady, O. and Forsyth, K. (2005) 'The Govan School Revisited: Searching for Meaning in the Early Medieval Sculpture of Strathclyde', pp. 135–58 in S.M. Foster and M. Cross (eds) *Able Minds and Practised Hands: Scotland's Early Medieval Sculpture in the Twenty-First Century* (Leeds)

Durkan, J. (2000) 'What's in a Name? Thaney or Enoch', *Innes Review* 51: 80–3

Edmonds, F. (2009) 'Personal Names and the Cult of Patrick in Eleventh-Century Strathclyde and Northumbria', pp. 42–65 in S. Boardman, J.R. Davies and E. Williamson (eds), *Saints' Cults in the Celtic World* (Woodbridge)

Edmonds, F. (2014) 'The Emergence and Transformation of Medieval Cumbria', *Scottish Historical Review* 93: 195–216

Edmonds, F. (2015) 'The Expansion of the Kingdom of Strathclyde', *Early Medieval Europe* 23: 43–88

Field, P.J.C. (ed.) *Sir Thomas Malory: Le Morte Darthur* (Martlesham, 2013)

Forsyth, K. (2005) '*Hic Memoria Perpetua*: the Early Inscribed Stones of Southern Scotland in Context', pp. 113–34 in S.M. Foster and M. Cross (eds) *Able Minds and Practised Hands: Scotland's Early Medieval Sculpture in the Twenty-First Century* (Leeds)

Foster, I. (1959) 'Culhwch and Olwen and Rhonabwy's Dream', pp. 31–43 in R.S. Loomis (ed.) *Arthurian Literature in the Middle Ages* (Oxford)

Fraser, J.E. (2009) *From Caledonia to Pictland: Scotland to 795* (Edinburgh)

Frescoln, W. (ed.) (1983) *The Romance of Fergus* (Philadelphia)

Frykenberg, B. (2006a) 'Lailoken', pp. 1081–3 in volume 3 of Koch 2006a

Frykenberg, B. (2006b) 'Myrddin', pp. 1322–6 in volume 4 of Koch 2006a

Frykenberg, B. (2006c) 'Suibhne Geilt', pp. 1633–5 in volume 4 of Koch 2006a

Frykenberg, B. (2006d) 'The Wild Man', pp. 1790–9 in volume 5 of Koch 2006a

Galyon, A. and Thundy, Z.P. (1990) 'History of the Kings of Britain', pp. 57–70 in P. Goodrich (ed.) *The Romance of Merlin: an Anthology* (New York)

Ginzburg, C. (1983) *The Night Battles: Witchcraft and Agrarian Cults in the Sixteenth and Seventeenth Centuries*. English translation by J. and A. Tedeschi of Ginzburg's 1966 original (Baltimore)

Glennie, J.S. (1869) *Arthurian Localities* (Edinburgh)

Goodrich, N.L. (1986) *King Arthur* (New York)

Goodrich, P. (ed.) (1990a) *The Romance of Merlin: an Anthology* (New York)

Goodrich, P. (1990b) 'Middle English Romances', pp. 129–78 in P. Goodrich (ed.) *The Romance of Merlin: an Anthology* (New York)

Goodrich, P. and Thompson R. (eds) (2003) *Merlin: a Casebook* (New York)

Gourlay, W.R. (1931) 'The Battle of Arthuret, c. 573 AD', *Transactions of the Dumfriesshire and Galloway Natural History and Antiquarian Society* 21: 180–204

Graham, T.B.H. (1913) 'Annals of Liddel', *Transactions of the Cumberland and Westmorland Antiquarian and Archaeological Society*, Second Series 13: 32–8

Grant, A. (1892) 'Scottish Origin of the Merlin Myth', *Scottish Review* 19: 321–37

Green, T. (2009) *Arthuriana: Early Arthurian Tradition and the Origins of the Legend* (Raleigh)

Grierson, E.W. (1910) *The Scottish Fairy Book* (London)

Griffiths, M.E. (1937) *Early Vaticination in Welsh, with English Parallels* (Cardiff)

Halsall, G. (2013) *Worlds of Arthur* (Oxford)

Higham, N.J. (1992) 'The *Regio Dunutinga* – a Pre-Conquest Lordship?', *Bulletin for the Centre of North West Regional Studies*. New Series 6: 43–9

Higham, N.J. (2002) *King Arthur: Myth-Making and History* (London)

Husband, T. (1980) *The Wild Man: Medieval Myth and Symbolism* (New York)

Hutton, R. (2007) *The Druids* (London)

Hutton, R. (2009) *Blood and Mistletoe: the History of the Druids in Britain* (New Haven)

Isaac, G.R. (1998) '*Gweith Gwen Ystrat* and the Northern Heroic Age of the Sixth Century', *Cambrian Medieval Celtic Studies* 36: 61–70

Jackson, K.H. (1940) 'The Motive of the Three-Fold Death in the Story of Suibhne Geilt', pp. 535–50 in J. Ryan (ed.) *Feilsgribhinn: Eoin Mhic Neill* (Dublin)

Jackson, K.H. (1951) 'A Further Note on Suibhne Geilt and Merlin', *Éigse* 7: 112–16.

Jackson, K.H. (1958) 'The Sources for the Life of St Kentigern', pp. 273–357 in N.K. Chadwick, K. Hughes, C Brooke and K.H. Jackson, *Studies in the Early British Church* (Cambridge)

Jackson, K.H. (1963) 'Angles and Britons in Northumbria and Cumbria', pp. 60–84 in H. Lewis (ed.) *Angles and Britons* (Cardiff)

Jackson, K.H. (ed.) (1969) *The Gododdin: the Oldest Scottish Poem* (Edinburgh)

Jankulak, K. (2010) *Geoffrey of Monmouth* (Cardiff)

Jarman, A.O.H. (1960) *The Legend of Merlin* (Cardiff)

Jarman, A.O.H. (1978) 'Early Stages of the Development of the Myrddin Legend', pp. 326–49 in R. Bromwich and R.B. Jones (eds) *Astudiaethau ar yr Hengerdd* (Cardiff)

Jarman, A.O.H. (ed.) (1988) *Aneirin: Y Gododdin* (Llandysul)

Jarman, A.O.H. (1991) 'The Merlin Legend and the Welsh Tradition of Prophecy', pp. 117–45 in R. Bromwich, A.O.H. Jarman and B.F. Roberts (eds) *The Arthur of the Welsh* (Cardiff)

Kelly, F. (1988) *A Guide to Early Irish Law* (Dublin)

Knight, S.T. (2009) *Merlin: Knowledge and Power through the Ages* (New York)

Koch, J.T. (ed.) (1997) *The Gododdin of Aneirin: Text and Context from Dark-Age North Britain* (Cardiff)

Koch, J.T. (ed.) (2006a) *Celtic Culture: an Historical Encyclopedia* (Santa Barbara)

Koch, J.T. (2006b) 'Arfderydd', pp. 82–3 in vol. 1 of Koch 2006a

Lacy, N.J. (ed.) (1996) *The New Arthurian Encyclopedia* (New York)

Legge, D. (1950) 'Some Notes on the Roman de Fergus', *Transactions of the Dumfriesshire and Galloway Natural History and Antiquarian Society* 27: 163–72

Lloyd, J.E. (1911) *A History of Wales* (London)

Lloyd, J.E. (1942) 'Geoffrey of Monmouth', *English Historical Review* 57: 460–8

Lloyd-Jones, J. (1948) 'The Court Poets of the Welsh Princes', *Proceedings of the British Academy*, 34: 167–97

Loomis, R.M. (1984) 'The Tale of Culhwch and Olwen', pp. 27–55 in J. Wilhelm and L. Gross (eds) *The Romance of Arthur* (New York)

Loomis, R.S. (1959) 'Layamon's *Brut*', pp. 104–11 in R.S. Loomis (ed.) *Arthurian Literature in the Middle Ages* (Oxford)

Lovecy, I. (1991) 'Historia Peredur ab Efrawg', pp. 171–82 in R. Bromwich, A.O.H. Jarman and B.F. Roberts (eds) *The Arthur of the Welsh* (Cardiff)

Lowe, C. (1999) *Angels, Fools and Tyrants: Britons and Anglo-Saxons in Southern Scotland, AD 450–750* (Edinburgh)

Lowe, C. (2006) *Excavations at Hoddom, Dumfriesshire: an Early Ecclesiastical Site in South-West Scotland* (Edinburgh)

Macquarrie, A. (1997) *The Saints of Scotland: Essays in Scottish Church History, AD 450–1093* (Edinburgh)

MacQueen, J. (1955) 'A Lost Glasgow Life of St Thaney (St Enoch)', *Innes Review* 6: 125–30

MacQueen, W. and MacQueen, J. (eds) (1989a) 'Vita Merlini Silvestris', *Scottish Studies* 29: 77–93

MacQueen, J. and MacQueen, W. (eds) (1989b) *Scotichronicon: Volume 2 – Books III and IV* (Aberdeen)

McClure, J. and Collins, R. (eds) (1994) *Bede: The Ecclesiastical History of the English People* (Oxford)

Miller, M. (1975) 'The Commanders at Arthuret', *Transactions of the Cumberland and Westmorland Antiquarian and Archaeological Society*, Second Series 75: 114–19

Miller, S.N. (1952) *The Roman Occupation of South-West Scotland* (Glasgow)

Mills, D. (2011) *A Dictionary of British Place-Names* (Oxford)

Morris, J. (1973) *The Age of Arthur* (London)

Morris-Jones, J. (1918) 'Taliesin', *Y Cymmrodor* 28: 1–290

Murphy, G. (1931) 'The Origin of Irish Nature Poetry', *Studies* 20: 87–102

Murray, J.A.H. (ed.) (1875) *The Romance and Prophecies of Thomas of Erceldoune* (London)

Ó Cuív, B. (1973) 'The Motif of the Threefold Death', *Éigse* 15: 145–50

O'Donovan J. (ed.) (1842) *The Banquet of Dun na nGedh and the Battle of Mag Rath* (Dublin)

Owen, D.D.R. (ed.) (1991) *Fergus of Galloway: Knight of King Arthur* (London)

Padel, O.J. (2006) 'Geoffrey of Monmouth and the Development of the Merlin Legend', *Cambrian Medieval Celtic Studies* 51: 37–65

Padel, O.J. (2013) 'Aneirin and Taliesin: Sceptical Speculations', pp. 115–52 in Woolf 2013

Parry, J.J. (ed.) (1925) *Vita Merlini* (Urbana)

Parry, T. (1955) *A History of Welsh Literature* (Oxford)

Pearson, M.J. (2000) 'The Creation and Development of the St Asaph Cathedral Chapter, 1141–1293', *Cambrian Medieval Celtic Studies* 40: 35–56

Pennar, M. (ed.) (1989) *The Black Book of Carmarthen* (Felinfach)

Pennycuik, A. (1715) *A Geographical and Historical Description of the Shire of Tweeddale* (Edinburgh)

Phythian-Adams, C. (1996) *Land of the Cumbrians: a Study in British Provincial Origins, AD 400–1120* (Aldershot)

Piggott, S. (1968) *The Druids* (London)

Pughe, W.O. (1873) *A National Dictionary of the Welsh Language*. 3rd edn. Volume 2 (Denbigh)

Renshaw, P. with Beall, T.S. et al. (2016) *Quest for the Thirteen Treasures of Govan and Glasgow* (Glasgow)

Rhys, J. (1888) *Lectures on the Origin and Growth of Religion as Illustrated by Celtic Heathendom* (London)

Ritchie, Anna (1997) *Meigle Museum Pictish Carved Stones* (Edinburgh)

Roberts, B.F. (1991) 'Geoffrey of Monmouth, *Historia Regum Britanniae* and *Brut y Brenhinedd*', pp. 97–116 in R. Bromwich, A.O.H. Jarman and B.F. Roberts (eds) *The Arthur of the Welsh* (Cardiff)

Ross, A. (1967) *Pagan Celtic Britain: Studies in Iconography and Tradition* (London)

Ross, A. (1989) *The Life and Death of a Druid Prince* (London)

Rowland, J. (1990) *Early Welsh Saga Poetry: a Study and Edition of the Englynion* (Cambridge)

Royal Commission on the Ancient and Historical Monuments of Scotland (1967) *Peeblesshire: an Inventory of the Ancient Monuments* (Edinburgh)

Sailer, S.S. (1998) 'Suibne Geilt: Puzzles, Problems and Paradoxes', *Canadian Journal of Irish Studies* 24: 115–31

Sandars, N.K. (trans.) (1960) *The Epic of Gilgamesh* (Harmondsworth)

Seymour, C. and Randall, J. (1997) *Stobo Kirk: a Guide to the Building and its History*. Updated edition, 2010. (Peebles)

Sharpe, R. (ed.) (1995) *Adomnán of Iona: Life of St Columba* (London)

Simpson, W.D. (1938) 'The Two Castles of Caerlaverock', *Transactions of the Dumfriesshire and Galloway Natural History and Antiquarian Society* 21:180–204

Skene, W.F. (1868) *The Four Ancient Books of Wales* (London)

Skene, W.F. (1876) 'Notice of the Site of the Battle of Ardderyd or Arderyth', *Proceedings of the Society of Antiquaries of Scotland* 6: 91–8

Smyth, A.P. (1984) *Warlords and Holy Men: Scotland, AD 80–1000* (Edinburgh)

Steer, K.A. (1960) 'Arthur's O'on: a Lost Shrine of Roman Britain', *Archaeological Journal* 115: 99–110

Stirling, S. (2012) *The King Arthur Conspiracy: How a Scottish Prince Became a Mythical Hero* (Stroud)

Tatlock, J.S.P. (1939) 'The Dates of the Arthurian Saints' Legends', *Speculum* 14: 345–65

Tatlock, J.S.P. (1943) 'Geoffrey of Monmouth's *Vita Merlini*', *Speculum* 18: 265–87

Thomas, A.C. (1968) 'The Evidence from North Britain', pp. 93–122 in M.W. Barley and R.P.C. Hanson (eds) *Christianity in Britain, 300–700* (Leicester)

Thomas, D.R. (1874) *History of the Diocese of St Asaph* (London)

Thomas, N. (2000) 'The Celtic Wild Man Tradition and Geoffrey of Monmouth's Vita Merlini: Madness or Contemptus Mundi?', *Arthuriana* 10: 27–42

Tichelaar, T. (2011) *King Arthur's Children: a Study in Fiction and Tradition* (Ann Arbor)

Tolstoy, N. (1983) 'Merlinus Redivivus', *Studia Celtica* 18–19: 11–29

Tolstoy, N. (1985) *The Quest for Merlin* (Sevenoaks)

Ward, H. (1893) 'Lailoken (or Merlin Silvester)', *Romania* 22: 504–26

Watson, W.J. (1926) *The History of the Celtic Place-Names of Scotland* (Edinburgh)

Weiss, J. (ed.) (2002) *Wace's Roman de Brut. A History of the British: Text and Translation.* (Exeter)

Wenthe, M. (2012) 'Mapping Scottish Identity in the Roman de Fergus', *LATCH* 5: 28–53

Williams, I. (ed.) (1938) *Canu Aneirin* (Cardiff)

Wilmott, T. (1997) *Birdoswald: Excavations of a Roman Fort on Hadrian's Wall and its Successor Settlements, 1987–92* (London)

Winterbottom, M. (ed.) (1980) *Gildas: the Ruin of Britain and Other Works* (Chichester)

Wood, J. (2009) 'The Arthurian Legend in Scotland and Cornwall', pp. 102–16 in H. Fulton (ed.) *A Companion to Arthurian Literature* (Oxford)

Woolf, A. (2007) *From Pictland to Alba, 789–1070* (Edinburgh)

Woolf, A. (ed.) (2013) *Beyond the Gododdin: Dark Age Scotland in Medieval Wales* (St Andrews)

INDEX